TRADITION VERSUS DEMOCRACY
IN THE SOUTH PACIFIC

CAMBRIDGE ASIA-PACIFIC STUDIES

Cambridge Asia-Pacific Studies aims to provide a focus and forum for scholarly work on the Asia-Pacific region as a whole, and its component sub-regions, namely Northeast Asia, Southeast Asia and the Pacific Islands.

Editor: John Ravenhill

Editorial Board: James Cotton, Donald Denoon, Mark Elvin, David Goodman, Stephen Henningham, Hal Hill, David Lim, Ron May, Anthony Milner, Tessa Morris-Suzuki.

R. Gerard Ward and Elizabeth Kingdon (eds)   *Land, Custom and Practice in the South Pacific*

TRADITION VERSUS DEMOCRACY IN THE SOUTH PACIFIC
Fiji, Tonga and Western Samoa

STEPHANIE LAWSON

Research School of Pacific and Asian Studies
Australian National University

CAMBRIDGE
UNIVERSITY PRESS

To
James, Richard, Katharine
and Elizabeth

CAMBRIDGE UNIVERSITY PRESS
Cambridge, New York, Melbourne, Madrid, Cape Town, Singapore, São Paulo

Cambridge University Press
The Edinburgh Building, Cambridge CB2 8RU, UK

Published in the United States of America by Cambridge University Press, New York

www.cambridge.org
Information on this title: www.cambridge.org/9780521496384

First published 1996
This digitally printed version 2008

A catalogue record for this publication is available from the British Library

National Library of Australia Cataloguing in Publication data
Lawson, Stephanie.
Tradition versus democracy in the South Pacific: Fiji,
Tonga, and Western Samoa
Bibliography.
Includes index.
1. Democracy – Tonga. 2. Democracy – Fiji.
3. Democracy – Western Samoa. 4. Tonga – Politics and
government. 5. Fiji – Politics and government. 6. Western
Samoa – Politics and government. I. Title.
320.496

Library of Congress Cataloguing in Publication data
Lawson, Stephanie.
Tradition versus democracy in the South Pacific: Fiji, Tonga, and
Western Samoa / Stephanie Lawson.
p. cm. – (Cambridge Asia-Pacific studies)
Includes bibliographical references and index.
1. Democracy – Oceania – Case studies. 2. Fiji – Politics and
government. 3. Tonga – Politics and government. 4. Western Samoa –
Politics and government. I. Title. II. Series.
JC423.L373 1996
320.995–dc20   95–32415

ISBN 978-0-521-49638-4 hardback
ISBN 978-0-521-06281-7 paperback

Contents

List of Maps	vii
List of Tables	vii
Preface	viii
Introduction	1
1. Tradition and Democracy	10
The Idea of Tradition	10
Tradition and Modernity	13
Tradition as Ideology	17
The Problem of Authenticity	20
Democracy	26
2. Constitutional Development, Chiefly Power and the Politics of Tradition in Fiji	37
Introduction	37
The Plural Society	42
Colonization and Indirect Rule	44
The Politics of Land and Indigenous Paramountcy	48
Fijian Sociopolitical Structures	53
The Background to the 1970 Constitution	57
The Rise and Fall of Labour	59
The 1990 Constitution	64
Party Politics and Elections in the Republic	70
Conclusion	75
3. The Monarchy Versus Democracy in the Kingdom of Tonga	79
Introduction	79
The Origins of the Political System	81
The Sociopolitical System	84
European Contact and Christian Conversion	88
Constitutional Development	90
The Reign of Queen Salote Tupou III	96
Transformations Under Tupou IV	98

The Pro-Democracy Movement   101
The Conservative Reaction   109
Conclusion   112

4. Preserving Tradition Through Democratization:
    The Introduction of Universal Suffrage in Western Samoa   117
    Introduction   117
    The Samoan Polity   120
    Samoa Before the Coming of Europeans   126
    From Contact to Colonial Rule   130
    Politics and Law after Independence: The First Twenty Years 138
    The Rise of Political Parties and Party Politics   146
    The Introduction of Universal Suffrage   148
    Fa'aSamoa and *Fa'amatai*   151
    The Village Fono Act of 1990   155
    Conclusion   157

5. Conclusion: Tradition Versus the West   160

Notes   175
Bibliography   206
Index   222

Maps

The South Pacific   xii

Fiji   36

Tonga   78

Western Samoa   116

Tables

1. Composition of the Parliament of Fiji 1970–1987   58

2. Ethnic Composition of Governments 1972–1987   59

3. Composition of Parliament under the New Constitution   65

4 Composition of House of Representatives after 1992 Election
   by Party and Communal Group   71

Preface

Over the last twenty years, a substantial body of literature has emerged on various aspects of cultural traditions in non-Western societies. Many of these works have celebrated the renaissance of indigenous cultural representations in the arts as well as in social life more generally, particularly in the context of post-colonial regeneration. Others, however, have been more critical of this renaissance, at least with respect to some of its important political implications. A number of studies in the latter genre have therefore scrutinized such processes as the 'invention of tradition', especially the way in which contemporary 'neo-traditional' formulations have been used as a means of legitimating certain forms of political authority. On the other hand, it has been pointed out that invention of this kind, as well as that which takes place in many other contexts, is an ineluctable feature of virtually all social and cultural life and that to imply otherwise is to deny the essentially dynamic nature of tradition itself. The present study acknowledges the value of both positions in several important respects. But it also takes a critical approach to contemporary assertions of tradition in the political sphere, not only in terms of the manipulation of cultural traditions for political purposes, but also in relation to the way in which a reified notion of tradition has often been used to mark off the 'West' from the 'non-West'. For this has tended to reproduce the insidious dichotomy erected by earlier generations of Western scholars in the form of 'Orientalism', but which has now been deployed in the service of some indigenous political elites.

These issues are particularly important in the context of discussions about the validity of Western democratic practices, values, and institutions in non-Western polities. In addition, they raise the usual problems of relativism, cultural chauvinism, epistemological imperialism, incommensurability, and so forth. The approach taken in this study, however, is one which defends certain aspects of Western democratic politics, not only against the 'argument from tradition' that implies the inherent unsuitability of Western forms of democracy in non-Western contexts, but also against the crude relativist notion (which often accompanies such arguments) that democracy can mean all things to all people. Most importantly, the present study will pursue this line of argument not simply from a 'Western' standpoint, but also from the perspective of those people in Fiji, Tonga, and Western Samoa who have called for greater democratization in their countries as against the continuing imposition of more authoritarian modes of government.

The choice of three substantial case studies which focus on elite expressions of traditionalism rather than a broader (but more superficial) coverage of the South Pacific region and the entire range of issues concerned with tradition means that the critique is necessarily limited in a number of ways. A comparative analysis which included Melanesia, for example, would have yielded additional perspectives on traditionalist discourses as well as on the experiences and legacies of colonialism that have influenced their development. Within the limits of the case studies, however, I hope to raise issues and problems that scholars concerned with other parts of the Pacific, as well as other parts of the world, will find useful or at least provocative.

Some of the arguments and other material used in this study are based on several earlier publications. Parts of the Introduction, chapter 1, chapter 2, and the Conclusion have appeared in 'The Politics of Tradition: Problems for Legitimacy and Democracy in the South Pacific', *Pacific Studies*, vol. 16, no. 2, June 1993; and in 'Constitutional Change in Contemporary Fiji: The Apparatus of Justification', *Ethnic and Racial Studies*, vol. 15, no. 1, January 1992. Parts of the Conclusion have also appeared in 'Culture, Democracy and Political Conflict Management in Asia and the Pacific: An Agenda for Research', *Pacifica Review*, vol. 6, no. 2, 1994. An earlier version of chapter 3 was presented to the conference of the Pacific Islands Political Studies Association, Rarotonga, Cook Islands, December 1993 and has been published as *Tradition Versus Democracy in the Kingdom of Tonga*, Discussion Paper no. 13, Department of Political and Social Change, Australian National University, 1994. A very much shorter article, based primarily on the Working Paper, has also appeared as 'Democratization in the Kingdom of Tonga: Problems and Prospects for Constitutional Reform' in *Legislative Studies*, vol. 8, no. 2, 1994. I am grateful to the editors of these publications for their permission to reproduce or draw substantially on this material here. Acknowledgement is due also to the Australian Research Council for the award of a Postdoctoral Research Fellowship and a number of grants to support the study. Additional financial and other research support has been provided by the Department of Politics and the Faculty of Arts, University of New England, as well as by the Department of International Relations, the Peace Research Centre and the Department of Political and Social Change, all in the Research School of Pacific and Asian Studies at the Australian National University.

A number of people in Fiji, Tonga, and Western Samoa have also been very helpful in discussing various issues with me or commenting on drafts of the case studies, or both, as well as providing additional material. In this respect I would especially like to thank Netina Galumalemana, Futa Helu, Aiono Fana'afi Le Tagaloa, Le Tagaloa Pita, Debbie Nitis-Mue, Masao Pa'asi, Akilisi Pohiva, Guy Powles, and Tui'atua Tupua Tamasese Efi. I remain grateful to Joeli and Sai Kalou for their generous hospitality in Fiji during earlier periods of fieldwork there which provided the basis for much of the background to chapter 2. Other colleagues have also given time or resources, or both, to assist with the project, and many thanks are due to Alastair Davidson, Donald Denoon, Rory Ewins, Greg Fry, Siosiua Lafitani, Brij Lal, Sione Latukefu, Ron May, Barbara McGrath, Guy Powles, Jan Preston-Stanley, Asofou So'o, Bill Standish, Carol Staples, Sandra Tarte, Robin Ward (who also compiled the index) and Christine Wilson. Finally, many friends have also given generous practical support. To Betts, Kev, Eric, Roland, Carolyn, Andy, Sally, Conall, June, Merilyn, and Fred, my special thanks.

Tradition is the living faith of the dead, traditionalism is the dead faith of the living ... it is traditionalism that gives tradition such a bad name.

Jaroslav Pelikan

I fell victim to the ... illusion that since the past exists only in one's memories and the words that strive vainly to express them, it is possible to create past events simply by saying they occurred.

Saleem Sinai (Salman Rushdie)

Truth is what the chief says, and history is what the highest chief says.

Elizabeth Wood Ellem

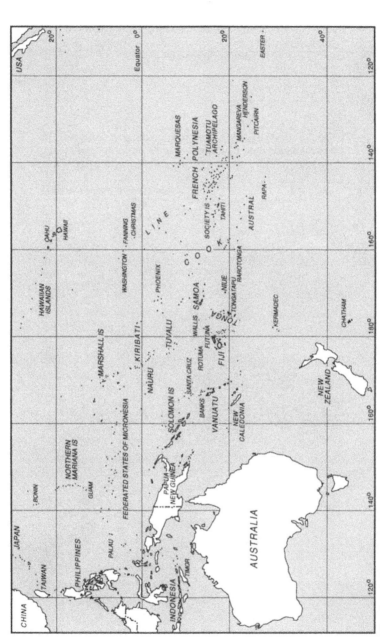

The South Pacific

Introduction

Throughout the Pacific, appeals to a reified concept of tradition, which incorporates such kindred concepts as culture, custom, ethnicity and identity, have been common for some time. These appeals have been used to serve a number of different purposes, depending on the context. Some of the ways in which the concept of tradition has been elevated have been seen as an appropriate and long-overdue response to the negative and racist images of Pacific peoples and their ways of life projected by Western colonialism in the region. One critic of colonialism, and a leading exponent of the romantic approach to traditional culture in the Pacific, stresses the negative aspects of the colonial legacy in these terms:

> Pacific islands religions, economic systems and other key elements of culture were either suppressed or destroyed and replaced by European ones. This naturally led to the loss of self-respect and diminishing confidence among the Pacific Islanders, who thus developed a sense of inferiority while the Europeans increasingly became self-righteous, seeing Pacific islands traditions and cultures as primitive and outmoded ... At constitutional independence ... between 1962 and the 1980s, Pacific Islanders ... began to reassert their eroding cultural identities and to reactivate some aspects of their lost or suppressed traditions and cultures in order to discover themselves once more.[1]

The images evoked by memories of colonialism in the Pacific, and contemporary responses to it, are comparable to the post-colonial experience elsewhere. In Africa, for example, the reassertion of traditional cultural values vis-à-vis Western values has been evident in a range of developments in the social and political spheres. Ironically, much of the currency of tradition with respect to political institutions and practices was due, at least initially, to colonial systems of indirect rule. These

1

systems tended to make a virtue of necessity in establishing political order on the basis of what were perceived to be existing hierarchies or methods of political and social organization. Furthermore, the language and forms of colonial administration, combined with the influence of earlier modes of political sociology and anthropology, and then with schools of thought associated with modernization and development, have combined to produce an image of 'tradition' that is construed conceptually in direct opposition to that which is thought to be 'modern' or 'Western', or both. In the Pacific of the 1980s and 1990s there has been a very noticeable growth of 'traditionalism' through which images of the distant, pre-contact, and definitely non-Western past have been evoked in terms of what Callick describes as the ultimate Pacific cliché – 'Paradise Lost'.[2]

The anti-colonial reaction is said to be part of the ideology behind the 'Pacific Way', a culturally as well as geographically oriented expression of identity that was launched on the international stage by Fiji's former Prime Minister, Ratu Sir Kamisese Mara, during an address to the United Nations General Assembly in 1970.[3] In elaborating the purposes of the slogan, Crocombe, in broad agreement with the quotation reproduced above, says that the colonial experience 'left a common unpleasant taste in the mouths of islanders: a common humiliation, a common feeling of deprivation and exploitation'; experiences which promotion of, and identification with, the 'Pacific Way' can help to ameliorate.[4] Similarly, the notion of a 'Melanesian way' has emerged as another specifically reactive force which, in the words of its foremost proponent, provides a basis for identity such that it is 'unnecessary for [Melanesians] to be perfect Englishmen or Americans'.[5] In an echo of these sentiments, another islander has argued along more specifically political lines that the 'dictates of a Westminster democracy must not be allowed to typecast our lives so as to require us to aspire to become prototype Englishmen'.[6]

These movements share many similarities with the *négritude* movement which in the Caribbean and, later, in Africa, sought to inspire a regeneration of African values to counter the legacy of oppression and racism left by the colonizers.[7] Although Aimé Césaire's original idea of *négritude* represented a wholesale rejection of essentialism, the influence of later figures like Léopold Senghor of Senegal is said to have transformed it into 'a backward-looking idealism, a falsely naturalized, consistent African mentality that tends to reinscribe the categories of a romantic, sometimes racialist European ethnography'.[8] For Senghor, *négritude* was the 'cultural heritage, the values and particularly the spirit of Negro-African civilization'.[9] But it was ahistorical and out of touch with the issues of class struggle that had been central to the anti-colonial movements. Instead, it sought to 'recreate a romanticized African and

Caribbean past which had little basis in social reality'.[10] Said's more general critique of the kind of 'nativism' found in such categories of thinking, exemplified by the idea of *négritude*, is especially pertinent to the present discussion:

> [To] accept nativism is to accept the consequences of imperialism, the racial, religious, and political divisions imposed by imperialism itself. To leave the historical world for the metaphysics of essences like *negritude*, Irishness, Islam, or Catholicism is to abandon history for essentializations that have the power to turn human beings against each other; often this abandonment of the secular world has led to a sort of millenarianism if the movement has a mass base, or it has degenerated into small-scale private craziness, or into an unthinking acceptance of stereotypes, myths, animosities, and traditions encouraged by imperialism. Such programmes are hardly what great resistance movements had imagined as their goals.[11]

The kind of thinking that characterized *négritude* ideas has also pervaded discourses about tradition and cultural identity in the Pacific. Carrier, citing Keesing's characterization of the Pacific rendering of *kastom* as 'an idealized reformulation of indigenous political systems and customary law', suggests that this is a method by which 'alien people' have created an essentialist notion of themselves – 'an ethno-Orientalism'.[12] Elsewhere, Keesing has also suggested that many aspects of these constructions, despite the counter-colonial character of their claims, are themselves derived from Western ideologies. He points to the apparent incorporation of Western structures, categories, and premises of thought in the 'counter-hegemonic' discourse espoused by those who promote idealizations of the pre-contact past.[13] While it is debatable whether these structures, categories, and premises really are peculiarly or uniquely Western, and have no counterpart in indigenous structures,[14] there is little doubt that a reactive process has been at work that has elevated the value of selected elements of cultural traditions 'as symbols of the contrast between those traditions and western culture'.[15]

One reason for drawing this out is to focus attention on the rather obvious dichotomy between 'traditional' and 'Western' ways which is produced in this process and to stress the point that Western values, practices, and institutions are very often a major focus of traditionalist criticisms. But on closer inspection we find that this too can be a very selective process, for not all Western values, institutions, and so forth are targeted in this way. As with cultural traditions themselves, only certain elements of Western ways are subjected to traditionalist critique. Further, and most importantly, there is more than one ideological component of such constructs as 'the Pacific Way' – the liberating ideas and ideals associated with the movement comprise but one aspect. Just as the search for an authentically African mode of politics resulted in the production of an ideology justifying the authoritarian one-party state in Africa,[16] so too has 'the Pacific Way' been employed at times as an instrument of social and political control by indigenous elites. This becomes evident when we examine more closely the positions occupied by the major proponents of the 'return to tradition' via 'the Pacific Way' – a trend which draws on the past as a source of legitimate political norms for the present and the future. These people have also frequently condemned Western democracy as an unsuitable form of political rule in the South Pacific, especially vis-à-vis pre-existing political systems. It is in this sense that 'tradition' is ranged against 'democracy' in a contest for conceptual or ideological supremacy.

One commentator notes that Mara's articulation of 'the Pacific Way' places a strong emphasis on the virtues of stability, tradition, and by implication, on the value of 'traditional' chiefly rule.[17] And despite much of the rhetoric against colonialism from South Pacific political elites, these same elites have been said not only to lead a life style that mimics that of their former colonial rulers, but also to 'exploit their own people, sometimes even worse than their colonial masters before them'.[18] Another critic has noted the extent to which the 'exaggerated mystique of custom' has been manipulated in a clearly instrumental manner as a means of legitimizing the aspirations and interests of ruling elites. He adds that many Pacific Islanders know this full well, and are not necessarily 'blinded by their own symbolism and rhetoric'. But the people who suffer most from the 'romantic approach' to tradition are the ordinary people of the region.[19]

In one of the most incisive attacks on the South Pacific's privileged classes, Hau'ofa has also identified the 'Pacific Way' as an elitist regional identity, sustained by various regional institutions and bureaucracies, which serve as something of a club for the region's political leaders. This elite has itself become increasingly homogenized as a distinct class in its own right. At the same time, its members have become distanced from their own indigenous cultures as well as from the ordinary people of the islands whom they purport to represent:

> As part of the process of integration and the emergence of the new society, the ruling classes of the South Pacific are increasingly culturally homogeneous. They speak the same language, which is English ... they share the same ideologies and the same material life-styles, admittedly with local variations due to physical environment and original cultural factors, but the similarities are much more numerous than the differences ...

> It is the privileged who can afford to tell the poor to preserve their traditions. But their perceptions of which traits of traditional culture to preserve are increasingly divergent from those of the poor, because in the final analysis it is

the poor who have to live out the traditional culture; the privileged can merely talk about it, and they are in a position to be selective about what traits they use or more correctly urge others to observe; and this is seen increasingly by the poor as part of the ploy by the privileged to secure greater advantages for themselves.[20]

Hau'ofa draws particular attention to parts of Polynesia where, under aristocratic rulers and certain Christian church traditions, ordinary people are at once urged to be more innovative and entrepreneurial so as to pursue 'development' strategies, while they are also expected to continue to live under the 'dead weight' of other traditions. These traditions are urged on the poor to maintain social stability; 'that is, in order to secure the privileges that [the elite] have gained, not so much as from their involvement in traditional activities, as from their privileged access to resources in the regional economy'. In this situation, Hau'ofa concludes, 'traditions are used by the ruling classes to enforce the new order'.[21]

It will be seen during the course of this study that the traditionalist emphasis on chiefly rule in Fiji, on the monarchy and aristocracy in Tonga and, to a lesser extent, on the *matai* system in Western Samoa – far from promoting a new kind of psychological liberation in the post-colonial era – can be criticized on many of the grounds identified above. It will be argued that the concept of tradition is one of the most important components of an ideological arsenal which has been used to counter the development of more democratic norms of political conduct and organization – norms that threaten the status of many elites in the region. In summary, then, one of the major purposes of the analysis is to demonstrate that the idea of tradition has been deployed not so much in defence of highly prized aspects of unique cultural identities, but in defence of elite power and privilege against growing demands for accountability in government as well as more extensive opportunities for participation by those without traditionally derived political or social status.

It is essential to any critical study of tradition in a political context that the motivations of those who invoke tradition are scrutinized closely. And, although some may grant a privileged status to 'insider' accounts of these issues, there is no reason to believe that these should be immune from external critiques, or that there is only one 'inside' view.[22] Furthermore, although 'tradition' and 'modernity' are central components of some of the most important contemporary political discourses, this does not mean, as Robertson and Tamanisau point out, that this should be equated with primacy. This can lead to the construction of the two components as absolute categories occupying the opposing poles of a rigid dichotomy.[23] This dichotomy poses further questions concerning the problem of cultural relativism. In the past, the notion of cultural relativism was exceptionally valuable in countering racist ideas. It implied that all cultures should be evaluated, not according to the arbitrary values and standards of a single dominant culture (such as our own), but in relation to each culture's own historical and social context.[24] In the present context, however, it poses considerable problems for attempts to criticize or evaluate anything that is different from, or outside, the commentator's own cultural milieu. In addition, it tends to reinscribe the essentialist framework.

This analysis takes the position that strong versions of the relativist argument lead to a conceptual as well as an ethical void in which virtually nothing of any critical value can be said. The rejection of relativism, however, does not entail adopting the equally untenable position of absolute universalism, especially with respect to political forms (including Western models of democracy). But it does entail some value judgements and in this respect I can only agree with the view that the true worth of study in the humanities or the social sciences is that it equips people to make value judgements, not to avoid them.[25] This is neither a popular nor a 'safe' position, but it will be defended not simply from the perspective of an 'external' supporter of democratic values, but also from the perspective of those in Fiji, Tonga, and Western Samoa who do not necessarily accept the eternal legitimacy of so-called natural indigenous hierarchies and who have provided the major internal impetus for movements promoting democratization. It is also undertaken in the spirit of criticism now promoted by a growing number of South Pacific writers, many of whom come from the most rigidly authoritarian and hierarchical society in the region – Tonga. The origins of this school of thought in Tonga will be discussed in more detail later, but it is worth noting here some of the broader implications of its project.

The approach of this new generation of indigenous critics is completely different from that of the proponents of the *négritude* style of anti-colonial critique and their successors. Although it affirms the worth of various aspects of indigenous culture, it nonetheless rejects all temptations to romanticization, and takes criticism of indigenous sociopolitical structures as a starting point for constructing a more positive approach to social, political, and economic problems. The leading exponent of this school in Tonga has said:

I fault Pacific cultures most harshly for not having criticism as part of their social morality. I have always maintained that criticism is a cornerstone of educational morality. And I take freedom, the openness, the toleration of, and the publicity of criticism and controversy to be the crowning achievement of a society's sociopolitical development.[26]

In the context of Tongan society, another commentator has mounted a critique of traditional socialization with respect to its almost complete suppression of the critical faculty in individuals, as well as its implications for authoritarian domination. He points out, first, that there is no equivalent of the European intellectual tradition in Tonga, and that the process of learning before the introduction of Western education is more correctly termed a socialization process which was highly authoritative, due to the rigid stratification of society.

> Consequently, the critical faculty of Tongan minds was undeveloped and enclosed. If it did exist, it did so quietly. The nature of Tongan society greatly contributed to this uncritical mindset of its members. Life without criticism is the life of a servant or slave. In Tonga a critical stance was suppressed and treated as unacceptable, if not rude. However, it can be said that this was an effective form of social control. Here the concept of *faka'apa'apa* [respect] is normally the justification, or in plain terms the cover-ups, given for authoritarian control ... This authoritarianism marks the difference between our intellectual tradition and the European one.[27]

The same commentator takes issue with representations of the past through oral histories in terms of their propensity, at least in the hands of authoritative elites, to justify present political structures. He says that these oral traditions have become powerful ideologies which have been used, for example, to justify past events such as 'brave Tongan chiefs and warriors invading other islands and subsequently ruling them' as well as 'the rise of the Tu'i Tonga and other kingly lineages'. Above all, their purpose is to fortify the prevailing sociopolitical structure and to maintain the status quo. In this respect, he concludes, most Tongans 'who make historical statements are more likely to be stating political rather than historical facts'.[28] As we shall see, much the same can be said about representations of the Fijian and Samoan pasts. It should be added, however, that although these remarks are accurate in many respects, they nonetheless tend to err in the direction of romanticizing (and over-generalizing) European intellectual thought. Intolerance and authoritarianism has long flourished in the West, and European histories are as much disposed towards stating political rather than historical facts as any others.

In considering the 'politics of tradition', particularly in relation to pressures for democratization, it is necessary to examine closely some basic ideas about tradition and traditionalism, and how these relate to political conservatism. The distinction between tradition and traditionalism is especially important because critiques of traditionalism can all too easily give rise to the impression that tradition per se is the target. It is also important to understand the extent to which tradition is an ineluctable element of all social life, and that it is not simply a residual, inert, and 'primitive' category of belief and behaviour. The first chapter, then, considers the notion of tradition and how it has often been misconstrued as an exclusive property of non-Western societies. This discussion also seeks to emphasize a number of features which are common, at least historically, to both Western and non-Western social and political contexts, but which are often overlooked or implicitly denied in the treatment of Western and non-Western polities, especially when it comes to discussions of the development of democracy in the West. The final section of chapter 1 raises some central concerns which are inevitably engaged in discussions of democracy in non-Western contexts, particularly the problems of relativism – both cultural and conceptual – and the difficulties that these pose for identifying the basic features of democratic political rule.

The three case studies outline some fundamental aspects of the history and sociopolitical traditions of Fiji, Tonga, and Western Samoa respectively, as well as their varying experiences with European imperialism. Although Tonga was never formally colonized, this latter aspect is as important for understanding Tonga's political development as it is for Fiji and Western Samoa. The historical accounts of the pre-contact period need to be understood as representing a synthesis of orthodox versions that are not necessarily accurate reflections of social or political 'realities'. There are no written records of earlier eras and the stories which survive as oral history, and which now make up a substantial part of 'official' histories, represent only very partial accounts. At the same time, I do not want to imply that written histories provide a record of indisputable 'facts'. In whatever genre histories are presented, the search for absolute historical truth 'is just as impossible as seeing into the future'. Furthermore, the narrative voice of the past is in many ways nothing more than the voice of the present, 'grafted onto the pieces of the historical record'.[29] Whether or not the accounts presented here are 'real' histories, however, they are nonetheless broadly accepted by members of the societies concerned as legitimate sources of historical, cultural, and political understanding. They therefore provide the necessary background for the discussion of certain political developments in each of the countries, especially as these relate to contemporary issues involving the juxtaposition of tradition and democracy.

In Fiji, the focus is concerned largely with the processes surrounding constitutional development and the role of the traditionalist emphasis on chiefly legitimacy, especially in a plural society. In Tonga, the rise of the Pro-Democracy Movement is considered against the background of an exceptionally conservative political order that has so far resisted all pressures for reform. Unlike Fiji and Tonga, however, Western Samoa has proceeded further along the path to democratization, although certain restrictions on political participation remain and are unlikely to be removed in the foreseeable future. Moreover, the move to universal suffrage in Western Samoa can in some ways be seen, not as a rejection of tradition in favour of more democratic norms, but as a means of preserving important aspects of traditional culture. In the light of the three case studies, the concluding section reconsiders the issues raised in the initial discussion of tradition and democracy. Athough some factors relating to external influences will be raised, the argument stresses the point that pressures favouring democratization in each of the countries are not so much imposed from outside, but come most forcefully from within the societies concerned.

CHAPTER 1

Tradition and Democracy

The Idea of Tradition

Although Pacific Island nations have vernacular expressions which broadly encapsulate the idea of a unique body of cultural traditions, the word 'tradition' (together with 'custom') is most commonly used, especially by political elites. We shall therefore explore the idea of tradition initially in terms of its anglophone understanding. The Latin root of the English word 'tradition' denotes several possible meanings, but its general understanding in contemporary English usage is related to processes involving the passing on of knowledge and doctrine from one generation to the next. Although this understanding carries no necessary normative force, it is nonetheless open to conveying, at the same time, a strong commitment to the idea that what has been transmitted from the past to the present is worthy of respect, and enjoins a duty of observance on the present generation.[1] Similarly, it has been suggested that a tradition of belief contains an inherently normative component which functions to elicit almost automatic affirmation of whatever state of affairs is apparently produced or endorsed by the tradition.[2] This implies that whatever has been received from the past is to be valued in the present, as well as carried forward by the generation which follows. Krygier has elaborated these ideas in the context of three essential characteristics which he ascribes to tradition. First, the contents of a tradition are imbued with a certain 'pastness' – or at least its participants believe that the origins of the tradition lie deep in the past. Second, there must be a belief that the presence of the past is authoritative in contemporary life. Third, the process by which the contents of a tradition are carried through time is understood as continuous. In other words, the norms, values and practices which make

10

up a tradition are not just resurrected from a past that is discontinuous with the present. It is further suggested that the assimilation of a 'living tradition' in this way is often largely unconscious – it is simply absorbed as a natural component of the world. Because of this, it may have a particularly powerful and pervasive presence.[3]

The concept of tradition is linked closely to culture and, in turn, to ideas about identity. The extension of tradition through culture and identity works to define a group as a political entity which may then claim certain privileges vis-à-vis other groups, including a pre-eminent political status and superior entitlements to resources. Some of the most obvious contemporary manifestations of politicized cultural identities are to be found in the ethnonationalist struggles of eastern Europe and the former USSR, but the phenomenon is also clearly evident in the assertion of Fijian nationalism as against the political aspirations of Fiji Indians. At the same time, Fijian 'tradition' is asserted as the essential component of an authentic Fijian identity which is often expressed strongly in opposition to Western political norms and values, and especially Western understandings of democratic politics. The situation in Tonga and Western Samoa differs in that there are no significant non-indigenous communities against which ideas about tradition, culture, and political identity can be affirmed. Nonetheless, the value of indigenous tradition and culture in these places has been asserted vigorously against the incursion of Western political values. This has occurred largely in the context of internal pressures for democratization which have gathered considerable momentum in recent years.

Since it is imbued with a strong normative force, the idea of tradition has long been recognized as an important source of political authority, and therefore of legitimacy. Despite the assumptions implicit in much of the literature that tradition is related almost exclusively to the under-developed world, it applies to the West no less than other parts of the globe. So just as anthropologists now recognize that all people and all communities are equally 'cultured',[4] so it must be acknowledged that 'the West' (however defined) is equally 'traditional'.[5] The idea of tradition is, in fact, an important part of the West's classical heritage of democratic thought. At the end of the sixth century BC, when the people of the Athenian *polis* adopted the word *nomos* (custom) to denote the law,[6] they demonstrated explicitly that their society was one in which the precepts of living traditions and patterns of customary social behaviour would play an important part in determining the basis of legal order and authority in the *polis*. This hardly precluded innovation and experimentation in political life – as the subsequent development of Athenian democracy in the following century so clearly attests.

As with the 'Pacific Way', however, there was another side to this development, for although the adoption of *nomos* was originally seen as a charter of freedom from the arbitrary rule of despotism, it came to be recognized as another possible type of tyranny – 'a series of customs and conventions imposed upon [people] who might not always wish to conform to them'.[7] Despite its restrictive capabilities, *nomos* nonetheless remained a largely depersonalized instrument of social control. This stands in contrast with many contemporary expressions of tradition as a legitimating force in the South Pacific, and especially in the three case studies considered here. In Fiji, Tonga and Western Samoa, there is a much stronger personalized element in the assertion of tradition since its most authoritative bearers are those whose status is largely (although not exclusively) ascribed. In other words, chiefly leaders in these places are generally held to represent the very embodiment of tradition, and the authority that they hold by virtue of their chiefly status is therefore attached firmly to personal status. Since a substantial part of the history of democratic development in the West has been about depersonalizing political power, and vesting it in impersonal institutions, the contrast is significant.

This brings us to one of the main concerns of the present discussion, and that is the extent to which the powerful symbolic force of a reified notion of tradition can be used, not just as an instrument of psychological liberation in the post-colonial context described earlier, but also as a means of subordinating the interests of ordinary people to those who occupy positions of high office by virtue of a traditional status system. This insight is not original, and there is now a substantial body of literature on the contemporary Pacific devoted to analyzing the manipulation of tradition by indigenous elites in ways that enhance their own legitimacy by sanctifying the political order to which they owe their privilege.[8] Analyses of the politics of tradition in Africa have produced almost identical findings,[9] while in at least one Asian country, political elites have attempted to resurrect Confucian political ethics in order to fortify their position at the expense of opposition groups.[10] Moreover, although indigenous elites in the South Pacific very often exhort the ordinary people to observe traditional practices, their own lifestyle is far from 'traditional'. Instead, many of these elites are themselves thoroughly Westernized, particularly with respect to education, living standards, and the ability to pursue commercial interests. Members of the Tongan nobility, for example, have been targeted for strong criticism by the Pro-Democracy Movement because of the enormous gulf that separates most of them from ordinary Tongans in the way they live, not to mention the amount of time they spend overseas.

It must also be stressed, however, that the use of tradition as a legitimating tool in politics is scarcely confined to non-Western cultures.

Indeed, one of the major points of this study will be to show that attempts to divide the West from the non-West, in this respect as in many others, are not only conceptually barren, but quite misleading in terms of ideas about incommensurability. It is especially important in addressing those arguments which deny the appropriateness of democracy in non-Western contexts because of its 'alien' properties. These issues are explored in more detail later. For the moment it is sufficient to note that the political use of the past as a legitimating device has been evident in practically all civilizations for which written records survive. Citing the propensity for maintaining genealogical records by ruling elites from antiquity to the present, Plumb emphasizes the extent to which the 'acquisition of the past by the ruling classes' and the 'exclusion of the mass' from its sanctifying prestige and charisma, has been widespread throughout recorded time.[11] Furthermore, the propensity to legitimate present political claims by fabricating suitable traditions is scarcely confined to relatively 'new' nations. Melman's study of the 'Anglo-Saxon tradition' highlights the fact that even in some of the oldest national communities, this process has been evident in the definition and redefinition of identity and of those who are entitled to claim membership in the group.[12] This indicates, among other things, that the simplistic portrayal of tradition as the logical antithesis of modernity and 'Westernity' is quite wrong, an issue addressed in the next section.

Tradition and Modernity

In post-Enlightenment thought, Weber's influential formulation of three major categories of authority and legitimacy, namely, traditional, charismatic, and legal–rational, brought about a significant change in the perception of 'tradition'. The manner in which Weber contrasted traditional authority with that derived from legal–rational sources relegated it to the realm of the intrinsically 'irrational' and placed it in direct opposition to ideas about 'modernization'.[13] Thus writers like Walzer have drawn explicitly on Weber in describing as 'traditional' the Western medieval worldview of political order which was conceived as hierarchical, organic, and unchanging. This order was also imbued with an emphasis on personal and particularistic relations which undermined any sort of 'independent political aspiration or initiative'.[14] This accords with general descriptions of feudal structures in which ideas about equality and legal rights were entirely absent and which embodied instead strictly personal and hierarchical notions of loyalty and duty.[15] In commenting on Walzer's position, Pocock points out that the conceptualization of 'traditional society' in this way – as the inert and pre-political antithesis of 'modernization' – is bound to dichotomize our thinking on the subject, no matter how carefully we try to refine it.[16] Pocock, however, is by no means prepared to defend a stance on political order and change that could be described, in Weber's sense, as 'traditionalist'. In terms of democratic or republican politics, he emphasizes that citizens (as opposed to subjects) are, virtually by definition, involved continuously in the process of public decision-making and must therefore acquire the cognitive capacity to go beyond the precepts of hierarchy and tradition.[17]

We can see that writers like Pocock, while critical of the traditional/ modern dichotomization, are no more prepared to give normative endorsement to a society which lives only by these precepts than Walzer is to his version of 'traditional society'. Rather (and to take the objection to Weber's account to its logical conclusion), it is the notion that whatever is 'traditional' in social and political life is, in some empirical as well as normative sense, opposed antithetically to something we call 'modern', that invites criticism. For this antithetical treatment of the concepts has given rise, inter alia, to the entirely mistaken idea that while everything that comes under the rubric of 'modern' is, practically by definition, 'rational', so everything that can be categorized as 'traditional' is 'irrational' or at best non-rational. More generally, the dichotomization of tradition and modernity has given an implicit positive endorsement to almost any kind of innovation on one hand, while on the other it automatically ascribes 'a negative connotation of backwardness and unthinking conservatism' to tradition.[18] In a similar vein, Wilson draws attention to the way in which the dichotomization has been rigidly empiricized so as to present an undialectical image of two 'sides' of the world – one standing for the rational, innovative West, and the other for the primitive, traditional Third World.[19] Furthermore, he points out that terms such as 'tradition' and 'the primitive' form the key concepts associated with our conceptualization of 'otherness' and 'the other'.[20] It is against this conceptualization that Said's passionate condemnation of Orientalism is directed.[21]

The emergence of studies inspired by the Orientalist critique has led to a great deal of academic introspection in the West, especially in the discipline of anthropology which has been labelled as little more than 'an academic accessory of British imperialism',[22] although this probably applies as readily to French imperialism and its own school of anthropology. In any case, it is a discipline which has provided the means by which Westerners have studied non-Westerners.[23] Citing some of Said's observations, Carrier notes that Orientalism was the means by which the Orient became essentialized, 'as eternally manifesting certain attributes simply because it was the Orient'. Furthermore, since this ontological essence was timeless, 'the past and the present collapse into each other'.[24] In response to Said's general critique, however, Carrier goes on to suggest that, regardless of the predisposition that may lead anthropologists to study alien societies, these societies need not be represented in an essentialist manner that 'heightens the sense of exotic difference and radical separation'.[25] It should also be recognized that Western anthropologists and other scholars are not the only ones who have proposed radical differences between Western and non-Western societies. This tendency can now be observed in the rhetoric of indigenous elites who speak in terms which highlight cultural difference and which seek to place Western political forms, and especially democracy, in opposition to their own 'natural' traditional forms. As Babadzan observes, the realm of custom 'is opposed in such an absolute way to the Western world that both worlds seem to have nothing in common'.[26]

Many writers have sought to expose the false or at least misleading nature of the tradition/modernity dichotomy and, especially, to demonstrate that neither tradition itself, nor its function as a source of authority and legitimacy, is necessarily at odds with rational or reasoned processes. Friedrich, for example, has argued that the very bases of reasoning and rational argument are grounded largely in tradition.[27] Similarly, Popper has shown in his work on scientific method that traditions, like scientific theories, are the means 'by which we try to bring some order into the chaos in which we live so as to make it rationally predictable'.[28] In another context, Jarvie has demonstrated that cargo cults can be understood as rational attempts, within their frame of reference, to achieve their particular aims.[29] And as McDonald and Pettit point out, the famous Hopi rain dances although 'manifestly ineffective in bringing about precipitation' may nonetheless function 'rationally' to consolidate group identity and promote social activity.[30] On a different level altogether, it is clearly evident that the program of rationalization envisaged by the modernization school of development studies for the now not-so-new states of Africa and Asia has been spectacularly unsuccessful in many vital respects.[31] Critics of enlightenment progressivism, and its implications for the antithetical treatment of traditionality on the one hand and rationality and scientific knowledge on the other, have also pointed to the dogmatism that can imbue the latter:

> Traditionality no more requires intolerance and dogmatism than do scientism, rationalism and secularism. In the twentieth century the most destructive acts of intolerance have been committed by revolutionary regimes, the progressivist revolutionaries being scarcely less intolerant than the reactionary ones. Dogmas are no less common among progressivists than they are among those who would give the benefit of the doubt to tradition.[32]

The consignment of all that is 'traditional' to the realm of the irrational has also, and in some ways deservedly, attracted the most scathing criticism and condemnation from proponents of conservative political philosophy. Oakeshott, for example, describes the rationalist as 'the enemy of authority, of prejudice, of the merely traditional, customary or habitual',[33] who commits the facile error of 'identifying the customary and traditional with the changeless'.[34] That this latter view had a profound impact on the way in which earlier schools of anthropology mistakenly viewed their subject societies, and identified tradition with 'fixism', can scarcely be doubted. So-called traditional societies were not necessarily 'prisoners of the past' and obviously had their own dynamics of change.[35]

Oakeshott's attack on rationalism in politics of course echoes Edmund Burke's classic dicta on the evils of radicalism and the more innovative styles of politics generated by the ideas of the Enlightenment which he so deeply abhorred. For Burke, tradition was to be exalted both politically and epistemologically as the more reliable embodiment of knowledge and practice, representing as it did the progressive experience of the species and the wisdom of the ages.[36] But innovative thinking and political action has never required abandonment of 'the partnership between present and past'. It merely requires that we recognize tradition, or any particular tradition, as something that is not immutable or immune from criticism or change. Quite apart from this, it is ridiculous to suppose that we can completely escape the past or free ourselves from its formative influences – even if it was thought desirable. Popper puts this point clearly.

[W]e could not live in the social world, did it not contain a considerable amount of order, a great number of regularities to which we can adjust ourselves. The mere existence of these regularities is perhaps more important than their peculiar merits or demerits. They are needed as regularities and therefore handed on as traditions, whether or not they are in other respects rational or necessary or good or beautiful or what you will. There is a need for tradition in social life.[37]

Popper goes on to suggest that in dealing with tradition, two main attitudes are possible. The first is simply to accept it uncritically – which often means that there is little or no awareness associated with such acceptance.[38] This is close to what some anthropologists might describe as 'simply living' a culture or way of life. The second attitude is critically aware, not only that something is a tradition but that it is subject to change. This may result in acceptance, rejection, or compromise, but at the very least it is thought about consciously. Accordingly, it is only when this level of critical awareness is reached that we are able to free ourselves from the taboos of a tradition, even if we can never entirely loosen its more generally encompassing bonds.[39] But it is at this point also that it becomes possible to reify, objectify, invent, or consciously construct tradition, to appeal to tradition, and to use the concept of tradition as a political legitimator. It is at this point, then, that a doctrine of 'traditionalism' can emerge and take on an explicitly ideological character that lends itself readily to instrumental manipulation. Rather than ameliorating or expunging the taboos of tradition, it can not only reinforce them, but can also create new ones.

Tradition as Ideology

We have seen that tradition exhorts its participants to an attitude of reverence and duty towards the practices and values that have been transmitted from the past. Where the imperatives of a body of tradition enjoin those who 'belong' to it to follow its dictates, the idea of tradition can acquire a status akin to that of a body of law. And where this acts to provide normative support for established political authority, tradition emerges as a vital adjunct to political conservatism. For it is implicit in the ideological rendering of tradition that established institutions are seen, not as a potentially alterable set of human constructions, but as a set of natural forms which command the automatic and uncritical allegiance of those who are implicated in them.[40] Of course, this is only one element of a larger ideological construct, for as Douglas points out, an ideology provides more than just a pattern for action. It also brings together evaluative, interpretive, and instrumental dimensions. Furthermore, it provides 'alternative strategies to be implemented selectively in action contexts and in the manipulation, negotiation and creation of social reality'.[41]

Traditionalist political ideology seeks to accommodate these wider dimensions primarily by preserving what is assumed to be a time-honoured structure of authority. This brings us back to the point that the authority structure, by virtue of its alleged antiquity, can be portrayed as the 'natural' locus of political power. This was a key element in much of the romantic backlash which followed the eighteenth-century revolution in European political thought, and which has been a persistent feature of Western conservative ideology. This is worth elaborating briefly because it illuminates some aspects of commensurability between important elements of Western political thought and those that pervade contemporary expressions of traditionalism in the South Pacific. In other words, although the latter are often constructed in diametric opposition to the West, they share much in common with conservative Western political thought.

Even before the age of revolution in Europe, organic theories of the state which assimilated established political structures to a pattern of order revealed in the so-called natural world were proposed in support of such institutions as absolute monarchy. Furthermore, this naturalistic pattern of order was grounded in the conception of a hierarchically arranged universe of which a properly integrated and unified society was a clear manifestation.[42] As we have seen, this was also a feature of European feudal arrangements. Similarly, it has been said that Polynesian mythologies interpreted 'the human order as a fixed projection of the natural order by which it is engendered'.[43] One implication to be drawn from these beliefs, at least in the European context, was that a normative pattern of political rule was supplied by the model of creation 'from which humankind could in no way depart', and this included the apparently universal pattern of human inequality in social, economic, and political life.[44] In addition, the descending thesis of government entailed in the idea of an immutable hierarchical order left those under the authority of the monarch with little choice except to obey the edicts issued from above, and to pass on the duty of obedience to those following after.[45]

Ullmann notes that the twin symbols of 'throne' and altar' came to express the established form of government.[46] Furthermore, they represented the mutual reinforcement of secular and ecclesiastical authority in a period that was beginning to grasp the more democratic implications of the ascending thesis of government, whereby legitimate political authority was seen as emanating from the masses below rather than being imposed from on high. This thesis, embodying such radical notions as popular sovereignty, was recognized as the real threat to the established order which reacted to protect its privilege by all means available. Tradition was on its side, and its legitimating symbols were employed to the fullest. Ullmann refers to the ceremonial attached to established institutions in the fifteenth century, such as 'the uninterrupted sequence of royal coronations, with their strong emphasis on the divine derivation of royal power ... every prayer text, symbol, gesture was highly charged with theocratic elements'.[47] Even with the weight of tradition behind the established order, however, arguments based on the right of people to oppose unjust political authority continued to gain ground.

The doctrine of the divine right of kings that developed in the sixteenth century, explicitly in opposition to the idea of popular rights, sought to reinforce the monarch as an object of unquestioned loyalty and obedience. The context of religious wars and civil unrest at this time, however, gave new meaning to expressions of popular resistance – especially to those in positions of privilege who came under threat. The idea of a popular right to resist was countered, through the doctrine of divine right, by a stronger version of the notion that subjects owe a duty of passive obedience to their rulers. Sabine shows how the old traditions emanating from religious beliefs were infused with new power at this time:

> The ancient phrases, almost meaningless in themselves, such as that kings are the vicars of God, thus got a new meaning: rebellion even in the cause of religion is sacrilege. The duty of passive obedience ... was sharpened by investing the king with a special sanctity.
>
> The divine right of kings in this new form was essentially a popular theory. It never received, indeed it was incapable of receiving, a philosophical formulation. But if the importance of a political doctrine depends partly on the number who hold it, the theory compares favourably with any political idea that ever existed, for it was believed with religious intensity by [people] of all social ranks and all forms of theological belief.[48]

It is fruitful to compare these broad developments with justifications for the duty of deference and submission owed to traditional leaders in the chiefly societies of the South Pacific, although these receive more detailed attention in the case studies. The power and authority of chiefly leaders in Fiji, Tonga, and Western Samoa, as well as the obedience enjoined on those below them, are also derived to some extent from normative concepts associated with divine authority. In describing (and defending) the traditional role of Fijian chiefs, for example, Ravuvu states that the explicit model for chiefs derives directly from divine sources and that power is ascribed only to those close to that source, while the 'relative powerlessness of others is clear by implication'.[49] In the contemporary context, the Christian god has of course largely supplanted the old gods of Fiji, but the nature of divinely sanctioned political authority remains much the same: 'For there is no authority except from God, and those [governing authorities] that exist have been instituted by God'.[50] The same arguments pervade conservative responses to calls for more democratic political practices in Western Samoa and Tonga. In the former, it is said that *matai* (chiefs) receive their titles from God,[51] while in Tonga the view persists that members of the ruling elite are 'divinely pre-conditioned' as social and political leaders.[52] Thus whatever other aspects of tradition are held up as unique components of cultural and political identity in opposition to 'the West', it is clear that some of the justifications used to support them have a counterpart in important historic aspects of European political thought linking secular political authority to a divine source.

To return again briefly to Europe, Edmund Burke, and others of his contemporaries (writing in the wake of the French Revolution and the body of Enlightenment thinking that had inspired the overthrow of the existing order), propounded a fresh corpus of conservative doctrine that stressed the extent to which political legitimacy and authority was a product of history and tradition. Indeed, Burke's view emphasized the character of national constitutions in terms that located their validity, not in the 'rationally' constructed documents favoured by disciples of the Enlightenment, but in the unique historical development of a particular society and its distinctive institutions. Similarly, Russian writers like Dostoevsky came to believe that their country had an 'historic, unalterable and "sacred" constitution' – thereby contributing, incidentally, to a lasting antipathy to Western values in Russia.[53]

Once again, there is little to distinguish these views from those of some contemporary proponents of particularistic identities in the South Pacific. The major proponent of the 'Melanesian Way', for example, has decried the estrangement and alienation produced by the intrusion of Western values and has urged as a remedy the establishment of 'a philosophical base, founded upon our ancient virtues' without which Melanesians 'stand to perish as a people of unique quality, character and dynamism'.[54] In Vanuatu, these sentiments have been echoed by a former head of state who, invoking the standard Western cliché, speaks of 'the boy from paradise' who wants 'his own identity' and 'his own cultural and traditional heritage' and, further, that '[t]he *European Way* is not the *Pacific and Melanesian Way*'.[55] In Fiji, the new constitutional arrangements, which are clearly contrary to democratic norms, are said to have been implemented in order 'to protect the proud traditions that are the core and essence of being a Fijian'.[56] In Western Samoa, cultural nationalism is expressed through the institutions of *fa'aSamoa* which are 'defended and perpetuated on the grounds that they are part of an ancient, authentic, indigenous Samoan cultural tradition'.[57] And in Tonga, the monarchy and aristocracy are also defended as constituting the essence of *anga faka Tonga* – the Tongan way – even though the institutions that sustain them are derived substantially from Western sources.[58] This latter point raises the issue of 'the invention of tradition' and ideas about cultural authenticity (and inauthenticity) that have dominated much of the debate about the politics of tradition in the South Pacific. This is especially relevant to the ideological deployment of traditionalism in opposition to Western forms of democracy, for notions of authenticity add considerable strength to its normative force.

The Problem of Authenticity

It is clear from the earlier discussion that the purpose of the present study is not to mount an attack on tradition per se, but to make a critical distinction between this and what Friedrich calls 'the normative theory of the importance of tradition'[59] that underscores the ideological and instrumental functions that the concept can serve. These are scarcely novel themes – Friedrich's study was published more than twenty years ago. At much the same time, Eisenstadt located the ideological rendering of tradition in the context of transitions to modernity in which he saw questions of authenticity or 'true traditions' arising frequently as adequate legitimators were sought for new patterns of social and political behaviour.

> As a reaction to the possibilities of erosion, the tendency known as 'traditionalism' can develop, preparing the soil for potential dichotomy between 'tradition' and 'traditionalism'. Traditionalism is not to be confused with a 'simple' or 'natural' upkeep of a given tradition. Rather, it denotes an ideological mode and stance oriented against the new symbols; it espouses certain parts of the older tradition as the only legitimate symbols of the traditional order and upholds them against 'new' trends. Through opposing these trends, the 'traditionalist' attitudes tend towards formalization on both the symbolic and organizational levels.[60]

Colson noted several years later that in colonial Africa anthropologists had found 'traditional' rules 'being invented on the spot to legitimate a course of action desired by the very realistic manipulators of the local scene'.[61] The context in which this took place is especially interesting, for the success of many of these appeals to tradition was apparently due largely to the resonance they struck with the British style of conservative thought that pervaded the colonial service.

> An appeal to tradition against impinging authority, of course, is effective only if those in authority are prepared to recognize the validity of other ways of life. It was a highly effective device in British colonies which were administered by officials who came from a country with a long tradition of common law, a respect for inherited position, and dominated by a Burkean belief in gradualism. It had less force in the French colonies. It had almost none in the United States with its policy of cultural assimilation where effective power was in the hands of the upholders of a particular tradition to which others were expected to conform. In Africa, therefore, we find local communities legislating under the guise of an appeal to tradition and also keeping at bay attempts to foist new programs upon them by arguments that the programs were alien to their traditions.[62]

Nearly a decade later, Keesing and Tonkinson edited a special issue of the journal *Mankind* on *Reinventing Traditional Culture: The Politics of Kastom in Island Melanesia*,[63] and Hobsbawm and Ranger published their provocative collection of essays on the invention of tradition.[64] Like Colson, Ranger found that in colonial Africa, invented traditions often received official endorsement because the colonizers thought that they were respecting age-old African customary practices.[65] But the colonizers

went further by introducing something that was clearly not in accordance
with traditional practice – the rigid codification of what were assumed
to be customary laws, land-rights, and political structures. The consequences were far-reaching.

> Codified tradition inevitably hardened in a way that advantaged the vested
> interests in possession at the time of its codification. Codified and reified
> custom was manipulated by such vested interests as a means of asserting or
> increasing control … Paramount chiefs and ruling aristocracies … appealed
> to 'tradition' in order to maintain or extend their control over their subjects.[66]

In some recent studies, the notion that 'invented traditions' have been
used for politically instrumental purposes has informed further analyses
of contemporary power struggles in the Pacific.[67] But the issue of
'invention' insofar as it implies 'inauthenticity' has provoked responses
from anthropologists who are concerned, inter alia, with the contrast
that is necessarily drawn between 'tradition as inheritance from ancestors' on the one hand, and tradition as the 'manipulative rhetoric of
contemporary politicians'.[68] Jolly objects to this contrast because of
its tendency to promote an essentialist view of Pacific cultures, because
it implies that only the advent of the West brought real social and economic change, and because authenticity is equated with unself-
consciousness and, as a logical corollary, that inauthenticity must be
equated with self-consciousness.[69] An acute self-consciousness, however,
is now seen as incumbent on all those whose studies concern 'others'.
Keesing, for example, urges more self-reflexivity in scholars of the
Pacific, arguing that they should recognize as problematic both 'the
implications and epistemology of our projects and representations' and
that the 'frame of certainty that surrounds scholarly expertise – like
mythical history – is less solid than it seems'.[70]

But this does not imply immediate surrender to the relativist void in
which critique becomes impossible. It simply recognizes that no one
epistemic position is especially privileged and that no observer can claim
to have captured the Archimedean vantage point from which the essence
of Truth can be grasped – and this applies to 'insiders' no less than to
'outsiders'. With respect to the latter, Keesing addresses an issue that
impinges on the whole question of epistemological imperialism.

> [S]pecialists on the Pacific do not best serve the interests of a less hegemonic
> scholarship or best support the political struggles of decolonizing and
> internally colonized Pacific peoples by suspending their critical judgement or
> maintaining silence – whether out of liberal guilt or political commitment –
> regarding mythic pasts evoked in cultural nationalist rhetoric. Our
> constructions of real pasts are not sacrosanct, but they are important elements
> in a continuing dialogue and dialectic.[71]

On a related theme, many anthropologists have drawn critical attention to some of the logical consequences of anthropology's revered doctrine of cultural relativism. Burling points out, for example, that although this doctrine rightly insists that judgements about 'other' cultures cannot be cast simply in terms of ethnocentric American or Western standards, the eagerness to counter vulgar assumptions of cultural superiority can all too easily lead to the permanent suspension of judgement about almost any activity or practice and to the doubtful conclusion that 'all human customs are equally defensible'.[72] Gellner's warning that we can be so blinded by an 'excessive indulgence in contextual charity' that we are unable to discern 'what is best and what is worst in the life of societies' is similarly apposite.[73] Returning to the specific problem outlined by Keesing, Jolly agrees that suspending critical judgement, maintaining one's silence, or being denied the right to speak at all, is hardly fruitful. But she does urge the abandonment of styles of writing which presume that 'we' have certain truths while Pacific politicians are in the business of 'perpetrating illusions or self-delusions'. This should enable scholars to turn their attention to more productive avenues of enquiry and analysis in the processes surrounding symbolic constitutions of tradition.

> Then our questions might cease to be those of persistence versus invention, of whether tradition is genuine or spurious. We probably cannot readily resolve the political conundra about whether and when to speak and write about Pacific traditions. But we might at least stop using the language of inauthenticity.[74]

Before responding specifically to this point, it is worth noting some other perspectives on the 'invention of tradition' debate. First, Thomas has pointed out that much of the work in this genre usually assumes that tradition is regarded as 'good' by those implicated in it. He further notes, however, that many people have actively criticized their 'own' cultural traditions and rejected some aspects in order to pursue other avenues deemed more rewarding. Thomas elaborates these points in the context of some Fijian examples:

> The stereotyping of foreigners as commercial individuals unconstrained by the burden of kinship is thus engaged in by some Fijians who want to modernize themselves and get rid of the shackles of custom and the chiefly hierarchy, by young urban women who are sick of arranged marriages – though of course 'arrangement' only became recognizable through the presence of another practice that could be taken as its opposite. Dissident Fijians refer to the same emblems of customary life as those who affirm the path of the land, rejecting rather than celebrating them.[75]

In contrast to these negative indigenous positions, and to emphasize the point that the idea of authenticity is, despite some of the problem with its application, nonetheless important to the study of tradition, it should also be noted that when something is identified as authentic, it often becomes more esteemed. The concern with authenticity can therefore entail 'a covert hierarchization and evaluation'.[76] This does not occur simply in the mind of the anthropologist or the tourist who wants to see the 'real thing'.[77] The hierarchical ordering of authentic traditional values and practices is also carried out in the minds of those living within the society, and is often done with political purposes in mind. It is in this context that the question of authenticity becomes particularly relevant to the politics of tradition in the Pacific. Most importantly, it is relevant not merely to 'outsiders' (whether academics, aid workers, diplomats, or foreign policy-makers) but to Pacific leaders and Pacific people generally in the conduct of their political activities. Take, for example, the following statement from the former Prime Minister of Vanuatu, Walter Lini:

> Traditional custom and culture, which are important and vital influences in our society, provide another challenge for us. Some people, mainly politicians, have used culture, custom, and custom chiefs for their own aims ... People have used the idea of 'custom' to totally contradict the idea of development and democracy in this country. On Santo and Tanna custom has been carried to extremes by people who incorrectly claim they respect traditional ways. It has become a political weapon and this has made it into something that is not Melanesian at all.[78]

Whatever we might say about the accuracy of Lini's claims and accusations, questions of authenticity, and inauthenticity, are obviously important to certain aspects of politics in Vanuatu. Further, it is Lini who is using the language of inauthenticity – not an 'outside' academic commentator. In other words, the 'spectre of inauthenticity' does not figure exclusively in the language of outsiders – it features regularly in the discourse of Pacific Islanders and clearly has political salience. Furthermore, it may plausibly be argued that the language of inauthenticity is perfectly acceptable in countering certain kinds of political rhetoric which attempt to use demonstrably false or misleading accounts of 'tradition' in order to enhance their own political power. As we shall see in the case studies, this is especially relevant to contemporary political developments since traditionalist rhetoric, and the ideology of traditionalism, have played exceptionally significant roles in shaping perceptions of national politics. So while we should avoid using the language of inauthenticity where it is clearly irrelevant, inappropriate, or otherwise unwarranted, to abandon it altogether is to deny its utility in understanding and criticizing important political phenomena.

Before taking these particular issues further, it is necessary first to spell out more precisely what is meant by 'tradition' or 'traditional' in the context of Pacific politics. We have seen that it is taken generally to denote continuity with the past. But a more subtle distinction must be made between the ways in which the past can be related to the present. Jolly explains this by sketching the two broadest extremes of the conceptual relation. On one hand, the past may appear to flow smoothly and continuously towards the present, whereas on the other it may be perceived as having suffered irrevocable separation from the present by means of a drastic rupture that can be bridged only through revival.[79] The point of rupture is especially important because in most parts of the Pacific the notion of tradition is often taken to imply the pre-colonial or at least pre-contact past, and this is reflected generally in academic references to what is 'really traditional' as well.[80] At least some responsibility for this treatment of tradition lies in the manner in which Western anthropologists have interpreted their material. To cite Carrier again, it seems that anthropologists have fostered the tendency to view the legitimacy of a practice primarily in terms of its longevity.

> Because the relatively new is the relatively inauthentic, there is pressure to treat as illegitimate those things associated with colonial administration or the emerging national state. Thus, the conventional anthropological approach is likely to result in a double predisposition to slight the effects of Western impact. Not only does their Western taint make them inauthentic, but the fact that the effects of this impact are recent also means that they are inauthentic.[81]

On a related point, Leach has observed that many ethnographers, even in the contemporary era, 'still have their eyes fixed on a kind of mirage, "the pre-contact traditional society", which they hope to uncover by some kind of time reversal process of "detransformation" '. This is driven by the powerful, romantic view that

> once upon a time there was a precontact, precolonial, era when human societies lying outside the ambit of European explorers, traders, missionaries, colonial administrators or whatever led an uncontaminated indigenous 'traditional' cultural existence which was what ethnographers would always like to have recorded but never did. What they did (and still can) observe is a version of such 'traditional' society, transformed by the processes of historical change ...[82]

However, the prevailing notion that what is genuinely (or authentically) traditional or customary is that which is unpolluted by Western influences is common not only among anthropologists and other outsiders but, as the case studies will show, among many Pacific Islanders as well. This view attributes a certain pristine quality to traditional life which accords well with aspects of the 'fatal impact thesis'.[83] Mulgan points out that this has given rise to the clichéd view of the South Pacific region as one that, at least historically, exuded unusual stability and peace. Although European in origin (and a product of eighteenth-century romantic revulsion against industrialization and puritan morality), the overall picture is congenial to many Islanders themselves.[84] In this context, 'tradition' has become a value-laden term, carrying with it a positive connotation of what is good (in social and political life) in specific opposition to that which is 'Western' (which can also be another way of saying 'modern'). In this way, the evaluative images of the dichotomy depicted earlier are inverted.[85] Moreover, it establishes a kind of moral high ground from which Western democracy can be attacked.

I argued earlier that although the evocation of indigenous values in opposition to those of the West, as well as idealizations of pre-colonial or pre-contact pasts, can be regarded as appropriate responses to the negative images engendered by the colonial experience, these must also be recognized as devices by which some political leaders can legitimate their own authority while suppressing political opposition. In addition, traditionalist appeals can often involve the retrospective homogenization of what were (and still are) quite diverse collections of communities. A homogenized or unitary image of 'the traditional way of life' is then held up as a suitable standard for contemporary political practice.[86] Viewed in this way, we can see that it is not so much a matter of bringing 'the past into the present' – that is, of resurrecting past practices and making them meaningful in the contemporary sphere – as it is a case of projecting some current state of affairs back into the past and thereby seeking to legitimate it by invoking the traditionalist refrain 'it has been this way since time immemorial'.

The past thus becomes something of an organic paradigm of the present, and its relevance as a serious political factor is dependent on its authentic reflection of the *volkgeist*.[87] As with classic conservative ideology and political romanticism, the idea of tradition here is linked closely to 'the natural order of things' which is upset only at great risk to the very fabric of society.[88] And just as the conservatives of Burke's time sought to preserve traditional institutions in the face of democratizing forces, so too do many of the South Pacific's political leaders seek to set tradition against demands for greater democracy. This leads us, finally, to consider the concept of democracy.

Democracy

The purpose of this section is not to set out a descriptive account of the institutions and practices of democratic politics. This has been done many times before, and the results are contained in a massive and ever-expanding body of literature. A number of standard texts also include discussions of how institutional practices vary over time and place, and canvass a number of problems associated with the gap between theory and practice. It should also be stressed that this gap is evident not only in non-Western contexts, but is just as problematic in the West where democratic institutions have largely failed to deliver on the promise of greater equality for the mass of ordinary people – a factor that also impairs the enjoyment of political liberty as well as undermining the sense of community that is meant to underscore a democratic polity.

So while the major focus of critique in this study is on a non-Western context, it should not be inferred that Western democracies are immune from criticism, nor that they have nothing to learn from countries with different political traditions. At the same time, it is argued that many of the practices and institutions that have been developed under the general theory of constitutionalism – practices and institutions which attempt to provide for a measure of self-government as well as for the protection of human and civil rights – are worth defending. This is not because they are necessarily the best possible devices, and cannot be improved on, but because they have yet to be replaced with something better. It should also be noted that this view is not one that only Westerners cleave to. Those arguing for a greater measure of democratic participation in non-Western authoritarian countries frequently do so by appeal to the normative framework of Western democracy.

Another major focus of debate has been the difficulty of 'transplanting' Western democratic institutions to non-Western polities. It has been suggested, for example, that democracy is a 'foreign flower', unable to take root and flourish in South Pacific soil.[89] This reflects the view, noted by Davidson, that South Pacific Islanders tend to view democracy as culturally laden (for example, with British culture).[90] Davidson also makes the point that British and continental European conceptions of democracy differ markedly with respect to the emphasis that each gives to culture. Whereas the British conception is indeed often tied to an anglocentric understanding of culture, the continental European is not. Rather, the latter conception is focussed more specifically on the procedural aspects of democratic rule. This is sometimes misunderstood as 'denying or ignoring cultural difference', whereas the real point of emphasizing procedural aspects is that these are, in fact, a response to cultural diversity as well as the means through which it can be protected.[91]

At the other end of the spectrum of debate, there have been claims of the 'democracy-as-indigenous' kind,[92] and these have figured in some debates about whether South Pacific island nations, or nations elsewhere for that matter, have pre-existing democratic traditions that can provide a better basis for contemporary political institutions than those imported from the West. Another argument (put forward in the context of the African experience) maintains that the post-independence societies there possess a democratic heritage derived from the struggle against colonialism itself. More specifically, it has been pointed out that the platforms of nationalist parties in Africa showed an allegiance to virtually the full range of democratic values and practices:

> [T]here was a strong commitment to democracy in terms of individual rights and liberties, popular participation in the affairs of government and accountability of the governors to the governed ... The democratic demands could [then] be summarized as follows: equality before the law, as opposed to the apartheid practices of the colonial state; citizenship and citizenship rights for all, irrespective of race, colour, sex, belief or ethnic affiliation – in other words, a secular, republican and democratic state; the right of citizens to elect their governors, including freedom to form parties, pressure groups, associations and interest groups in the process of articulating political preferences; an ethic and practice of social justice in matters of development and the entitlement of citizens to equality within the public realm.[93]

Another issue raised by the cultural context is whether the Western world, broadly construed, has some moral monopoly over 'correct' interpretations of democracy, let alone the right to make prescriptive pronouncements. In countries where the experience of Western colonialism is still fresh in the memories of a large proportion of the population, questions of this kind may have a particularly sharp resonance with feelings of historic injustices arising from domination. But the picture is not consistent with respect to the three countries dealt with here. In Western Samoa, colonial rule was resisted strongly and feelings against the colonial regimes (of both Germany and New Zealand) at times ran very high, giving such impetus to the local independence movement that Western Samoa became the first country in the region to gain independent status. In Fiji, however, it was independence rather than colonial rule that was resisted – at least by chiefly leaders. Tonga was never formally colonized, but European domination of the Pacific region generally has been instrumental in the adoption of some anti-Western attitudes.

One of the ironies of Western colonialism, of course, is that although colonial powers often left a democratic legacy in the form of constitutional government under a written constitution at independence, colonial rule itself was far from democratic. Crown colony governments, although relatively benign in places like Fiji, were nonetheless authoritarian. To refer again to the African experience, there has been a 'legacy of indifference to the fate of democracy' – an attitude that has its roots in the era of colonial rule when political discourse 'excluded democracy'.[94] The main point, however, is that issues concerning institutional legacies, in the form of introduced structures, remain relevant to many concerns about epistemological imperialism, and will be addressed later. A related concern involves the problems of cultural and ethical relativism – problems that are intimately bound up with aspects of tradition and cultural politics. These particular concerns take on greater salience in the contemporary world where the word 'democracy' has been adopted as the ultimate regime legitimator and it is in this context that the problem of conceptual relativism will be explored.

It is now a commonplace that the moral prestige of the word 'democracy' enjoys an unprecedented ascendancy in the late twentieth century, a position that it has not achieved in any other era, either ancient or modern. Never before has democracy been embraced by so many of the world's nations as the most desirable form of political life. This trend has been evident at least since the end of the Second World War, when a world-wide survey by UNESCO evidently 'showed the concept of democracy to be sufficiently elastic to allow every nation to applaud it'.[95] Even in those cases where dictatorships have seized control of the state, this has often been justified 'as necessary for the regeneration of the polity to allow for stable and effective democratic rule'.[96] In the South Pacific, all of the island states claim to be democratic, regardless of whether their parliamentary structures, including their systems of elective representation and other mechanisms for participation, conform to basic democratic institutional norms.

The current wave of 'democratization' in various parts of the world has clearly brought some welcome relief to those suffering the burden of political oppression. Some of its other legacies, however, are far less attractive and although the point of this discussion is not to elaborate on the excesses of ethnic nationalism and free market forces which now beset some of these places, they are nonetheless worth noting. They are worth noting, in particular, because the former phenomenon may perhaps be confused with democratization to the extent that the idea of an ethnocratic state is sometimes conflated (at least in the ethno-nationalist imagination) with a democratic state. Similarly, although certain economic freedoms are clearly compatible with democratic theory, there is an unfortunate tendency to equate democracy with capitalism and, as a consequence, to deny the state any valid interventionist role in dealing with problems of distributive justice. The main point of this section, however, is to emphasize that although the word 'democracy' has received almost universal acclamation, neither its institutions nor the values that sustain it have achieved the same level of esteem.

I therefore argue that many of those principles that first gave democracy pride of place as the most desirable form of government are largely absent in the political practice of many countries, including those in the present study. It follows that the position taken here denies that democracy can mean all things to all people. To state the relativist position in this way is to pose it in its most extreme form. And at first glance it may seem that the alternative is also an extreme, namely, that there is only one set of institutions and practices that can give proper expression to the values of democracy. It must be emphasized, however, that I do not assume that there is only one 'correct' universal form, nor that the institutions of democracy cannot be adapted legitimately to suit particular circumstances. But there are limits to its elasticity, both conceptually and empirically. In setting out the argument I first review the emergence of democracy and how it has been understood in classical as well as modern periods.

It has been noted already that the desirability of democracy is almost universally acknowledged, but that this is only a fairly recent development. Even in its original birthplace, the *polis* of the ancient Athenians, democracy was much criticized by the ancient philosophers and it was something of an anomaly among the Greek city-states of the fifth century BC.[97] In modern times, from the seventeenth century to the twentieth, critics could voice their opposition to democracy without risking derision. Indeed, before the present century, to call something a democracy was still usually to disparage it, and even the famous Levellers did not claim to be democrats.[98] Further, until about the end of the Second World War, there was little dispute in the international context about the proper application of the word in describing actual forms of government[99] – fascist regimes were proudly described *as* fascist by their proponents, and the word democracy was spoken by them with contempt.

So whereas the terms 'democracy' or 'democrat' were frequently used as words of abuse in the past, today, clearly, they are words of praise and are essential props in regime legitimation. In short, democracy is an evaluative word of the kind that unquestionably performs a commendatory speech act.[100] Certainly, democracy as a form of rule in the fifth century BC was clearly understood empirically. In Athens, the *demos,* the body of ordinary citizens, took an active part in the everyday government of the *polis,* and decided major policy matters collectively in the Assembly through the device of a simple majority vote. Many public officials, including the President of the Assembly, were chosen by sortition (that is, by lot) to perform various duties and offices. The most powerful public office holders, the *strategoi,* were elected by the assembly. It was a system of government controlled and operated by the many, rather than by the few, let alone by a single person. It contrasted clearly with monarchy and tyranny (the rule of one), and with aristocracy and oligarchy (the rule of the few). Then, the distinctions were transparent enough and, whatever disagreement there was as to its merits, there was little disagreement as to what a democratic system meant.

In ancient Rome, too, there was little doubt about what democracy meant, and some of its important elements were repudiated, along with monarchy, through the development of the republican form of government. In fact the republic was specifically designed to keep effective political power away from the allegedly capricious mass of the people. Following the Roman tradition, the founding fathers of the American constitution adopted the republican form for their own national government – it was informed directly by the Roman model – and in so doing quite consciously and unashamedly rejected a number of the norms and principles associated with popular power. James Madison, arguably the foremost figure in the Constitutional Convention of 1787, and one of the founders of the original Republican Party, declared that 'democracies have ever been spectacles of turbulence and contention; have ever been found incompatible with personal security or the rights of property; and have in general been as short in their lives as they have been violent in their deaths'.[101]

Today, however, the adjective 'democratic' is the ultimate ornamental trope with which so many official styles of government are embellished. But, largely because of the compelling force of its commendatory illocutionary performance, there are now significant differences of opinion about the meaning of democracy. One of modern democracy's many apparent paradoxes, then, is that the universal acclaim which it now enjoys has made the concept of democracy 'all the more controversial and contestable as a result',[102] and 'its range of contemporary senses ... confused'.[103] Indeed, as 'the appraisive political concept par excellence', democracy has come to enjoy the status of an 'essentially contested concept'.[104] These quotations, then, indicate the extent of agreement over the extent of disagreement. A perceptive remark by Orwell indicates one reason for this state of affairs:

> In the case of a word like democracy, not only is there no agreed definition but the attempt to make one is resisted from all sides. It is almost universally felt that when we call a country democratic we are praising it: consequently the defenders of every kind of regime claim that it is a democracy, and fear that they might have to stop using the word if it were tied down to any one meaning.[105]

This directs attention to the idea of democracy as 'an essentially contested concept'. As formulated by Gallie the notion of 'essential contestability' seems, at first glance, both straightforward and persuasive.

In the case of democracy, it denotes that a highly appraisive concept endowed with a very strong positive performative force is likely to provoke any number of competing interpretations. There can be little argument with this. Gallie then goes on to mount a case for essential contestability that denies the possibility that conceptual disputes of this kind are capable of rational resolution. Again, this seems a reasonable and indeed a compelling position, especially for a democratically-minded person who should always be prepared to admit her fallibility and to concede that there is no possibility of attaining a God's-eye perspective of the world from which the truth of the matter can ultimately be determined. To do otherwise would be dogmatic at best, and smacks of absolutist pretensions at worst. Embracing fallibilism, however, does not entail conceding that every interpretation is of equal worth, for that leads to the relativist (or skepticist) void which is equally dogmatic.[106] But that is precisely where Gallie's position takes us when he urges that no rival uses of a concept can be regarded as 'anathema, perverse, bestial or lunatic'.[107]

It is quite unfashionable to take a stand on anything as complex and appraisive as the word 'democracy'. This is particularly so in the current postmodern mood, one strand of which supports a hermeneutic passion that is most clearly evident in some zealous manifestations of anti-ethnocentrism (which can often be read as anti-eurocentrism) in many contemporary anthropological writings.[108] Before proceeding on this issue, however, I wish to emphasize that the criticism I intend to launch against some aspects of postmodernist thought does not entail condemnation of the whole body of thought that is generally associated with poststructuralism, deconstruction, semiotics, and so forth. After all, much of the analysis engaged in throughout this book has a markedly deconstructive character because it is directed against the 'master narrative' of traditionalism. Furthermore, it must be recognized that post-modernists do not necessarily share a common political agenda, and that there are many different political orientations that can be taken within the general framework of postmodernism.[109]

To return now to the main problem, it should be noted first that the intellectual history of concerns about relativism, ethnocentrism, and socially constructed beliefs and values goes back at least as far as the ancient Greek debates on *physis* and *nomos*. But in its present form it can be traced most directly to the prominence of issues concerning value-freedom in modern social science theorizing. Sartori identifies several versions of the 'freedom-from-value' issue, that is, the moderate 'value-fairness' version, the extreme 'value void' version, and the weak 'value avoidance' or 'value-shyness' version.[110] Proponents of postmodern hermeneutics generally take up a position within the latter varieties. In

an effort to purge all traces of ethnocentrism, and especially eurocentrism, some scholars have indulged in the kind of theorizing that
rejects all standards as arbitrary, and are therefore led to the position
where concepts like democracy can indeed mean all things to all people.
As Gellner notes, not only does a hermeneutic account of a political
system leave us wondering 'whether we have been offered an explanation
of social order, or merely a description of its atmosphere', it is also
accompanied at times 'by a certain facile and self-congratulatory
relativism' through which 'systems of meaning are credited not merely
with a magical potency and efficacy, but also, each in its own zone, with a
kind of automatic legitimacy'. He continues:

> I can accept neither a murky relativism nor a semiotic mysticism. For one
> thing, I am none too impressed by … 'epistemological hypochondria' … I have
> much sympathy for genuine Hamlets and real doubts, but the recent fashions
> [seem] marked less by their apparent skepticism than by their real dogmatism.
> The argument tends to be: because all knowledge is dubious, being theory-
> saturated/ethnocentric/paradigm dominated/interest linked … etc., there-
> fore the anguish-ridden author can put forward whatever [s/he] pleases …
> What is really at issue is the denial of relativism.[111]

Keesing has articulated similar concerns in the context of the politics
of tradition in the South Pacific. With reference to the body of critique
that takes issue with representations of cultural identity and nationalism,
he notes that this has drawn protests from those who advance
postmodern arguments against the privileging of any representations as
authentic, promoting instead the view that 'the insider position of Pacific
Islanders gives them a primary right to advance representations of their
cultural past'.[112] Apart from noting that this hermeneutic device (as well
as that which takes the extreme relativist position in denying a privileged
status for *any* account of the past or the present) can also be subjected to
a deconstructive and political critique, Keesing further notes that the
articulation of political ideologies is usually carried out 'by those insiders
who have the power to make themselves heard and have interests to be
served by doing so'.[113] It should come as no surprise, then, that conservative political agendas are often to be found at the heart of relativist arguments. Keesing offers a perspective that targets extreme versions of
postmodern relativism with regard to representations about the past. In
a manner that follows very closely the fallibilist position, he says that
while there is no single 'truth' about a community or society, or about
the past, there is nonetheless a vast universe of non-truth that can be
uncovered.[114] Similarly, in seeking a way out of the relativist impasse,
critical theorists have maintained that although knowledge is historically
and socially conditioned, it is possible nonetheless to adjudicate truth

claims in an 'independent moment of criticism' that occurs outside immediate social or class interests.[115]

To deny relativism is to take a stand against a position that is at least as dogmatic as a rigid universalism. In the present context, it is to take an intellectual stand against the appropriation of the word 'democracy' by all comers. No-one can legislate for the correct use of words – nor would that be desirable in any case, for that would only be supporting another type of authoritarian mentality. The denial of relativism in the form of an intellectual stand, however, does not amount to a call for enforcement. Rather, it calls for resistance to the idea that words are mere conventions and that they can be employed at the stipulatory whim of any speaker.[116] Nonetheless, defenders of cultural relativism would argue that the denial of relativism leads to the arbitrary imposition of outside standards on 'native' values. They might also argue that the denial of relativism also constitutes a form of epistemological or cultural imperialism that some-how attacks or interferes with the cultural 'sovereignty' of other places, other people, or other systems of politics and government. This is precisely what some defenders of non-democratic systems in the South Pacific have done in promoting the validity of indigenous traditions against Western ideas about democracy. The case studies and the con-clusion discuss this in more detail, but for the present purposes it is important to foreshadow a response to these positions.

It has been suggested that arguments invoking cultural relativism and cultural sovereignty against various forms of conceptual imperialism are based on a misunderstanding about what value judgements entail, and that the metaphors of imperialism and sovereignty in this context are simply inappropriate. In arguing a case for evaluative universalism and against cultural relativism, Nathan proposes that:

> Evaluation is an intellectual act, not an act of coercion; an act of communication, not of excommunication. It is the opposite of the kind of denigration labelled by Edward Said as 'Orientalism'. A value judgement is a way of focussing discussion, not ending it. It involves defining, defending, and applying a value so that others may be informed of it and may respond if they wish. Applying values in which one does not believe, were it even intellectually possible to do so, would defeat the process of communication.[117]

The stand taken here, then, is basically in terms of the application of evaluative universalism, through which it is argued that democracy is the name of a form of rule that derives from an identifiable set of values and embodies a certain set of norms and principles. It has an ethos that is clearly distinct from authoritarian modes of rule, and to the extent that we can define democracy at all, it can at the very least be understood as a form of rule that stands in contradistinction to the principles of autocracy. Thus democracy has been defined, minimally, as a system in which no person can arrogate to him or herself unconditional or unlimited power.[118] This statement embodies a strong version of the idea, noted earlier, that democratic politics is characterized by the depersonalization of political power. It is also important to note that this cannot be demonstrated merely by reference to institutions. Very little insight is needed to recognize the fact that constitutions, elections, parliaments, and so forth, which are very often taken to embody the values of democratic practice, have often constituted nothing more than a facade for a great many of the world's repressive regimes. Adam may have named the tiger because it looked like a tiger,[119] but it is hardly adequate to name something a democracy simply because it looks like one on the surface. So although the presence or absence of certain institutions can be taken as a guide, they are scarcely enough to establish its operation in practice. In other words, they are necessary but not sufficient conditions for the practice of democratic politics.

Let me now return to the broad problem of conceptualizing what is involved in the use of particular appraisive words like democracy. Skinner says that to apply such a term correctly, the range of reference needs to be understood so that there is 'a clear sense of the nature of the circumstances in which the word can properly be used to designate particular actions or states of affairs'. Further, to grasp the criteria for correctly applying it is to understand the sense of the word.[120] It is not suggested here that politicians who use the term 'democracy' in such titles as the 'Sovereign Democratic Republic of Fiji' have necessarily failed to grasp the appropriate criteria. It is more than likely that in applying it they understand the criteria very well. What they are attempting to do in some cases is to revise and relativize the concept of democracy in order to make it fit their preferred style of rule – a style that purportedly incorporates authentic traditional structures of sociopolitical organization. Then in defending the new revised version against external criticism, they can employ a hermeneutic tactic that effectively turns the tables by accusing these critics not only of errors in cross-cultural understanding (for example, 'you just don't understand our traditions'), but of ethnocentrism, epistemological imperialism, cultural chauvinism and so forth. This amounts to an appeal to relativism of the dogmatic kind since its purpose is to foreclose criticism and therefore to stifle meaningful debate. And if it is conceded that problems of cross-cultural interpretation constitute an insurmountable barrier to communication, then the very possibility of discourse is denied. For although debate does not presuppose agreement, let alone the attainability of Truth, it does presuppose the possibility of shared understanding.

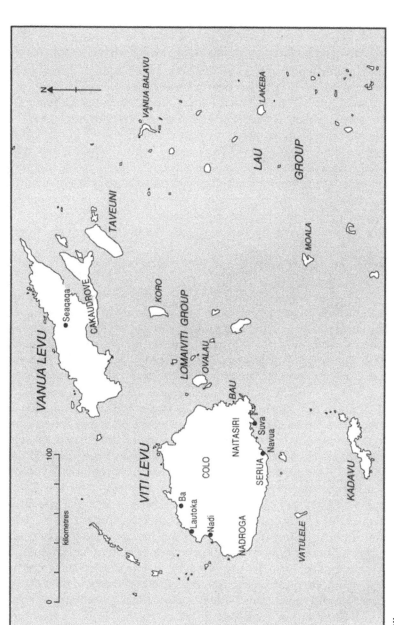

Fiji

CHAPTER 2

Constitutional Development, Chiefly Power and the Politics of Tradition in Fiji

Introduction

Fiji consists of approximately 320 islands which are scattered over an area of 650,000 square kilometres in the south-west Pacific. About 150 are inhabited. The total land area is just over 18,000 square kilometres, making Fiji one of the largest states in the region. The islands of Viti Levu and Vanua Levu are the two largest land masses in the group and together comprise almost 16,000 square kilometres. Indigenous Fijians are usually described as Melanesian, although there is ample evidence of a long-standing Polynesian presence not only in physical terms, but in some of the most important sociopolitical structures. This is especially so in the eastern regions of Fiji which lie closest to the Tongan and Samoan groups. Fiji is now home to around 700,000 people, just under half of whom are descended from settlers who arrived in successive waves of migration from about 1500 BC, as evidenced by the presence of Lapita pottery fragments in a number of sites which date from this time. Archaeological and linguistic evidence supports the hypothesis that the early Lapita people were the forebears of the Fijians as well as the Polynesians. In Fiji, linguistic research also indicates that there was a break in the dialect chain in the later history of the islands between the western and eastern regions. Routledge has argued that internal histor- ical developments of this kind are more important to the understanding of Fijian society than those which focus on external antecedents and affiliations. This is because close attention to intra-Fijian development reveals the fundamental heterogeneity of the Fijian people and their cultural practices – a feature that has too often been overlooked in some accounts of Fijian social structures.[1]

Chiefly authority and Fijian 'tradition' can often be treated synonym- ously because the former is so frequently taken to embody the latter.

More specifically, however, the apotheosis of chiefliness has centred on the eastern provinces of the Fiji islands.[2] Since before colonization by Great Britain in 1874, and throughout the colonial era until independence in 1970, as well as for most of the period since then, Fijian politics has been dominated by chiefs from these areas. In the later period, the most prominent of these chiefs included both of Fiji's governors-general, Ratu Sir George Cakobau and Ratu Sir Penaia Ganilau (the latter continued to serve as president of the republic until his death in December 1993), as well as Fiji's longest-serving prime minister, Ratu Sir Kamisese Mara. Having held the position of chief minister in the colonial government since 1966, Mara went on to lead the country as prime minister following independence until his party's defeat in the general elections of 1987 – a defeat that precipitated a military coup less than six weeks later. He then returned as prime minister in the interim regime and stepped down only before the first post-coup elections in 1992 when he became deputy head of state. Following the death of Ganilau, Mara was appointed president. The leader of the coup, and the present prime minister, Sitiveni Rabuka, is a commoner but nonetheless a member of a high-ranking eastern descent group[3] of which Ganilau was paramount chief.

Not only have these easterners (and many others serving in less conspicuous posts) dominated political institutions, but the structures and values surrounding chiefly power and privilege in the east have been promoted as the model of tradition for the whole of Fiji, despite the diversity of pre-colonial structures throughout the islands. Some of this diversity has atrophied under the homogenizing influence of the dominant eastern structures, and there is of course a very real sense of common identity among indigenous Fijians, especially in the presence of a significant non-Fijian population. So while a reified notion of 'tradition' in many other South Pacific nations is most often posed in contradistinction to that equally reified entity known as the 'West' (and of course Fiji is no exception to this ubiquitous contraposing), understandings of tradition in Fiji have received an added dimension in that it is also construed in opposition to Fiji Indians. This has assisted in producing Fijian 'internal nationalism' which many Fijian leaders have exploited as a means of enhancing their political claims. It is in the nature of this ideology that the 'nation' is also understood in reified terms – terms that posit a unified cultural/ethnic entity. Individual Fijian interests and political aspirations have thereby been subsumed, at least conceptually and rhetorically, in the collective. In the years since the military coup, however, the diversity of political interests and aspirations among Fijians has become evident in the failure of the eastern chiefly establishment to consolidate Fijian support through a range of constitutional and extraconstitutional devices. This has struck a major blow at the foundations of the 'grand Fijian tradition' embodied in the structure of eastern chiefly power.

Although the masking of cultural diversity is now wearing thin in many respects, Fiji's colonial and post-colonial history still stands as a monument to the successful promulgation of a myth of cultural homogeneity among Fijians – a myth which had considerable success in binding the majority of Fijians together under what was perceived to be traditional chiefly authority.[4] Political myths of this kind, however, cannot be sustained effectively in the absence of solid institutional support. A number of concrete structures have long supported the more ethereal aspects of the myth of cultural homogeneity and, in turn, the grand tradition of eastern chiefly power. The establishment of the Great Council of Chiefs, the Native Administration, and a codified land tenure system in the early years of colonial rule set the pattern for the remainder of the colonial era and into independence. The growth of the party system in Fiji contributed further to the gathering together of all Fijians under the conceptual mantle of chiefly power and legitimacy. At the broadest level, the 1990 Constitution of the Sovereign Democratic Republic of Fiji sought to establish Fijian tradition at the very centre of political life. For most non-indigenous Fijians, this amounts to relegation to political subordination. Although the relegation of 'others' in this manner seems to imply the elevation of indigenous Fijians to a position of considerable privilege in the new order, we shall see that this is by no means straightforward. Another noteworthy development in recent years is that many of the most powerful Fijian political actors are no longer the bearers of chiefly status, although they purport to support and protect Fijian tradition.

The Constitution of the Sovereign Democratic Republic of Fiji was promulgated in July 1990 just over three years after the elected coalition government, led by a Fijian commoner, Dr Timoci Bavadra, was overthrown in a military coup led by another Fijian commoner, Lieutenant-Colonel Sitiveni Rabuka, then the third-ranking officer of the Royal Fiji Military Forces, on 14 May 1987. Although based superficially on the Westminster system, this constitution, which replaced the more democratic constitution adopted at independence in 1970,[5] contains a number of discriminatory racial and other non-democratic provisions. These features have been justified by the post-coup regime largely on the grounds that they were essential for the protection and enhancement of indigenous Fijian rights and interests vis-à-vis other communities, especially the Fiji Indian community. These were precisely the same reasons given by coup leader Rabuka for the overthrow of the elected government in 1987, and the 1990 constitution can therefore be seen as having secured his primary objectives, at least at the level of formal institutional structures.

The justifications put forward for both the May 1987 coup and for the discriminatory provisions of the 1990 constitution are underscored by two further related claims. Taken together, these promote the view that Western democratic principles and practices are unsuited to Fiji's political environment. First, it is claimed that the nature of Fiji's 'plural society' is a prima facie barrier to the kind of democratic politics practised in Western nations. The latter are said to be heterogeneous but not characterized by such sharply delineated ethnic groups. This argument was employed on numerous occasions both before and after independence, usually during times when Fijian leaders and the British colonial rulers sought to undermine Fiji Indian claims for greater political equality. It has been used less explicitly since the coup, but is nonetheless an important underlying theme in debate over constitutional change. Phrased in these terms, it is not so much an argument from tradition as a claim about the 'objective conditions' of a plural society under which democracy can, or cannot, be managed successfully. The second justification is related to the first, but is more explicit in rejecting Western democratic principles and practices on the grounds that they are inappropriate in the context of Fijian politics. The essence of the argument here is that the relatively democratic political institutions established in the 1970 constitution represented the imposition of values alien to a pre-existing, and therefore more legitimate, traditional political framework. It is this framework that the post-coup regime purported to resurrect in the new constitution – together with a quasi-democratic façade.

The new constitution is therefore meant to be understood, at least by those responsible for its promulgation, as an instrument that better reflects the genuine cultural and political values of Fijian tradition as well as providing for their protection and enhancement. These justifications rest, of course, on an assumption that the military coup and subsequent developments were prompted primarily by factors concerned with ethnicity and with the safeguarding of indigenous Fijian rights. Most academic commentators on these events, however, have argued strongly against the notion that ethnic factors were the essential cause of the 1987 coups and, more specifically, against the idea that indigenous Fijian rights were at risk under the Bavadra government.[6] An impression nonetheless persists that the ethnic issue, together with some kind of threat to Fijian rights, was the major motivating force behind the military intervention. This impression has, of course, been reinforced at every turn by supporters of the coups, whose rhetoric has been put most strongly in these terms. Similarly, the post-coup regime's move to promulgate a new constitution, which purports to ensure a paramount political position for indigenous Fijians as a whole, also involved an appeal to the ethnic factor for its major justification. Indeed, the constitution of the Sovereign Democratic Republic of Fiji refers explicitly to the coup (and, by implication, to the ethnic factor) in the preamble:

> AND WHEREAS events in 1987 in Fiji led to the abrogation of the 1970 Constitution;
> AND WHEREAS those events were occasioned by widespread belief that the 1970 Constitution was inadequate to give protection to the interests of the indigenous Fijians, their values, traditions, customs, way of life and economic well-being; ...

Chapter III of the new constitution sets out certain provisions for the promotion and safeguard of 'the economic, social, educational, cultural, traditional and other interests of the Fijian and Rotuman people' and directs the government 'to adopt any program or activity for the attainment of the said objects'.[7] In the longer term, however, it is unlikely that the new constitution will do much to advance the rights and interests of the majority of the indigenous population except in a superficial sense. It provides no greater protection of, for example, Fijian land rights than did the 1970 constitution. Rather, the institutions established by the new constitution reflect the determination of a political elite to retain political control. Shortly after the constitution was promulgated, a meeting of the deposed Labour/NFP coalition denounced it for its 'racist, undemocratic, authoritarian and feudalistic features ...'.[8] This may be party political rhetoric, but it does not detract from the accuracy of the statement.

The 1990 constitution thus represents a clear move away from democratic norms towards a regime which not only precludes meaningful political participation by Fiji Indians, but denies also the basic political integrity of ordinary Fijian people in the name of Fijian tradition. This is not a new problem for Fijians – they have long been tied to separate institutions such as the Fijian administration which is purportedly based on tradition, but which has operated to their disadvantage in many ways. In relation to this it is worth noting here the critical findings of one of Fiji's most respected anthropologists:

> There is a limit to the amount of authoritarian direction which people will accept, but in a situation where they have no choice of alternative affiliation and where their membership and participation are enjoined automatically on their birth, this limit may be reached sooner rather than later – particularly if alternative solutions can be seen but not legally chosen ... While the idea of building on traditional institutions is a noble one and undoubtedly sound, its value may be quickly lost in a situation of change; it may develop ideas based on old patterns which may become quickly obsolete, for the people are

continually working out new patterns, alternative ways of ordering their lives, which they judge to be more advantageous in the new conditions.[9]

Since the idea of Fijian tradition has been constructed and defended largely in the context, not only of opposition to Western norms and values, but also of indigenous Fijian rights in a plural society, we examine first the idea of the plural society and its implications for constitutional change in Fiji.

The Plural Society

Plural societies are characterized generally as displaying an immutable systemic disassociation between culturally distinct groups which are themselves assumed to be relatively homogeneous. In Fiji politics, for example, the respective communities of indigenous Fijians and Fiji Indians have frequently been depicted as monolithic, unified cultural/ethnic entities. Strength of attachment to these groups by their respective members is reinforced by the very existence, within the boundaries of the nation-state, of the 'other' group, which thereby produces a 'two-nation ideology'. M.G. Smith says that pluralism 'simultaneously connotes a social structure characterized by fundamental discontinuities and cleavages, and a cultural complex based on systematic institutional diversity'.[10] This serves to distinguish plural societies from those which are simply heterogeneous or 'pluralistic' (of which the United States, Great Britain, and Australia are often cited as examples). Another characteristic emphasized by plural society theorists that arises directly from the unintegrated nature of the communities, and their consequent (or assumed) lack of cross-cutting affiliations, is that the nation as a whole lacks a fundamental 'social will' to hold it together, therefore necessitating a relatively high degree of coercive authority on the part of the rulers in order to maintain political stability.

Critics of plural society theory have identified a number of false or misleading assumptions in its formulation. First, the theory fails to acknowledge the extent to which political unity and consensus on national goals may be achieved despite social or cultural disassociation between groups. It therefore places undue emphasis on the necessity for political coercion to hold the state together. Put another way, the degree of 'social will' essential to maintaining political cohesion at a national level, without resort to authoritarian measures, is not necessarily dependent on a high level of social or cultural homogeneity within the nation (although this may be a facilitating factor). Further, and as we have seen, plural society theory tends to depict the constituent groups as monolithic and internally homogeneous thereby relegating to insignificance cross-cutting associations between the groups as well as ignoring diversity within them. On a related point, conceptual confusion can arise in terms of distinguishing class interests from, say, ethnic interests when conflict arises.[11] Horowitz also draws attention to the fact that since plural society theory focusses almost exclusively on whole groups, 'it ignores the specific contributions that elites make to ethnic conflict, just as it ignores their contribution to norms of moderation'.[12] This point is especially relevant to the role of the Fijian chiefly elite in the now defunct Alliance Party whose tactics in retaining political authority after independence depended, in part, on fostering Fijian fears of an 'Indian takeover'.

An important consequence of the 'plural society problem', as depicted by plural society theorists, is the apparent inability of these societies to institute and maintain stable forms of democratic rule. Nicholls notes that 'one of the most widely held theses in comparative politics is that a segmented society is likely to be both unstable and violent'.[13] To the extent that a much higher degree of coercive power is said to be necessary in maintaining the stability of the state (in the assumed absence of a unifying social will), governments in plural societies must therefore resort to the construction of (relatively) authoritarian national institutions. The more authoritarian the institutions then, ipso facto, the less democratic they are.

One further point that needs to be drawn out here concerns the assumed immutability of cleavages within a plural society, which I have elsewhere described as the 'plural society syndrome'.[14] This gives rise to the notion that conflicts and problems for political organization and control in plural societies are capable only of management and not of resolution. In 'managing' these problems, the tendency is to reinforce the cleavages rather than attempt to break them down and 'de-pluralize' the society or, more accurately, to turn it from a plural into a simply pluralistic or multicultural society. In turn, the reinforcement of cleavages serves to strengthen further the plural society syndrome.[15] A parallel consequence of these kinds of developments is that the arguments associated with them lend themselves to the powerful and manipulative rhetoric of demagoguery – as exemplified by the instrumental fostering of Fijian fears by chiefly leaders. Political discourse in Fiji has long been characterized by this kind of rhetoric, but it has received additional force following the events of 1987 and the subsequent process of constitutional review.

Shortly before the 1990 constitution was promulgated, coup leader Rabuka voiced unambiguously his views on race relations in Fiji, which reflected very clearly the thinking that is characteristic of the plural society syndrome. Referring to what he claimed were efforts by Ratu Mara to develop a peaceful, multiracial society under the old Alliance government, he said that Mara had tried 'to achieve something that was

impossible'.[16] Rabuka's views on the place of modern democratic politics
in Fiji are equally uncompromising, and also form an important part of
his justification for the overthrow of parliamentary democracy. Following
the 1987 coups, he claimed that his Western critics (especially those in
Australia and New Zealand) were virtually blinded by their ethnocentric
attachment to democratic forms. 'They do not understand Fijian society.
I believe they are judging Fiji according to European standards. As far as
I am concerned, we are not a European society.'[17] Nonetheless, it seems
that Rabuka feels compelled to pay lip-service to the normative idea that
democracy is a universal good. However, this leads inevitably to a revision
of the concept in terms suitable to Rabuka's thinking and the situation
he has created in Fiji. 'I think democracy is a relative term ... What is
democratic in a European society might not be democratic in our system.
We have our own system of democracy.'[18] But Rabuka's view of 'Fijian
democracy', which is reflected in the new constitution, clearly precludes
a meaningful political role for the majority of Fiji's citizens.

In terms of entrenching authoritarianism and reinforcing the
boundaries between the ethnic groups in Fiji, as well as endowing Fijian
nationalism with much of its ideological force, the constitution-makers
have used the powerful rhetorical resources associated with chiefly power
and status. Again, political discourse in Fiji, at least on one side of
politics, has long been imbued with appeals in support of chiefly
authority. The nature and implications of this issue are best understood
in the context of certain aspects of Fiji's colonial history and the Fijian
sociopolitical system.

Colonization and Indirect Rule

European contact first occurred in the seventeenth century, and continued largely through the activities of explorers and traders. Of the
latter, the majority came from the Australian colonies rather than
Europe, and the same holds true for much of the western Pacific.
Capitalist penetration of Fiji commenced when the sandalwood stands
found in the southwest of Vanua Levu and harvests of bêche-de-mer were
incorporated into the trade network.[19] The traders were followed in the
nineteenth century by missionaries who first arrived in the islands in
1835 via the Wesleyan mission in Tonga, and who settled initially in the
eastern areas.[20] Previous Tongan migration from the northern Vava'u
group to the Lau region of eastern Fiji had established a strong Tongan
presence which assisted the advance of the missionaries. It was shortly
after this that the Tongan warrior Ma'afu, cousin to the powerful
Taufa'ahau (who became the first of Tonga's 'modern' monarchs),
consolidated his position in the Lau group and assumed the title 'Tui
Lau'[21] – a title now held by Ratu Sir Kamisese Mara.

British colonization in 1874 followed a period of internal strife in the Fijian islands, much of which involved rivalries between Ma'afu and the powerful Bauan chief, Ratu Seru Cakobau. Bau was one of three eastern confederations, or *matanitu* (the others being Lau and Cakaudrove), which had come to dominate all of the small islands off the north and east coasts of Viti Levu and Vanua Levu, as well as significant areas of the main islands themselves.[22] The strife, however, was not simply a matter between islanders, and European interests were very much involved in the political turmoil. With the aid of European groups, various forms of government, usually purporting to exercise authority over the whole of the Fiji islands, were attempted under the leadership of Cakobau, with suitable concessions to Ma'afu, but these attempts were largely unsuccessful. Apart from the disruptive activities of some Europeans, a major factor in their failure was the lack of sociopolitical unity among Fijians.[23] Given that there was no sense in which a 'national' polity existed in Fiji at that time, and that there were quite different practices and structures throughout the Fiji islands, this is hardly surprising. The solution to the problem of government and control, not only over Fijians but also over many unruly Europeans, was finally found in an act of unconditional cession to the British Crown. Of the Fijian chiefs whose signatures appear on the Deed of Cession, including Cakobau, Ma'afu, and ten other high chiefs, only one was not from the east.[24] Fiji was thus brought under the mantle of British colonialism through the agency of eastern chiefs, and it was these Fijians who, by and large, were to benefit most from colonial rule and who were able to carry many of those benefits through to the independence period.

Colonization did much to unify the various groups of Fijians, at least in institutional terms. First, and most obviously, the diverse communities were brought together as a single political entity to form a British Crown Colony – and one which, following the urgings of the Earl of Carnarvon (then Secretary of State for the Colonies in the Disraeli government), was 'of a rather severe type'.[25] Although representative government was introduced by degrees over the next ninety years, the initial (and most severe) form of Crown Colony government meant that executive responsibility was vested exclusively in the governor who was responsible only to the cabinet in London.[26] Fiji's first substantive governor, Sir Arthur Gordon, came to the new colony with very firm, paternalistic ideas about how colonized people should be treated. He was particularly concerned that indigenous Fijians should not suffer the same fate as many colonized peoples elsewhere, especially with respect to the erosion of their customs and land ownership at the hands of European entrepreneurs. Gordon was primarily reponsible for establishing the institutions and practices which are now held up as the essential foundations of Fijian tradition. They were designed, in part, to reflect the new 'national character' of the island group and were necessary as much for administrative convenience as for fulfilling Gordon's stated desire of establishing a form of indirect rule in order to support traditional chiefly authority.[27]

One such institution was the Council of Chiefs,[28] now regarded as one of the foremost symbols of a homogenized Fijian tradition. Although there had been some gatherings of chiefs before colonization (mostly in the larger political units of the east), the council is unquestionably a colonial artifact, brought into being under colonial rule. Since it has existed now for over one hundred years, it can clearly be called traditional in some sense. But it is certainly not traditional in the pristine, pre-colonial sense described earlier, nor can it be said to have endured since 'time immemorial'. The same applies to a number of other important colonial practices and institutions, which together may be termed 'neo-traditional' impositions.

One of the most important neo-traditional bodies established in Gordon's time was the Native Administration – later renamed the Fijian Administration. In keeping with Gordon's philosophy, as well as the exigencies of colonial bureaucracy, the administration was to operate through what was thought to be the traditional chiefly system, with certain modifications to ensure compatibility with the functions of colonial government. It was also both logical and convenient for Gordon to turn initially to the most powerful chiefs with whom relations had already been established by traders and missionaries, and these were the paramount chiefs of the eastern regions. The system which emerged was therefore based very largely on the sociopolitical structures characteristic of the east which were, relative to the central and western regions, much more authoritarian and highly stratified.[29] In this way, 'Fijian traditional structures' were redefined to meet the criteria of uniformity as well as to legitimate the new system, in much the same way as had occurred in parts of British colonial Africa.[30]

The Fijian Administration, which effectively set up a form of local government through indirect rule for Fijians alone, persisted throughout the colonial era and into independence. Between 1915 and 1944, however, the mode of rule was much more direct, with traditional chiefs taking a lesser role in the management of Fijian affairs. But the system was revitalized in the mid-1940s, largely under the influence of Ratu Sir Lala Sukuna, a paramount chief of the eastern province of Bau. Sukuna's generally conservative attitudes, with respect to both the chiefly system as well as the suitability of democratic institutions in the Fijian context, were highly influential in setting the tone of debate in later years. In introducing the Fijian Affairs Bill in the Legislative Council in 1944,[31] he argued strongly for the retention of chiefly power, and against the introduction of more democratic institutions in the colony which, he believed, were unsuitable to the Fijian cultural milieu.[32] In an earlier communication, he had critically assessed the suitability of democracy in terms of plural society ideas. These remarks, however, were prefaced by a generally negative assessment of the democratic mode of rule, through which he maintained that 'men of low attainments, without instruction in the art of government and without the sense of responsibility that comes from great inherited traditions' would come to dominate the legislature. Invoking the conventional wisdom of plural society theory, he further described democracy as a 'form of government experience has shown to be suited to Dominions politically and racially homogeneous but rejected in Colonies peopled by small numbers of whites alongside preponderantly native communities that differ from Europeans in language, culture and religion'.[33]

In the later colonial period, the Fijian Administration came in for a great deal of informed criticism, most notably from two reports commissioned by the Legislative Council. The Spate Report covered many areas of Fijian development (or lack thereof), and was especially critical of the role of chiefs – a role that Sukuna had earlier defended with vigour.

> The functions of the chief as a real leader lost much of their point with the suppression of warfare and the introduction of machinery to settle land disputes, but constant emphasis seems to have led to an abstract loyalty in vacuo, to leaders who have nowhere to lead to in the old terms and, having become a sheltered aristocracy, too often lack the skills or the inclination to lead in the new ways. Hence, in some areas, a dreary negativism: the people have become accustomed to waiting for a lead which is never given.[34]

The second report was issued just one year later and echoed many of the concerns of the Spate Report. One recommendation was to give ordinary Fijians a direct voice in the Legislative Council, on the grounds that the chiefly appointees, and the Council of Chiefs which was primarily responsible for nominating them, was not fully representative of Fijian opinion.[35] This was eventually achieved, but not without strong opposition from the Council of Chiefs which agreed to endorse the change only by a narrow minority.[36] So although some recommendations of the reports were taken up, the Fijian Administration remained the primary institution for managing and directing virtually all Fijian policy under chiefly leadership. In the 1970s, Nayacakalou's equally critical work on Fijian leadership was published. Nayacakalou highlighted the opportunities missed by Fijians, especially in terms of economic development, in clinging to a system that had demonstrably failed to provide tangible benefits. He drew particular attention to the fact that the Fijian Administration rested on fixed beliefs about the role of chiefs, as well as on the proper channels of authority and communication 'which assumed that the people were bound to their chiefs and to their land in unalterable ways which were defined once and for all by their birth'. He continued:

> The Fijian Administration claimed to be based on the traditional system and yet to have the aim of development into a modern institution. It was the most important single source from which was derived the framework of ideas associated with 'building on traditional institutions', 'adaptation', and change 'within the framework of traditional culture'. This is a powerful set of ideas in which the Fijians believe firmly. But it contains a basic contradiction in that one cannot change and preserve at the same time ...
>
> It seems to me that one of the greatest obstacles facing the Fijians today is the failure to recognize that there is a contradiction; they must make the momentous choice between preserving and changing their 'way of life'. The belief that they can do both is a monstrous nonsense with which they have been saddled for so many years that its eradication may be very difficult to achieve.[37]

Little has changed, for the dominant Fijian political party that succeeded the Alliance after the coup has based its philosophy of economic development for Fiji very largely on the same 'monstrous nonsense'.

The Politics of Land and Indigenous Paramountcy

Another important policy initiated under Gordon's administration concerns the land. Again, uniformity of land tenure practices under chiefly control throughout Fiji was required for the purposes of colonial management through indirect rule. In this area, however, attempts to discover a uniform 'tradition' were frustrated for some decades and the system that was finally adopted, and which persists to this day, represents one of the most distorted bodies of so-called traditional Fijian practice. In this respect, it is important to note that traditionalist interpretations of ideas about *vanua* (literally 'land'), which incorporate a host of mystical values as well as more practical aspects of land ownership and usage, developed strong normative links with eastern chiefly authority and came to constitute a powerful political symbol subject to intense, instrumental manipulation. The mystical elements which are said to resonate among Fijians, especially when told of real or imagined threats to their *vanua*, have been most clearly expressed by a conservative Fijian anthropologist in the following terms:

> [The land] is the place where [their] ancestors preceded [them] and in which their spirits or souls linger and watch over the affairs of those who come after

them. The vanua contains the actuality of one's past and the potentiality of one's future. It is an extension of the concept of self. To most Fijians, the idea of parting with one's vanua or land is tantamount to parting with one's life.[38]

This romanticized interpretation of sentiments about the land, however, does not reflect the realities of pre-colonial practices, nor, for that matter, some contemporary practices. Furthermore, to the extent that this interpretation has any validity, it relates quite specifically to male prerogatives. It has been pointed out, for example, that on marriage a woman was effectively separated from both her land and her ancestors.[39] The recent work of Ward[40] gathers together a mass of evidence to demonstrate the variety of practices relating to land, both before and after colonization, which indicate very clearly that Fijian groups were able to detach themselves from the land both materially and spiritually. In the nineteenth century, for example, there is much evidence to suggest that the Fijian population was highly mobile:

> The tukutuku raraba, the histories of groups of people recorded by the Native Lands Commission, tell of frequent moves from one settlement site to another, the splitting of yavusa or mataqali [clans], the relocation of the different parts, and the coming together of groups which may or may not have had prior kinship links. The distances involved in these moves were often considerable and took people into areas where they did not have prior land claims but where they obtained land by a variety of mechanisms.[41]

It has also been found that with the tendency of groups to move around, land was often transferred temporarily from one group to another, and sometimes alienated permanently. Ward also notes that the evidence gathered by the Land Claims Commission (when it was attempting to assess European claims to land in the period after colonization) shows that 'in many parts of the country the appropriate chief could transfer and sell lands to others, Fijian or non-Fijian, if he so wished, and that such actions were accepted as legitimate by his people'.[42] On this point, Ward concludes that the concept of the inalienability of Fijian land was 'invented' in the 1870s and became enshrined through a 1912 Ordinance.[43]

In a seminal book on the subject of land and the fixed understandings that have evolved in this context about Fijian tradition, France also traces the development of powerful colonial orthodoxies that tie many of the most important concepts associated with land to chiefly legitimacy.[44] This is reinforced in Ward's work which elucidates the context within which chiefly status may be enhanced by links to the land. Ward points out, first, that traditional social and political status was not necessarily related to the size of land holdings. Rather, chiefly power was derived from the authority exercised over people in their capacity as both a labour force and a fighting force. This could be managed through a combination of diplomatic manoeuvres, the forging of alliances, and through the exercise of personal abilities rather than through control of land as such. He also notes, however, that linkages with legendary events and sacred places could work to bolster the validity of chiefly authority and that 'myth and tradition linking people to place could be moulded to fit current realities'.[45]

Another recent analysis explores these concepts specifically in the context of 'Fijianness' in that they have acted to constitute the basis of 'identity and authenticity in Fijian culture'.[46] And again, Ward's study articulates the context of power relations and ethnicity within which this is set in contemporary politics:

> The retention of an unreal ideal of native land tenure is now a basic component of the creation and maintenance of Fijian identity as set against that of Fiji Indians, other Pacific Islanders and the people of other nations. One frequently stressed component of Fijian public identity is the sense of community, communal responsibilities, and the respect for chiefs and their role in the social structure. Land is an integral part of this complex both because the codified model of land tenure is based on that structure, and because nominal authority over a group's land is one of the foundations of chiefly status. The inalienable control of land had become an icon of ethnic distinctiveness. It is what Fijians have and other ethnic groups do not.[47]

The political implications of these issues have been expressed in a classic statement on the link between the land and Fiji's leading chiefs that was reported in the press during the 1987 election campaign. One prominent Alliance politician (and chief) charged the Coalition with attempting to destroy the inseparable link between the *turaga* (chiefs) and the *vanua*. At the same time, a warning was issued concerning the dire consequences for the future of Fijians: 'The Turaga and the Vanua were one – one could not exist without the other – the chiefs were a bulwark of security for all and custodians of Fijian identity, land and culture'.[48] This suggests, of course, that in the absence of a strong, working chiefly system, indigenous Fijians would lose all their important rights, especially in relation to land, and therefore virtually cease to exist as a unique community.

In a commentary on some of my previous arguments on the subject of Fijian land and the myths and distortions associated with it (which are similar to those outlined above),[49] Carens has highlighted several important normative issues that have not been adequately acknowledged or addressed in the critique of traditionalism as it pertains to land. In my earlier work, for example, several advantages (as well as the disadvantages) of the colonial tenure system were noted, especially the extent to which an influx of European settlement was discouraged by the strict control of land. This meant that Fijians could not be pushed further and further off their lands to accommodate white settlement and 'development' as had occurred in the neighbouring colonies of Australia and New Zealand.[50] So, as Carens points out, the preferable historic course for Fijians seems clear, for whatever other economic and social costs were borne by Fijians under the colonial plan for land ownership and tenure, these 'pale beside the costs of the alternative suffered by the indigenous people of Australia and New Zealand'.[51]

There can be little argument against this perspective, but this does not mean that the tenure system in place today is immune from critique, especially in terms of the way in which its internal operations work against the interests of many ordinary Fijians, as well as the many Fiji Indians whose economic security also depends on access to land. The continued reservation of land ownership entitlements for Fijians does not preclude devising an equitable system through which the needs of both indigenous Fijians and Fiji Indians can be met and which may result in greater economic benefits for Fiji as a whole. And it is too often forgotten that the problem of land is not simply one of Fijian interests versus Fiji Indian interests. This implies not only that their interests are mutually exclusive, but also that all Fijians have the same interests. The prime beneficiaries of the present tenure system are chiefs who collect a disproportionately large share of land rental monies, while ordinary Fijians get very little return. Reform of the land tenure system, therefore, may result in a reduced return to chiefs, but a greater benefit to ordinary Fijians.[52]

The issue of land clearly gains much of its political salience with the presence of Fiji Indians, and this brings us to another of Gordon's early policies. In order to establish a firm economic base for the colony while preserving customary ways of life against the usual depredations that followed the use of indigenous labour for plantation work, Gordon decided to introduce indentured labourers from India. The first of these labourers arrived in 1879, and many more followed until the scheme was abolished in 1916. Of the 60,000 Indians transported to the Fiji islands under indenture, some 20,000 later returned to India while the rest, together with a smaller number of free immigrants, remained as settlers. By 1945, the number of people of Indian ancestry in the colony outnumbered indigenous Fijians for the first time.[53] Indigenous Fijians and Fiji Indians now make up over 90 per cent of the population with small numbers of Europeans, part-Europeans, Chinese, and other Pacific Islanders making up the balance.[54] As suggested earlier, this demographic configuration is one that can be described in terms of classic plural society theory, the tenets of which endorse essentialist notions about the internal unity, boundedness, and exclusivity of cultural/ethnic groups.

The period of rapid Indian population growth in the early part of this century was, as Lal points out, of more than statistical significance. It also signalled a very profound transformation in the social, cultural, and psychological basis of the Indian community. In the earlier days of immigration under the indenture scheme, Indians tended to be 'socially isolated, economically dependent, culturally disoriented, and politically disorganized and voiceless'. Furthermore, they were expected to 'accept as permanent and proper their place at the bottom of the Fiji social hierarchy'.[55] It is within this context, and the general framework set by plural society ideas, that another important doctrine, also initiated in the time of Gordon, developed in Fiji. Briefly, this doctrine holds that the rights and interests of indigenous Fijians with respect to their lands and customs are virtually inalienable. Most importantly, these rights and interests are to be held as paramount over and above those of any other community in Fiji. The paramountcy doctrine arose at the time of colonization and rested on a loose interpretation of the Deed of Cession. It was nowhere codified but became nonetheless another powerful orthodoxy in the ideological arsenal of chiefly power, especially after the introduction of Indian labourers and their subsequent struggle for political rights.

Although its initial purpose was to prevent European encroachment on indigenous rights, the most important consequence of the doctrine for contemporary politics is that it relegates Fiji Indians to a subordinate status in the hierarchy of rights and interests. This underscores the notion, implicit in the new constitution, that Fiji Indians (either individually or as a group) have no legitimate claim to the exercise of political power on a basis of equality with indigenous Fijians.[56] This is despite the many assurances given to Fiji Indians that their status, as British subjects, would be equal to that of any other colonial subjects. The earliest statement of this intention, known as the Salisbury Despatch, was made in 1875 in the general context of Indian indentured labour in British colonies:

> Above all things, we must confidently expect, as an indispensable condition of the proposed arrangements, that the Colonial laws and their administration will be such that Indian settlers who have completed the terms of service to which they agreed as the return for the expense of bringing them to the Colonies, will be in all respects free men, *with privileges no whit inferior to those of any other class of Her Majesty's subjects resident in the colony.*[57]

In the specific context of Fiji, a later report affirmed the rights to which Fiji Indians were entitled:

The present adminstration [of Fiji] itself fully recognizes the value of Indians
as permanent settlers, and is willing to concede them the enjoyment of equal
civil rights. The whole tenor of the correspondence between India and the
Colony shows that it was on this condition that indentured immigration has
been allowed in the past, and any measures directed towards lowering the
political status of the immigrants or reducing their economic freedom would,
in our opinion, involve a breach of faith with those affected.[58]

The growth of the colony's broader political institutions (as distinct
from those provided specifically for indigenous Fijians) was influenced
decisively by the doctrine of Fijian paramountcy as well as the general
philosophy surrounding the system of indirect rule. Fiji Indians were
never to enjoy effectively the same political rights as others in the islands,
even though the 1970 constitution provided a more equitable form of
parliamentary representation than other constitutional instruments
before or since.

Fijian Sociopolitical Structures

Since the earliest days of Rabuka's post-coup regime, the notion that
Fiji's chiefly elite is the only proper and legitimate focus for the political
loyalty of indigenous Fijians has been asserted repeatedly. One of the first
actions of the regime was to convene the Great Council of Chiefs which,
predictably, endorsed Rabuka's intervention thereby giving it some
semblance of legitimacy. The role of Fiji's chiefly elite in the process of
constitutional change following the coup was a prominent one, at least at
the level of endorsing the wishes of Rabuka with respect to the
'objectives' of his coup. In June 1990, the Great Council of Chiefs
reconvened to approve the new constitution. Again, this approval was a
key part of the process of legitimation.[59] This directs attention to the
nature of chiefly authority and the basis of traditional (and neo-
traditional) Fijian leadership.

Chieftainship as a political institution providing traditional leadership
for indigenous Fijians is structured formally around kinship groups and
is based, through these, largely on principles of seniority and patrilineal
descent. There are other factors, however, that qualify this rule because
genealogical knowledge is poorly developed in Fiji, especially when
compared with Tonga and Samoa. Nayacakalou reports that genealogies
may be avoided or sometimes varied 'in order to facilitate the direct
interplay of forces in selecting leaders on the basis of personal qualities,
or of the political power of the groups which support them'. He adds that
it is impossible now to observe the free operation of the traditional
system for selecting chiefly leaders because of the rigidity introduced by
British exercises in codification.[60] Nonetheless, a hierarchical grading of

chiefs can be seen to be linked to a progressive set of sociopolitical units based on the *i tokatoka* (extended family group), the *mataqali* (a larger primary kinship group), and the *yavusa* (clan). Several *yavusa* combine to form a larger territorial unit – the *vanua* (which is also the literal word for 'land'), and this is usually the largest patrilineal group. In the eastern regions, political networks were wider still and here, beyond the *vanua*, was the *matanitu* (which is translated more or less as 'state' and is also used for the modern rendering of 'government').

Chiefly positions featured at all these levels, and the most powerful chiefs were naturally those who headed the larger units. The differentiation of chiefs from commoners was (and is) determined by the special position of chiefs in relation to the structures described above – a position through which they are given, according to tradition, 'precedence, loyalty, obedience, authority, privilege and respect' and which was reinforced through rituals and ceremonies which symbolize the subordination of the commoners to their chiefs.[61] This is a simplified description of what is understood to be the traditional position of chiefs vis-à-vis commoners, and it is important to emphasize that the status of chiefs and the nature of sociopolitical structures generally varied throughout Fiji, especially as between the eastern regions and the central and western areas. These differences require at least a brief elaboration.

A number of ethnographic studies have highlighted the relatively hierarchical structures of chiefly power and control in the eastern regions, which more closely approximate a Polynesian model, and have contrasted these with the lower level of stratification found in the central and western areas of Viti Levu.[62] Arguments about the contextual significance of these differences, especially in terms of their importance in analyzing the events of 1987 and other developments, have been canvassed in more recent literature, with writers like Scarr attributing no special political importance to intra-Fijian cultural or sociopolitical differences.[63] This view accords with the tendency of plural society theorists to treat the broader categories of ethnic groups as internally homogeneous. Others recognize that there has been considerable resentment among Fijians from the central and western areas of Viti Levu about the predominance of eastern chiefly power and that this resentment is related, among other things, to sociopolitical differences in 'traditional society'.[64] The major points to be noted here are that there are tangible differences between the east and the central and western regions, that these are based on linguistic and other cultural factors (including the institutions associated with chiefly power), and that they still carry some political salience despite the homogenizing effects of colonial institutions and eastern chiefly hegemony.

One other point to be noted here is the effect of Christianity on the traditional chiefly system, especially in terms of the synthesis worked out in practice between Christian principles and pre-Christian beliefs in some areas. In a study of contemporary Fijian understandings of tradition in the context of religious beliefs and practices, it has been argued that the 'light' brought by missionaries is perceived not as a violation of pre-existing practices, but as a means by which the 'inherent Christianity' of the Fijian people was revealed. This study identifies the ways in which chiefly hierarchies, which are posited as the guiding principle of social order, are seen to be divinely sanctioned. Indeed, the Christian god stands at the very peak of the Fijian social hierarchy.[65] Another study of political hierarchies in Cakaudrove, which examines both the historical and contemporary contexts of chiefly power there, shows that many of the pre-Christian taboos have simply been 'Christianized' and continue to provide an ideological basis for chiefly legitimation in modern politics:

> The head of the vanua Cakaudrove, the Tui Cakau, who was a member of the i Sokula lineage, was the paramount of the matanitu. Subordinates of the Tui Cakau thought of them ... as sacred, the descendants and representatives of the ancestor-gods and as such gods themselves. This ideology asserted they ruled by right ... and Fijian paramounts are believed, still, to hold their position because their right has been prescribed. To prove this the Bible may be quoted: 'For there is no authority except from God, and those [governing authorities] that exist have been instituted by God'.[66]

It is evident that chiefly power in contemporary Fiji derives in part from pre-colonial institutions, and much of the legitimacy with which chiefly leaders seek to bolster their status in the modern state rests on this foundation.[67] We have seen also, however, that the notion that contemporary chiefly power and the institutions which support it are 'purely traditional', is quite misleading. Of course, the mere demonstration that these sociopolitical practices are, in many ways, distortions of pre-colonial traditions and patterns of chiefly authority is in itself unremarkable. After all, tradition is never static, and the point that its continuous reconstruction is a feature of virtually all social life has been well established.[68] What gives contextual significance to neo-traditional transformations is the extent to which they serve the interests of chiefly legitimation in contemporary Fijian politics. This is especially so with respect to the transfer of legitimacy from the traditional to the contemporary national sphere. It is significant also in relation to the rejection of Western democratic values, in favour of (neo)traditional political authority, which is reflected in the new constitution. What is really at issue, then, is the evocation of political symbols as ideological tools, and whether they have been used as 'instruments of liberation or of oppression'.[69] For that reason, the account of the colonial construction of tradition in Fiji given here is not simply or even primarily concerned with exposing inauthenticities, but more with understanding the processes by which they have acquired authenticity.[70]

To summarize, it has been shown that certain colonial institutions and practices in Fiji, such as indirect rule through a separate administration, the establishment of a uniform land tenure system, as well as early missionary activity, brought about important transformations in the power relations between the various traditional polities. The most significant of these was the degree to which the mantle of eastern chiefly authority was extended over the entire island group, at the same time subsuming many pre-existing sociopolitical formations in other regions. Many eastern chiefly leaders were incorporated into the new colonial institutions, thereby enhancing both their dominance and legitimacy in the new order. And, as Kaplan points out, the adoption of eastern norms and values as the standard model for indirect rule meant that customary practices in the other regions were necessarily viewed as 'illegitimate and disorderly'.[71]

By independence in 1970, the reins of the ruling Alliance Party were firmly in the hands of eastern chiefs. Many members of the same chiefly elite remain at the helm of the Sovereign Democratic Republic of Fiji. In other words, these chiefs were able to transfer their legitimacy, and therefore a certain political authority, from one sphere to the next, first from the dominant pre-colonial polities to the 'national' colonial polity, then to the government of the independence period from 1970 to 1987, and then again, after the coup, to the interim government of the republic. The only hiatus in continuous eastern chiefly dominance was during the very brief tenure of the Bavadra government. The general elections of 1992 and 1994, however, have seen some changes in the distribution of power among Fijians, and these will be discussed shortly.

A major point of the discussion so far has been to show that the impression of a unitary Fijian society was achieved, inter alia, by the spread of eastern chiefly authority and sociopolitical structures and that this has been vital to the differentiation of political groupings as well as to the rise of Fijian nationalism in contemporary politics. More specifically, the unitary view of Fijian society and culture has been an essential device in maintaining a high degree of political solidarity among Fijians, as opposed to Fiji Indians (whose interests are represented as necessarily antipathetic). This has created the conditions under which Fijian leaders have been able to appeal rhetorically to assumed group interests – also an important ingredient in the plural society syndrome. Further, by aggregating assumed Fijian interests under the mantle of their 'protection', the chiefly elite added an important dimension to their own political legitimacy among Fijians. The Alliance, for example, had long held itself out as the only party capable of protecting the special rights and interests of indigenous Fijians from the ever-present threat of encroachment by Fiji Indians, and rhetoric of this kind was prominent during the 1987 election campaign – as indeed it had been ever since political parties were first formed in the 1960s. Moreover, as we shall see in the next section, the Alliance had been concerned to stress its close connections with traditional Fijian chiefly rule as a further important aspect of its ability to protect indigenous interests.

The Background to the 1970 Constitution

Political organization in Fiji has always been based on ethnicity, and representative institutions clearly reflected this from the earliest colonial times. In the first Legislative Council, instituted in 1904, only European members were elected while indigenous Fijians were appointed from among the ranks of chiefs from a list of nominees submitted to the governor by the Council of Chiefs. From 1916, one Fiji Indian member was appointed by the governor until 1929 when the Fiji Indian community was granted a franchise to return three members on communal rolls separate from those for Europeans. These communal rolls were introduced and retained despite constant pressure against the system from politically active Fiji Indians and, until the 1930s, from the government of India. Until 1936, Europeans held as many seats as the Fijians and Fiji Indians combined. In 1936 a superficial parity of representation was attained with the three major population groups being allocated five seats each. Europeans and part-Europeans then numbered 4,023 and 4,574 respectively, while indigenous Fijians numbered 97,651 and Fiji Indians just over 85,000.[72] The franchise was not extended to any women until 1963. Indigenous Fijians received the franchise in the same year but, in keeping with previous practice, were placed on communal rolls of their own.

Fiji Indians opposed the system of separate communal rolls largely because they resented the inferior position it assigned them vis-à-vis the small but influential European community. Throughout the colonial period Fiji Indian political leaders sought, unsuccessfully, to introduce some form of a common electoral roll. Europeans opposed a common electoral roll because they feared it would lead inevitably to political and economic domination by the Fiji Indians whose numbers were, of course, very much greater. But it was in relation to the position of indigenous Fijians, and the doctrine of Fijian paramountcy of interests, that Europeans put forward their major justification for separate rolls.

Table 1:   Composition of the Parliament of Fiji 1970–1987

House of Representatives

Fijian Communal	12	Fijian National	10
Indian Communal	12	Indian National	10
General Elector Communal	3	General Elector National	5
Total = 52			

Senate

Council of Chiefs' Nominees	8
Prime Minister's Nominees	7
Opposition Leader's Nominees	6
Council of Rotuma's Nominees	1
Total = 22	

Notes: The system of voting and organization of electorates for the return of members to the lower house was exceptionally complex. Each voter had four votes, one in a communal electorate and three (one for each racial grouping) in a national electorate. A Fijian voter, for example, would vote for a Fijian candidate in the appropriate communal electorate, and cast three additional votes, one for a Fijian, one for a Fiji Indian and one for a General Elector in the appropriate national electorates. The method of voting was first-past-the-post. The term 'General Elector' was introduced to categorize Europeans, Part-Europeans and 'other races', such as Chinese.

Europeans in the Legislative Council claimed that the Fijian people had ceded their country so as to be governed by the British race, and held themselves up as protectors of the Fijians against the threat of 'Indian domination'. Furthermore, Europeans encouraged Fijians in the belief that any extension of political rights to Fiji Indians via a common roll would endanger their land ownership. Despite the fact that Fijian lands (constituting some 83 per cent of all land in Fiji), had been vested permanently in Fijian kinship groups and made legally inalienable, these fears persisted in a susceptible Fijian population.[73] In later years, the ever-present bogey of an Indian land grab – impossible though it was under the 1970 constitution – was used to great effect by the Alliance to maintain its Fijian support base as well as by Rabuka and the Taukei movement to whip up Fijian support for their activities.[74] As a corollary, the land issue gave the Alliance the basis on which to mount the claim that the interests of the Fiji Indians were essentially antipathetic to those of the indigenous Fijians which is, of course, another key factor in the plural society syndrome.[75]

In the lead-up to independence, a more complex system of communal representation was introduced. This allowed a little more movement in the otherwise inflexible racial categorization of electors and candidates.

Table 2:   Ethnic Composition of Governments 1972–1987

	1972 Alliance	1977(a) Alliance	1977(b) Alliance	1982 Alliance	1987 NFP[†]/Labour
Fijians	22	14	20	17	7
Fiji Indians	7	4	8	5*	19
General Electors	7	6	8	6	2
Totals	36	24	36	28	28

[†] NFP = National Federation Party
* This number increased to 6 in a by-election in 1985.

Nine 'crossvoting' or 'national' seats were introduced in addition to the existing communal seats and, although three of these were allocated to each of the ethnic groupings in keeping with the idea of ethnic parity, the candidates were to be returned by all the ethnic groups voting together in the special electorates created for the purpose. The essential basis of communal representation was retained at independence, but several more modifications were introduced in the 1970 constitution. The total number of members for the new House of Representatives was increased to 52 as set out in Table 1.

While providing marginal flexibility in terms of ethnic voting, the retention of such a large number of strictly communal seats virtually ensured that the parliamentary party of governments elected under the system would comprise many more members of one of the major ethnic groupings than the other. This is evident in Table 2 showing the ethnic composition of all governments elected under the 1970 constitution.

Another point to be emphasized in relation to the communal system is the scope that it provided for ethnically-oriented appeals for votes – a problem that has long been recognized as inherent in communally-based systems of representation.[76] Electoral contests throughout the post-independence period in Fiji were characterized by appeals to communal interests. This created considerable difficulties for the Fiji Labour Party (and later the Coalition), in its attempts to confront the plural society syndrome by opening a new multi-ethnic discourse and, especially, in establishing its legitimacy as a political party capable of representing Fijians and Fiji Indians simultaneously. We next consider the party system in Fiji and the difficulties posed for its development by the plural society context and chiefly power.

The Rise and Fall of Labour

Since divisions between Fijians and Fiji Indians were fostered by institutional and political developments in the early-to-mid-colonial

period, these were inevitably reflected in the emergence and consolidation of the party system in the last decade before independence. The
National Federation Party (NFP) had its origins in the predominantly Fiji
Indian canegrowers' unions in the early 1960s but quickly established a
wider support base among Fiji Indians due, among other things, to
popular grievances against European (not Fijian) class domination and
political privilege.[77] On the Fijian side, the major vehicle for the political
dominance of the eastern chiefly establishment, from before independence until the 1987 coup, was the Alliance Party. Established in 1966 as
a response to political organization among Fiji Indians, the Alliance was
led from its inception by Mara. Its major component was the Fijian
Association, an organization formed a decade earlier for the purpose of
protecting the political rights and interests of indigenous Fijians under
Fijian leadership.[78] The Alliance also included two other small groups –
the Fiji National Congress (composed of Fiji Indians opposed to the
major Fiji Indian party) and the General Electors' Association (made up
of the small numbers of Europeans, part-Europeans, Chinese and
others). The ethnic basis of organization evident in these groups was a
reflection of the electoral system in which each and every voter was
designated as belonging to a particular ethnic group. Until the emergence of Labour and its subsequent coalition with the NFP, electoral
contests between the Alliance and the NFP were characterized by the
kind of ethnically oriented rhetoric described earlier.

It is important to emphasize that neither the Alliance nor the NFP
were ever entirely monolithic in the sense that they drew their support
exclusively from just one of the two major ethnic communities, and this
is because neither community is homogeneous. As we have seen, there
are significant sociopolitical differences between eastern and western
Fijians and, similarly, the Fiji Indian community has long been divided
along religious, linguistic, and socioeconomic lines.[79] Despite the intra-
communal divisions, however, party leaders were able to maintain a
relatively high degree of cohesion in their respective bases of communal
support by manipulating anxieties about the so-called hidden agendas of
the other party in relation to issues such as land. Such techniques were
particularly effective among indigenous Fijians due to beliefs about the
dangers posed for them by the large Fiji Indian community. After
independence, Alliance rhetoric persisted with precisely the same tactics,
and this acted as an effective source of fear in reinforcing the apparent
desire of Fijians to remain politically united, to maintain their separate
institutions and distinctive traditions and to view these as differentiating
emblems of ethnic identity.[80]

The focal point of these institutions and traditions is, of course, the chiefly system which remained one of the most dominant forces in post-independence politics. Chiefly connections were used to great effect by the Alliance, not only to bolster its status, prestige and legitimacy, but also to attack parties opposed to it by depicting criticism of the Alliance as a direct attack on the chiefs and therefore an insult to all Fijians and their traditions. These factors had made the task of the NFP as an opposition party especially problematic since their criticisms of the government frequently met with facile accusations of anti-Fijian motivations and insulting attitudes towards the chiefs and 'their people'. A prime example of this type of politicking was evident in the campaign for the 1982 elections after the NFP had distributed for public viewing a videotape recording of an Australian television program which contained, among other things,[81] 'insulting' remarks about Fijian chiefs – especially Ratu Mara. In the opening segment, Mara was shown, together with some of his colleagues, while the narrator's voice-over said:

> Britain bequeathed the Westminster system of government to Fiji and it has worked for the 12 years since independence in spite of the lingering remains of an old feudal system: Government by *the descendants of the Great Chiefs who clubbed and ate their way to power in these islands centuries ago.* The democratic chief of Fiji for the past 12 years is such a descendant. A Ratu, a Chief, and a Knight too, Sir Kamisese Mara.[82]

This remark was interpreted by the Alliance as 'a deadly insult' not only to Mara and his immediate chiefly colleagues, but to the entire Fijian people. Because of the NFP's role in disseminating the videotape, the remark was turned against the party by suggesting that its action was 'anti-Fijian'.[83] The election campaign, from this point on, was diverted from attention to any other substantive issues. Instead, the remainder of the election period was dominated by an avalanche of Alliance rhetoric to the effect that the entire Fijian people had been ridiculed 'in a fashion never to be forgotten or forgiven'.[84]

After its defeat in these elections, the NFP seemed to lose its way, a situation not helped by internal dissent and leadership instability. In the next several years, however, the party system underwent some significant changes, most notably with the formation of the Fiji Labour Party in 1985. This added a new dimension to politics as well as to the general conduct of political debate in Fiji. Labour's formation was inspired essentially by a growing discontent with the economic and related policies of the Alliance and by the NFP's increasing ineffectiveness in opposing them. This soon led to a call for a new party oriented more towards the concerns of lower socioeconomic groups, regardless of ethnic identities.[85] Labour therefore set out to appeal to groups across the ethnic spectrum and to divert the old racially-oriented emphasis of political discourse in Fiji to a broader consideration of economic class and social justice issues. Labour performed well in its first electoral contest in the Suva City Council elections in December 1985, winning eight of the twenty seats. It narrowly missed defeating both the NFP and the Alliance in a by-election for a seat in the House of Representatives three weeks later. Following the latter contest, however, it became apparent to both Labour and the NFP that the first-past-the-post method of voting could well ensure a resounding victory for the Alliance in the next round of general elections. Despite some dissent from within the ranks of both parties, a formal coalition was established by the end of 1986, thereby consolidating the major opposition forces.

The new coalition was clearly capable of presenting a significant threat to Alliance hegemony. The Alliance's response was to continue to warn Fijians against the dangers of a non-Alliance government. In 1986, the year before the next general elections, Alliance leaders and spokes-people concentrated on land and related issues, with Mara once again asserting that unless proper Fijian leadership was supported by the body of Fijian people, rights to land would be endangered.[86] Another senior Fijian argued that: '[T]he chiefs represent the people, the land, the customs. Without a chief there is no Fijian society. When Fijian chiefs are attacked or criticised in whatever capacity – personal or political – it is the Fijian *vanua* which is also being criticised'.[87]

In the campaign for the general elections which followed in 1987, the Coalition attempted to address issues in a manner that transcended narrow questions of ethnic interests. Alliance rhetoric, however, re-mained explicitly directed at creating fear and uncertainty among Fijians in relation to their special rights, and emphasized the legitimacy of the chiefs – especially those connected with the Alliance – as the 'natural' rulers of Fiji. But the Coalition had one significant advantage over parties and coalitions that had previously opposed the Alliance. It was led by a highly respected Fijian who, although not himself a chief, was nonetheless a member of a prominent chiefly family from the west of Viti Levu. In addition, his wife, Adi Kuini Bavadra, had chiefly status in her own right. All the same, Bavadra faced a formidable task in terms of establishing his own legitimacy among Fijians in the face of decades of eastern chiefly predominance, especially as the leader of a coalition that drew much of its support from Fiji Indians. His public statements highlighted some of the major difficulties:

> In the contest that democracy provides us, one person's vote is exactly the same as another's. A chief, be he ever so high in the traditional system, does not have five votes where his people have four ... In previous elections, the

Alliance fear tactic used to include asking people whether they wanted an Indian Prime Minister; now ... the leader is a Fijian, so the question is whether a non-chief should be Prime Minister.

One could thus imagine that if an equivalent chief from another province challenged Ratu Sir Kamisese, the Alliance question would be: 'Can we let a Prime Minister of Fiji come from any province but Lau?'[88]

But the question of chiefly power and status, as well as the perennial questions concerning security of Fijian rights under a non-Alliance government, were not the only issues in the campaign. One of the other major issues, and one that had been raised by Labour over the past two years, concerned corruption among Alliance leaders and their dealings with prominent businesspeople, in which Mara himself was implicated. Another involved more general problems with the structure and administration of the Native Lands Trust Board, since it had long been evident that few ordinary Fijians were reaping any significant benefits from their much-vaunted land-owning privileges. Rather, it was said that land rental monies were appropriated largely by chiefs and that in many areas little was distributed to those below them.[89] Moreover, the level of bureaucratization involved with managing and leasing land had left individual *mataqali* members with very few effective rights.[90]

Opinion polling is virtually non-existent in Fiji, and there is no way of telling which particular issues carried the most salience among Fijian voters. But in the one poll that really counts – or usually counts in a democratic parliamentary system – the Coalition was able to win over a sufficient number of Fijian votes to give it 28 seats to the Alliance's 24 in the House of Representatives. For the first time since independence, the Alliance and its chiefly leaders were relegated to the opposition benches. Within less than six weeks, however, Fiji's brief experiment with democratic succession of government was destroyed by Lieutenant-Colonel Sitiveni Rabuka on the floor of the parliament, thereby resolving the crisis of legitimacy created for the tradition of Fijian chiefly rule by the Alliance's electoral loss.

In the weeks and months following the coup, violence and civil disorder in Fiji reached levels previously unheard of. Most attacks and assaults were initiated by informally organized groups of Fijians and were directed against Fiji Indians and their property. There was also a dramatic increase in crime, and between mid-May and mid-July the normal rate had doubled. In the weeks leading up to Rabuka's second military intervention, violence and threats of violence appeared to be linked most clearly with the Taukei movement which had emerged as an extremist Fijian nationalist movement immediately after the elections.[91] To the outside world, these troubles may have appeared to confirm the notion that Fiji's political problems were indeed the result of deep-seated ethnic animosity. But it must be emphasized that increasing violence (ethnic or otherwise) became a problem only after the initial propaganda campaign by the Taukei movement in the aftermath of the election, and that it escalated further under Rabuka's regime. Indeed, Rabuka's own propaganda campaign can only be interpreted as a manipulation to maximum advantage of the plural society syndrome. One of the areas in which this was most evident was in Rabuka's use of religious divisions within Fiji – the majority of Fijians are Christian but most Fiji Indians are Hindu.[92] Rabuka had even linked a threat to Christianity with his justification for the coup. Dean and Ritova report that he had a concern that the 'immigrant race' of Indians were 'threatening the Christian principles, culture and heritage of the Fijian people'.[93]

Rabuka aimed to unite Fijians against the Coalition through the chauvinistic assertion of nationalistic rights, interests, and prejudices. But he achieved a great deal less success than he had hoped for. Fijian support for his actions was by no means united and the months between the coups were marked by protests and organized dissent among both Fijians and Fiji Indians. Moreover, many of the nation's older, established political leaders like Ratu Mara were now involved in negotiations with Coalition members over setting up a bipartisan caretaker government pending constitutional review. They were, in Rabuka's eyes, far too moderate. Rabuka later conceded that he had 'little confidence in the ability of the politicians to come up with an agreed formula that would also ensure that the coup "objectives" were attained'.[94] On 25 September, Rabuka reasserted his authority with a second 'coup' and on 7 October declared Fiji a republic. A quasi-civilian interim government was installed on 5 December, with Ratu Mara returning to the helm as Prime Minister and Ratu Ganilau assuming the presidency. Any hope of reintroducing a constitution based on genuine principles of parliamentary democracy, such as equitable representation, was now even more remote.

The 1990 Constitution

The original draft constitution was published on 23 September 1988 and combined proposals made by the Great Council of Chiefs and a Constitutional Review Committee (CRC) established by the interim government. It was then referred to another new body, the Constitution Inquiry and Advisory Committee (CIAC) which, after inviting and considering public submissions, submitted its report in late 1989. A revised draft constitution was eventually submitted to the Great Council of Chiefs in June 1990 and subsequently received its endorsement. The new constitution of the Sovereign Democratic Republic of Fiji was promulgated, to take immediate effect, on 25 July 1990 by President Ganilau without first being

Table 3: Composition of Parliament under the New Constitution

House of Representatives	
Fijians	37
Indians	27
General Electors	5
Rotumans	1
Total = 70	

Senate of Chiefs	
Fijian Chiefs	24
Rotumans	1
Other Communities	9
Total = 34	

released for public scrutiny.[95] Of special importance to the present discussion are the provisions concerned with the composition of the legislature, the structure of the electoral system, and the way in which each of these combine to entrench chiefly power.

The distribution of seats in this manner means that all members of the House of Representatives are elected communally. Of the 37 Fijians, 32 are returned on a provincial basis and the remaining five from urban areas. No provision is made for any cross-voting to take place. In other words, there is no way in which a Fijian voter, for example, can cast a vote for a Fiji Indian candidate (or vice-versa) as was possible under the 1970 constitution. With respect to the Senate of Chiefs, the 24 chiefly members are to be appointed by the president on the advice of the Great Council of Chiefs, the Rotuman member is appointed on the advice of the Council of Rotuma, and the remaining nine members representing 'other communities' are appointed by the president 'acting in his own deliberate judgement', although the president is directed to 'take into account the special interests of the minority communities'. This allows the president, who must be a high-ranking chief, to determine who will represent the 'other communities', including Fiji Indians.

Another important issue with the new constitution concerns the definition of who, and who is not, an 'authentic' Fijian. Section 156(a) states that for the purposes of the Constitution:

[A] person shall be regarded as a Fijian if and shall not be so regarded unless his father or any of his male progenitors in the male line is or was the child of parents both of whom are or were indigenous inhabitants of Fiji and his name is registered or eligible to be registered in the Vola ni Kawa Bula and includes persons who are registered or eligible to be registered in the Vola ni Kawa Bula by virtue of custom, tradition, or practice.[96]

Since the constitution was promulgated, the practical application of this section has produced many anomalies. Some people, who for years believed that they were Fijian, were suddenly confronted with the fact that since a paternal forebear was found to have belonged to another race, they were no longer regarded as Fijians. One of these cases concerned an elderly man whose paternal grandfather was a Solomon Islander. He was excluded from the roll of Fijians even though all his other forebears were Fijian and he had lived (and voted) as a Fijian all his life. Others with far weaker claims to 'Fijianness', however, were allowed to claim Fijian status using the clause which referred to recognition 'by virtue of custom, tradition and practice'. One case which was dealt with under this clause concerned a prominent businessman whose father was Chinese, but who was nonetheless granted Fijian status. One of the greatest ironies of the provisions was highlighted when some western Fijians pointed out that many eastern Fijians – including some of the highest chiefs in the region – were descended directly from Tongans who had invaded the area in the nineteenth century.[97]

The primary intention of the parliamentary structure is clearly designed to exclude Fiji Indians as a group from any meaningful share of political power. Given previous patterns of communal voting, and the fact that no crossvoting seats (which had proved the downfall of the Alliance in 1987) were included, it is almost impossible for any Fiji Indian candidates to be returned directly as members of a majority party and therefore as members of a government. The only way in which this can happen is if a majority Fijian party invites Fiji Indian members to join a government. Also, the inflated number of Fijian communal seats, combined with the strictly communal voting restrictions, means that governments can be formed without the support of a single Fiji Indian voter or, for that matter, a single voter from the 'other communities'. It seems to have been anticipated that in any electoral contest under this system, the dominant Fijian party (although this was not expected to be the Alliance in its old form), would be unbeatable. The version of Fijian 'democracy' reflected in the new constitution, then, appears to represent a form of political apartheid on the one hand, and the attempted institutionalization of a one-party state on the other.

It is worth emphasizing at this point that although there is no one institutional form that can be claimed to give ideal or exclusive expression to the practice of democratic politics, there are nonetheless certain features which are essential to its character. The constitutional relegation of any part of the citizenry to a position of virtual political irrelevance, whether this is a minority or a majority group, is quite obviously contrary to the character of democratic rule. Further, the institution of a system that attempts to guarantee the permanent domin- ance of a single political group destroys one of the most basic features of modern democracy, and that is the function of a constitutional political opposition. Where there is no possibility of the opposition becoming the government (at least through peaceful processes), no amount of constitutional or parliamentary window-dressing can obscure the non- democratic nature of the regime.

The consignment of Fiji Indians and members of other minority communities to virtual political oblivion, however, is not the only feature of the new constitution that has significant consequences for the conduct of politics. The way in which the constitution provides for the election of Fijians also bears close scrutiny, as do its provisions for enhancing and entrenching chiefly power. All but a small number of the Fijian constituencies are provincially based – an arrangement that is meant to reflect 'traditional' Fijian political organization, although these pro- vinces are in fact based on colonial administrative structures. The bias towards provincial representation discriminates heavily against the growing number of urban Fijians – whose voting patterns showed a marked trend away from the Alliance in the 1987 elections and were partially responsible for their defeat. At the provincial level too, there is discrimination against some of the more heavily populated western and central districts in favour of eastern constituencies. When the draft constitution was first released in 1988, dissent from western Fijians was most marked, as it had been following the coup.

Western Fijian dissent has also been reflected in efforts there to establish a new Fijian confederacy to counter the dominance of eastern chiefs, especially in the reconstituted Council of Chiefs (referred to in the new constitution as the Bose Levu Vakaturaga or BLV), which is now based on the eastern-dominated Fijian confederacies of Tovata, Bure- basaga, and Kubuna. The west, following the colonial construction of administrative practices, is currently divided between Burebasaga and Kubuna.[98] Several submissions, representing diverse interests among Fijians, were made to the CIAC, one of which came from a group of conservative western chiefs (and supporters of the old Alliance) led by the Tui Vuda. The submission proposed that a fourth confederacy for the Yasayasa–Vakara provinces be established – a move that would acknowledge the separate standing and interests of western Fijians. But the CIAC, anxious not to become involved with intra-Fijian dissent of any kind, concluded that:

[I]n view of the delicate and special nature of the subject, the question of admission of the 'Yasayasa–Vakara' provinces as a separate traditional confederacy is a matter on which the Great Council of Chiefs would need to make its pronouncements.[99]

It has been argued that the proposal for a fourth confederacy expressed political dissent in only a very narrow sense because it was not associated with the Fiji Labour Party and because its leadership was in fact largely pro-government (and, by implication, pro-chief).[100] It may not be pro-democratic dissent, but it indicated at the very least that Fijians were not united in support of the neo-traditional colonial structures on which the present arrangements are based. Another clear indication of dissent was the establishment in June 1991 of a new western-based political party, the All Nationals Congress (ANC), under the leadership of Apisai Tora.[101] There also emerged other dissenting groups in the west that were not only anti-government (and pro-Coalition), but were openly hostile to the efforts of the constitution-makers to strengthen neo-traditional authority. One of these, the 'Twelve-Member Committee of the Western Confederacy', articulated a clear challenge to developments of this kind:

While evoking an almost sacred call to preserve Fijian tradition, the proponents of the draft constitution seek to codify for their own benefit an oppressive, authoritarian system of thought and action that will usher in a new era of exploitative insular imperialism that augurs ill for Fiji and the Fijians.[102]

One of the major concerns of this group, expressed during the period of public comment on the draft constitution, was with the allocation of constituencies within the provinces. Attention was drawn to the fact that the relative value of votes in many of the western, central, and urban areas (which together comprise the majority of the Fijian population) was significantly lower in comparison with a number of provinces in the east. The most extreme example was the allocation to Naitasiri province in central Viti Levu, with a population of around 50,000 Fijians, of only two constituencies, while the province of Bua on the island of Vanua Levu, which has a population of around 10,000 Fijians, was also allocated two constituencies. A vote in Bua, therefore, has five times the value of a vote in Natasiri.[103] Malapportionment in the provinces is paralleled by a similar gerrymander against urban Fijians. The allocation of only five constituencies to these Fijians, who make up about 32 per cent of the Fijian population, effectively reduces the value of their votes to around one-third of the value of an average provincial vote. If the urban value was compared again with the value of a vote in some of the eastern constituencies, the disparity would be even greater. Rabuka had acknowledged early in the process of constitutional review that problems may well arise in terms of dissatisfaction with the allocation of Fijian seats, and admitted the 'likelihood of the Fijian members of parliament splitting up along provincial lines and creating a chasm'.[104]

These gross disparities in Fijian representation, which were clearly designed to favour the eastern Fijian provinces, signalled an unambiguous intention on the part of the chiefly establishment to consolidate their control, not merely at the expense of Fiji Indians, but at the expense of the majority of the Fijian population. This was to be reinforced further by the eastern-dominated Council of Chiefs. But none of this has worked out in practice as smoothly as the constitution-makers may have hoped. Both the 1992 elections and the events surrounding the 1994 elections demonstrate many of the difficulties that have been encountered in keeping Fijians united in the name of Fijian tradition, and these will be discussed shortly.

One factor that has changed the nature of political discourse in Fiji is that the political relegation of Fiji Indians has blunted much of the force of plural society rhetoric, thereby weakening an important rallying point for the old chiefly establishment. This has been reinforced to some extent by the general decline in numbers of the Fiji Indian population which has come about through a falling birthrate and, since the coup, a higher than usual level of emigration. Nor should it be forgotten that the deposed Coalition government did find some common ground on socio-economic issues between Fijians and Fiji Indians. Taken together, these factors have favoured the development of further intra-Fijian political disunity leading in turn to the formation of more rival Fijian parties. One of the long-standing minor Fijian parties, the Fijian Nationalist Party, is certainly anti-establishment and has a lengthy record of grievances against eastern chiefly privilege. Indeed the Fijian Nationalist Party argued in its submission to the CIAC that the chiefly system should be abolished altogether.[105]

In an effort to consolidate their position against a growing number of Fijian splinter groups, the chiefs formed a new party in 1990 which, in many ways, was simply a resurrection of the old Alliance. Called the Soqosoqo ni Vakavulewa ni Taukei (SVT), its constitution and manifesto state that it was formed by 'the Fijian people' following a decision by the BLV in June 1990 that a Fijian political party be established. Its objectives, inter alia, are:

> To promote the interests of the indigenous Fijians, their advancement, the protection of their rights and interests and to provide means of social, economic and political development in association with other ethnic communities in Fiji.[106]

More specifically it was reported as intending to:

> facilitate, promote and stimulate the accelerated promotion of the Fijian
> people in business, commerce and industry [and to] facilitate, promote and
> stimulate the economic and social development of the Fijian people in their
> villages, districts and provinces and protect, strengthen and promote the unity
> of the Fijian people and the consolidation of their tradition and culture.[107]

Although the chiefly system has been strengthened and further
entrenched at a formal institutional level, both constitutionally and
through party organization, this has not guaranteed that their long-term
grip on power has remained unchallenged. In fact, at the level of SVT
leadership, the reins are no longer held personally by a chief. Instead,
following Mara's retirement from active involvement in party politics and
his subsequent appointment as deputy head of state, the SVT was to go
into the next elections under the leadership of the commoner Rabuka.
The results of the two elections that have now taken place under the new
constitution provide the best indicators of the direction in which Fijian
politics have moved since the coup.

Party Politics and Elections in the Republic

At the opening of the 1992 election campaign, there was a general
expectation that the SVT was virtually unbeatable. As the official 'party of
the chiefs', and with an electoral system skewed clearly in its favour, the
SVT no doubt anticipated an unambiguous electoral victory. The
campaign itself was relatively quiet, partly because of restrictions imposed
by the electoral office on party advertising and promotional activities, but
also because it seemed as though an SVT majority was a foregone
conclusion. The range of ideological alternatives facing most Fijian
voters was narrow. Apart from the SVT itself, other minor Fijian parties
and independents displayed one brand or other of Fijian nationalism in
order to attract support. In the absence of any national seats, which had
previously required parties to pitch their manifestos to a multiracial
electorate, there was little incentive for Fijian politicians to do anything
other than appeal to purely Fijian interests.

The Fiji Labour Party, which had earlier decided to boycott the
elections and had changed its mind only a few weeks before the election,
attracted little support in the few Fijian seats that it contested. In the
Indian constituencies, however, it was remarkably successful, considering
the very short campaign that it ran, and managed to win 13 seats to the
NFP's 14. No other other Indian party or independent candidate
managed to win a seat. Table 4 sets out the results in all seats.

Table 4:   Composition of House of
Representatives after 1992 Election by
Party and Communal Group

Party	Number of Seats
SVT	30 Fijian + 1 Rotuman
FNUF	3 Fijian
STV	2 Fijian
Independent	2 Fijian
NFP	14 Indian
Labour	13 Indian
GVP	5 General

Source: Fiji Times, 1 June 1992.

These results show that Fiji Indian voters were divided evenly between
the NFP and Labour, and that the effect of minor parties and independents was negligible. Labour may have been even more successful had it
contested all Indian seats. As it was, it failed to field candidates in Nadi
and Bua, and these went almost automatically to the NFP. Labour's
results in the Suva urban area, however, showed that it had lost
considerable support there and the end result was that all of its seats were
based in the rural cane-growing areas.[108] The results in the General
Electors' seats showed that little had changed to shake the conservatism
in this constituency since the previous election or, indeed, since
independence. In all previous contests, General communal seats had
been won, without exception, by Alliance candidates. After the Alliance
had been formally disbanded, the General Electors' Association was
reconstituted as the General Voters' Party (GVP). After making a clean
sweep of the Generals' seats in 1992, its members aligned themselves with
the SVT, thereby carrying on an unbroken tradition of support for the
Fijian establishment.
    Although the outcome in the Fijian constituencies showed strong
support for nationalist sentiments, this did not ensure an unqualified
victory for the SVT. Rather, the results indicated that regional rivalries
played an important part in voter affiliations. This resulted in the SVT
gaining only 30 of the 37 Fijian seats, well short of an absolute majority.
Not surprisingly, SVT support was strongest in the chiefly establishment's
eastern heartland. In Cakaudrove, home to both Rabuka and Ganilau,
the SVT won around 98 per cent of the vote, while in Bua and Kadavu
the SVT candidates were returned unopposed. Lau, where the SVT
polled 96 per cent, was only slightly behind Cakaudrove. More
surprisingly, however, the vote in the urban Fijian constituencies, where

Labour had collected crucial Fijian support in 1987, favoured the SVT with 77 per cent of the overall Fijian vote. But in the west of Viti Levu, both rural and urban Fijian voters had shunned the SVT. Urban returns showed a relatively low 45 per cent for the SVT while in Ra it sank to only 21 per cent. The only province in the region which showed a majority in favour of the SVT was Ba where the party managed 52 per cent. When compared with the Alliance's record in all the pre-coup elections, the SVT's showing was quite poor. Indeed, with only 63 per cent of the whole Fijian vote, the SVT's results in 1992 were worse than the Alliance's all-time low in the March/April elections of 1977 when it polled only 66 per cent of the Fijian communal vote.[109]

The 1992 elections showed that the SVT, although by far the most successful of the Fijian parties, had failed nonetheless in its call for united Fijian support behind the party operating under chiefly patronage and sponsorship. One media report described the result for the SVT as a 'mauling', and also pointed to a number of implications that followed:

> Born with high hopes in the aftermath of the 1987 coups of uniting the Fijians under one roof and blessed with the prestige of so august an institution [as the Council of Chiefs], it must face the fact that it failed to win – as expected – the 37 seats ... the significance of the loss of the seven Fijian seats lies in the fact that they were provincial rather than urban seats. They were won by parties ostensibly standing for traditional values associated with the Fijian chiefly system but who, on closer inspection, actually represented radical departures from such a system.[110]

If the SVT represented the Fijian tradition of chiefly rule in principle, in practice the new government was relatively thin in chiefly numbers. Of its 30 parliamentary members following the elections, only seven bore the honorific 'Ratu' while the remainder were commoners who had risen through the ranks. Furthermore, Mara's son, Ratu Finau Mara, although elected to parliament via the SVT, had a relatively low political profile and was never a contender for the SVT leadership. It is evident, therefore, that despite all the rhetoric about the sacrosanct nature of the Fijian chiefly system and normative beliefs concerning its pre-eminence in Fijian politics, commoners by this stage had claimed the leading role in parliamentary politics. The results of the second set of general elections since the coup confirm this trend.

Rabuka's SVT government lasted only 19 months before it fell in the face of a budget defeat in the House of Representatives in November 1993. The fall was precipitated by the defection of seven SVT parliamentarians led by Rabuka's earlier rival for the prime minister-ship, Josevata Kamikamica (also a commoner). This followed a period of internal dissent and instability within the SVT that had been exacerbated in 1993 by Rabuka's role in the 'Stephens affair', especially when Rabuka was found to have acted improperly, and prima facie illegally, by agreeing to pay compensation for wrongful imprisonment to a businessman with a criminal history.[111] In the wake of the government's defeat, Mara, as acting president, took the opportunity during the opening speech to a meeting of the Great Council of Chiefs to urge political unity among Fijians. Mara was also reported as saying that chiefs should be wary of who they chose as candidates for the SVT.[112] As the campaign period started, however, Mara and other Lauan chiefs were soon shown to have adopted a position in support of the breakaway Fijian group.

The defecting group of SVT members, which included two ministers, quickly formed a new Fijian political party, named the Fijian Association Party (FAP), which fielded candidates in 25 of the 37 Fijian seats for the February poll, thereby threatening to split the Fijian vote further. But despite the rupture within its ranks, and the continued rivalry of the more strident Fijian nationalists as well as other minor parties and independents, the final result for the SVT was again 31 seats with only five going to the FAP and one to an independent. In the greatest blow to the FAP, Kamikamica failed to retain his seat in the Tailevu constituency. On the other hand, prominent SVT member, Fillipe Bole, lost his seat in Lau to Ratu Finau Mara who had been among the defectors forming the core of the new FAP. The other major Fijian losers were the more militant nationalists. Long-time leader of the Fijian Nationalist Party (and critic of the eastern chiefly establishment), Sakeasi Butadroka, failed to retain his Rewa seat and no other nationalist candidate succeeded against either the SVT or the FAP. The SVT also polled relatively strongly in the western rural and urban areas, winning seven of the eight Fijian seats in the region, although its support there was still much weaker compared with that in Cakaudrove.[113] The results in the west may indicate an easing of Fijian resistance in the region to the predominance of eastern Fijians, although the very short period of time for effective political organization before the elections could also be counted as a factor in the weaker showing against the SVT.

The SVT victory was heralded by some as a sign of continuing strong support among Fijians for the chiefly system. One of the three successful SVT candidates for Tailevu, Ratu Timoci Vesikula, interpreted the election results in these terms, attributing his win to the fact that the people in his electorate 'still respected and supported the chiefly system'. On the other hand, he depicted the slippage of around 3,000 votes to the FAP in the constituency as indicative of a move by some 'against the chiefly system'.[114] The leading chiefly SVT candidate in Tailevu, Adi

Samanunu Cakobau Talakuli, reinforced Vesikula's principal claim, stating that the electorate's rejection of Kamikamica and the FAP 'proved that chiefs kept and held the people together'.[115] Given the present context of electoral contests in the Fijian constituencies, however, these claims are rather simplistic. First, the dictates of the strictly communal system which enforces a very narrow choice for Fijian voters must be taken into account. Second, even within these constraints, it is evident that the chiefly establishment generally is far from united. The emergence of the FAP and its success in gaining all three of the Fijian seats in the eastern chiefly heartland of Lau, where it was formally endorsed by the Lau Provincial Council (of which Ratu Sir Kamisese Mara is the Chair), indicates a serious split within the ranks of the Great Council of Chiefs which first sponsored the SVT. Third, despite continuing rhetoric from the SVT about the importance of chiefly control, the SVT leadership, the parliamentary party, and cabinet remain dominated by commoners.[116]

With the strict enforcement of communal voting under the new constitution, the results in the Fiji Indian electorates, as in the previous election, had virtually no bearing on the formation of the new SVT government, which incorporates four GVP members[117] and two Fijian independents, giving it a total of 37 seats in the 70-member parliament. But the results in the Fiji Indian constituencies saw a return to outright predominance of the NFP, which took 20 seats to Labour's seven, indicating that Fijian Indians generally favoured its relatively moderate approach to resolving their grievances in contrast with the more confrontational stance adopted by Labour's leadership. NFP leader, Jai Ram Reddy, has had a reasonable working relationship with Rabuka, while the latter has frequently indicated a desire to establish dialogue with Reddy on the formation of a 'national unity' government incorporating some NFP members. Some have speculated, however, that Rabuka's overtures may have as much to do with political dissension among Fijians as with 'a change of heart towards the Indians'.[118] Given the narrow margin by which Rabuka and the SVT have held onto power, it is possible that he may have to look to some Fiji Indian support in the future, although persuading the SVT's sponsoring body, the Council of Chiefs, to make the concessions necessary to achieve this will be no easy task. Should Rabuka pursue this strategy, it will be one of the greatest ironies of the post-coup political situation. Nonetheless, it remains highly unlikely that any significant constitutional reform will take place. Fiji Indians are a marginal political force in parliament and their ability to influence political developments will remain tied to their perceived value as allies in intra-Fijian struggles for political control.

Conclusion

Although the constitution of the Sovereign Democratic Republic of Fiji sets up a form of elective parliamentary rule, even the most generous of interpretations cannot disguise the non-democratic nature of its political institutions. Neither procedural nor substantive democratic political practices are given any real force or meaning under its provisions. We have seen that, at one level, justification for the abandonment of these practices is linked superficially to the doctrine of Fijian paramountcy of interests and the notion that Fijian rights and interests were not sufficiently protected under the 1970 constitution. At a deeper level, however, justification clearly rests on certain assumptions about Fiji's plural society, the value of 'tradition', and the inappropriateness of 'introduced' democratic institutions. It is also clear that those chiefs who reject democratic norms are themselves committed independently to more authoritarian modes – namely those of their own 'traditional' culture from which their status is ultimately derived.

A major purpose of this discussion of tradition versus democracy in Fiji has been to demonstrate that the justification for the 1990 constitution rested largely on claims which were self-servingly false (with respect to threats to Fijian rights), while at the same time disguising the real motivation for the new constitution, namely, the attempted consolidation of chiefly authority. In the wake of the military coup, the essential mechanism of this apparatus was developed through a heightened sense of Fijian nationalism that was constructed in opposition to Fiji Indians, as well as to important elements of Western democratic principles, and expressed through the traditionalism of the chiefly elite. The implications of these factors for all the people of Fiji are clearly negative. In commenting on post-independence constitutional development in Fiji, Ghai has drawn attention to the manner in which both the 1970 and 1990 constitutions, with their heavy communal orientation, have contributed to the aggravation of inter-ethnic tension, suspicion, and mistrust. While constitutional instruments are obviously not the only relevant factor, the framework established by them is nonetheless crucial to the conduct of politics and the policy making process. Ghai further points out that political leaders have had neither the incentive nor many real opportunities for learning and understanding the anxieties and aspirations that move members of other ethnic communities. And in the absence of an inclusive political system which brings together the entire community, little has been done to develop a common perspective on pressing issues concerning the economy, education, industrial and infrastructure policy, and general social well-being. Instead, there is a widespread perception that security lies only within the bounds of communalism, and that people's interests 'are best served by inter-communal competition rather than inter-communal cooperation'.[119] This is a legacy of cultural politics and the deployment of traditionalism as a means to a political end.

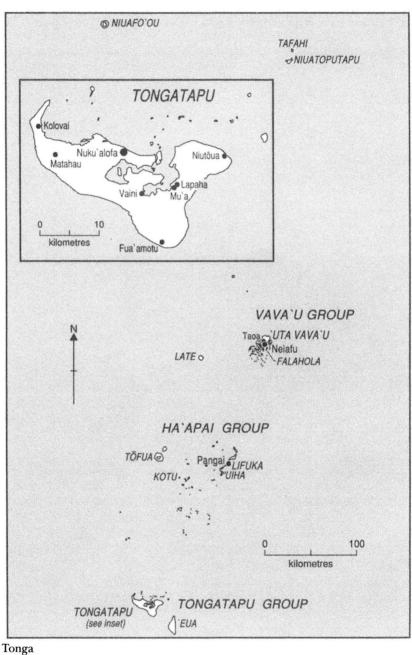

The map contains these labels:

◎ NIUAFO'OU

TAFAHI
↵NIUATOPUTAPU

TONGATAPU

Kolovai
Nuku'alofa
Matahau
Niutōua
Lapaha
Vaini
Mu'a
0   10
kilometres
Fua'amotu

VAVA'U GROUP
Taoa 'UTA VAVA'U
Neiafu
LATE ○
FALAHOLA

N

HA'APAI GROUP
TŌFUA ◎
Pangai
KOTU
LIFUKA
'UIHA

0   100
kilometres

TONGATAPU TONGATAPU GROUP
(see inset) 'EUA

Tonga

CHAPTER 3

The Monarchy Versus Democracy in the Kingdom of Tonga

Introduction

The islands which constitute the Kingdom of Tonga lie in three major groups (with numerous smaller islands around them) in the southwest Pacific region – southeast of Fiji and southwest of the Samoan islands – and yield a total land area of just under 700 square kilometres. Excluding the small outlying islands, the three main groups comprise the Tongatapu (southern) group; the Ha'apai (central) group; and the Vava'u (northern) group. Out of a total of around 160 islands, some 36 are inhabited and these sustain a population of about 95,000 people.

Until relatively recently the image of Tonga which struck most outside observers was one which exuded stability, contentment, and durability. The only remaining kingdom in the entire Pacific, Tonga had also been the only island country in the region to escape formal colonization during the period of European expansion in the nineteenth and twentieth centuries and was therefore spared the turbulence which has typically accompanied most moves to decolonization. It is widely accepted that Tonga's ability to remain independent had been achieved largely through the development of a unitary, centralized political system, presided over by an indigenous monarch, and which incorporated major elements of traditional sociopolitical organization. This system was entrenched through the promulgation in 1875 of a formal written constitution establishing the monarchy and a landed nobility, and codifying a set of principles and practices designed to sustain them as a ruling class. The superimposition of certain Westminster-style institutions, such as a prime minister, cabinet, legislature, judiciary, and electoral system, as well as a declaration of rights, gave the system some additional legitimacy in the European-dominated sphere of nineteenth-century international politics, although these by no means added up to

79

a democratic system of responsible government. The concentration of power in the hands of the monarch, and the extent of privilege granted to the nobility under the constitution, enshrined instead the basic principles associated with the descending thesis of government. In this respect, there is little doubt that the provisions of the 1875 constitution resonated very clearly with traditional Tongan sociopolitical notions concerning the proper locus of political authority and legitimacy.

Writing in 1983, one commentator held that 'if "politics" is defined as a "struggle for power", there is comparatively little of it in Tonga'.[1] This accords with the image of stability referred to above and, at the time, was a reasonably accurate comment on the dynamics of Tongan politics. A decade later, however, a struggle for power has emerged, spearheaded by a determined pro-democracy movement which is pushing for significant reforms to the political system. There has so far been considerable resistance on the part of the ruling elite to these later developments, and the kind of democratic reforms advocated by the movement are unlikely to be realized in the immediate future. A much more remote possibility, however, is that the pro-democracy movement will simply wither away. The most recent general elections, held in early 1993, indicated growing support for its reformist aspirations – a trend which is unlikely to be reversed and which is bringing increasing pressure to bear on the ruling elite.

Although its protagonists were originally concerned with a set of specific issues concerning corruption and accountability, the pro-democracy movement is now presenting a significant challenge to the whole basis of government in Tonga and the system of privilege which it supports. While having no wish to dispense with the monarchy per se (indeed, loyalty to the monarch remains something of an article of faith), the movement and its supporters are seeking to reform the political system to bring it into line with a much more democratic form of constitutional monarchy and responsible government. Apart from corruption and the almost complete lack of accountability in the present system, proponents are also concerned with wider issues of social justice and equity for ordinary Tongans in terms of access to land, equal opportunities, and public welfare. The response of the privileged establishment (that is, the royal family and the nobility) has ranged from merely attempting to ignore the movement and the pressures that it is bringing to bear, to some attempts at repression, persecution of pro-democracy leaders, intimidation, and misleading propaganda.

Some justifications for maintaining the status quo are based on standard conservative arguments concerning the 'tried and tested' nature of long-standing institutions and the dangers inherent in meddling with these. Koloamatangi, reporting one conservative Tongan view on the viability of the present system, says that the supporting 'evidence' consists of little more than 'the fact that the system has survived for over a thousand years'.[2] Other arguments which emphasize the uniqueness of Tonga's political institutions, and its basis in an equally distinct body of tradition, clearly draw on nationalistic sentiments. While it may be acknowledged that this past was not entirely exemplary, it is nonetheless valued as a repository of important icons through which the romantic imagery so essential to nationalism can be evoked. The emphasis on distinctively Tongan images reflects the universal tendency of nationalist thinking to exalt the parochial elements of national differences and national individualities.[3] Another strong nationalistic rallying point, and one which has helped to shroud present constitutional arrangements in a mantle of sanctity, is the notion that these arrangements were historically instrumental in securing Tonga against foreign domination in the past and should therefore be defended as a matter of pride, gratitude, and loyalty in the present.

At the core of many of these arguments lies an appeal to 'tradition' which supports the view of Tongan culture purveyed through nationalist images and which seeks to anchor the legitimacy of the present political system in the remote past. As one observer has noted, however, Tongan 'tradition' is neither timeless nor homogeneous, and this is clearly evident in the record of internal struggles for power which characterized the centuries preceding the formal unification of Tonga in 1875.[4] Many of the internal ruptures and changes were not the result of external influences, but arose almost entirely within Tonga's own political dynamics, thereby illustrating the point that pristine traditional systems do not necessarily, if ever, enjoy a state of natural equilibrium. Another commentator holds that the apparent stability of Tongan politics throughout most of the twentieth century is not a legacy of the distant past, 'but merely the projection and amplification of an image which is historically shallow'.[5] This raises once again the question of authenticity and the problem of invented as opposed to genuine traditions, the salience of which lies in the way the past may be used as a source of allegedly inviolable norms of political conduct in the Tongan present. The critical evaluation of present arguments centering on the issue of tradition and democracy in contemporary Tonga must therefore be grounded in what is thought to be the Tongan past.

The Origins of the Political System

Archaeological evidence, derived from the earliest radiocarbon-dated material so far discovered, indicates that the Tongan islands were probably inhabited no later than 1,140 BC. Like the Fijians, the earliest inhabitants of Tonga were makers of the distinctive, elaborately decorated Lapita pottery.[6] There are no Tongan migration myths to account for the first settling of the islands. Rather, the myths convey the belief that the earliest Tongan people were created in Tongatapu and that they were 'small, black and descended from worms'.[7] Other myths concerning the genealogical origins of the ruling dynasty say that the Tu'i Tonga line, through which the present monarch and many of the nobles trace their ancestry, commenced with 'Aho'eitu, believed to have descended from the skies following the union of his divine father with his Tongan mother.[8] Although, as one observer notes wryly, his method of arrival is questionable,[9] orally preserved genealogies support 'Aho'eitu as the actual founder of the dynasty in the tenth century AD.[10]

Although there is little to tell us about the sociopolitical relations of the earliest Tongans, there are indicators pointing to the probability that the Tu'i Tonga line was founded by alien chiefly lineages penetrating the group and superimposing a non-indigenous hierarchy on an earlier system. This is supported in part by the myth of 'Aho'eitu as a progeny of the sky which implies the supremacy of an invading ruler, as well as by aspects of local chiefly customs which suggest the survival of forms from the pre-Tu'i Tonga era.[11] Robert Williamson's account of Tonga's early political system refers to a group of conquering 'Tangaroans' who, having subjugated the original 'pre-Tangaroan' people, adopted the posture of divinity while at the same time assigning commoner origins to the soil – hence the belief that they were created from worms.[12] The alien origin of the ruling Tongan dynasty is further supported by anthropological studies which have elaborated the theory of the 'domesticated stranger-king'.[13] It should be noted here that the stranger-king phenomenon was evident elsewhere. Sahlins, working largely in relation to Fiji, but also noting the extent of the phenomenon in other parts of Polynesia (including eastern Polynesia), observed that this type of archaic kingship

> makes its appearance from outside the society. Initially a stranger and something of a terror, the king is absorbed and domesticated by the indigenous people, a process that passes by way of his symbolic death and consequent rebirth as a local god.[14]

Another commentator on Tonga proposes that the idea of 'descent from the sky' was commonly applied to any foreign arrival, including that of the early explorers and missionaries. It is further suggested that the divinity of the Tu'i Tonga line may not have been properly established in local lore until the late eighteenth century when a new myth, implying supernatural legitimacy, became necessary to bolster the weakening authority of the incumbent title holder. Thus the 'descent from the sky' trope may have been transformed from one which simply referred to a foreign arrival to one which attributed divine origin to the Tuʻi Tonga line.[15]

Whatever the precise origins of the Tuʻi Tonga line and the nature of the myths surrounding the ruling dynasty, it is certainly clear that a hierarchy of chiefly control developed from the eleventh century onwards and extended throughout the islands. The pattern which emerged, and which has left its traces in contemporary Tonga, indicates that a number of chiefs exercised effective control at the various local levels while paying homage and allegiance to the Tuʻi Tonga. Convention has it that this figure, standing at the apex of the entire system, retained the spiritual and secular leadership of the islands as a whole.[16] Marcus describes the pre-contact Tongan polity as 'a highly stratified kingdom, which, along with ... Hawaii, is conventionally cited as an extreme case of the hierarchical social organisation considered typical of Polynesia'.[17] It was under this system that the early Tongans also engaged in various 'imperial' adventures around the region and the twelfth century has been described as the high point of a so-called Tongan empire. Campbell says that although nothing certain is known about this empire, various places are mentioned in legends indicating that the Tongans ranged as far afield as ʻUvea, Futuna, Samoa, various parts of Fiji and Tuvalu, Rotuma, and even Vanuatu. There is nothing to suggest, however, that this amounted to an empire in the sense that Tongan rulers actually established direct control over the populations in these places.[18] Even in the case of Samoa, about which it is commonly asserted that Tongan invaders ruled directly, Campbell says that this does not imply more than that a Tongan lived and ruled in Samoa (and in any case, perhaps by invitation rather than force), and was later driven away after proving himself objectionable.[19] What the oral histories and legends do establish is that Tongans and Samoans had relatively extensive contact with each other in this early period.

To return to the early sociopolitical system in Tonga, the standard accounts suggest that the system lasted as a fairly well-centralized, unitary system until the closing decades of the fifteenth century when the twenty-third Tuʻi Tonga, Takalaua, was assassinated. Although assassinations may well have occurred before this time, thereby altering balances of power and the institutions that supported these, no oral histories of such events survive.[20] It is generally agreed, however, that Takalaua's son, Kauʻulufonua, was the major figure responsible for initiating the important changes in the political structure of the fifteenth century which were designed to avoid a recurrence of violence aimed at the person of the Tuʻi Tonga. He split the duties of the Tuʻi Tonga by creating a new title, Tuʻi Haʻatakalaua, which he gave to his younger brother. This title was to carry with it the responsibility for the secular, practical aspects of government. In a retreat from the more dangerous role of political leader, Kau'ulufonua retained only his religious functions, although he preserved all the honour and privileges that accrued to the rank of Tu'i Tonga. Nonetheless, the separation of power meant that the position of the Tu'i Tonga was weakened. As Goldman remarks, power was an attribute of hierarchy as well as a means by which hierarchy was sustained. When power balances were disturbed, therefore, as in the division of the Tu'i Tonga's powers and responsibilities, the end result was not its preservation, but rather the opposite.[21]

Further important developments occurred in the seventeenth century when the sixth Tu'i Ha'atakalaua created another new title, Tu'i Kanokupolu, which he assigned to his son, Ngata, with the intention that he exercise firmer control over the troublesome Hihifo district. Through a combination of internal tensions, as well as some influence from increasing contact with external forces, this tripartite system began to disintegrate in the eighteenth century. By the nineteenth century, far-reaching formal constitutional changes took place. These were more clearly the result of missionary influence (by now firmly established in the islands), and had the effect of breaking down much of the localized traditional chiefly system.[22]

The period of internal political instability and change described above was accompanied by a decline in traditional religious practices. Cummins writes that:

> The modifications of the Kingship in the fifteenth century into sacred and secular divisions highlights the radical political and religious changes that were taking place. The murder of Takalaua was itself a desperate act of irreligion. Kau'ulufonua, the son who avenged the assassination of Takalaua, is reputed to have entrusted his back to the protection of the gods in a battle, and when wounded exclaimed: 'The gods are fools'. During the civil disturbances at the close of the eighteenth century sacred houses were in some instances destroyed, sanctuaries violated, gods and priests abused and ignored, and the Tu'i Tonga himself opposed in battle by his subjects.[23]

The Sociopolitical System

Like other Polynesian societies, Tongan society to the time of the 1875 constitution was based on a complex, hierarchical system of chiefly rule. Its monarchical structure under the headship of the Tu'i Tonga, however, was quite unique in the Pacific, and some find it comparable only with distant systems of the kind that supported the Dalai Lama and the Japanese Emperor.[24] From all accounts, the chiefly system was one of the most rigid and severely authoritarian in the region. One commentator remarks that Tonga had the character of a 'chain of islands bound together by the battles of warrior chiefs who could at will, and with impunity, club any commoner to death'.[25] Another points to the degree of chiefly control in terms of resources: 'The chiefs owned all the land and could take what they pleased from their tenants and even kill them', and further: 'The arbitrary power and cruelty of some of the chiefs is manifest from the early accounts. The Tuʻi Kanokupolu Tukuaho cut off one arm from each of his cooks and Ulukalala tortured and drowned his political enemies.'[26] Goldman's analysis holds that in order to demonstrate its awesomeness, chiefly power was often exercised to the very margins of propriety and that the requisite meekness of the lowly orders provided a suitable contrast with displays of power by the higher strata.[27]

On the other hand, Latukefu notes that the key to the socio-economic system was an underlying principle of reciprocity which, when operating at its best, provided a stable and relatively peaceful lifestyle. He also says that by virtue of the fact that commoners served their chiefs with loyalty and devotion, and made their tributes as required, chiefs in these circumstances would find it difficult to deprive their people of land or otherwise abuse their authority.[28] The reciprocity of obligations and duties (*fatongia*) on the part of the chief lends a more humane touch to the less appealing images described above.[29] Furthermore, others have detected an underlying theme of chiefly status by achievement rather than pure ascription, as well as a populist dimension to chiefly power. Biersack, following Latukefu, says that a chief who neglected the people, or who actively exploited them, may himself have been abandoned or even assassinated, regardless of his pedigree, thus leaving open the constant possibility of usurpation.[30]

These sanctions, however, do not really amount to a system of status by achievement rather than ascription – it seems more accurate to depict it as a system which embodied an element of achievement as necessary for retaining effective chiefly status that still rested largely on ascription. Furthermore, the essence of the order was undoubtedly a matter of total, unquestioning obedience (*fakaapaapa*) on the part of Tongan commoners.[31] In this, there is virtually no trace of an egalitarian ethos in which legitimate dissent could be expressed by the lower classes: '[C]riticism was taboo. It was an anti-value'.[32] We shall see in the next chapter that the traditional form of a village meeting in Samoa, the *fono*, was a place at which extensive discussion took place (even if this was – and still is – only among *matai*, or chiefs). In Tonga, however, the *fono* did not function to provide this sort of forum. It was never more than a meeting where instructions were issued by chiefs to those below them.[33] The structural inequalities with which the sociopolitical system was suffused reached into every aspect of life. The forms adopted in art, for example, reflected and defined unambiguous dimensions of social inequality. They permeated the entire range of artistic activities which included music, dance, tattooing, woodwork, and the production and decoration of bark cloth, mats, baskets and ornaments.[34]

Given these factors, it is hardly surprising that contemporary democratic principles have little resonance with traditional ones. Helu argues that values such as equality and social justice have therefore been enormously difficult to approach in practice. This is reflected in a Tongan expression that encapsulates the anti-equality ethic very clearly: *Oua e tangi ke tatau na'a 'ita 'a Taufa'ahau* (Do not aspire to be equal lest Taufa'ahau be angered).[35] At times, however, others have pointed to concepts that resonate with more liberal ideas. Hau'ofa, for example, maintains that the word *fa'iteliha* (unrestrained) is a unique Tongan term which expresses something of a democratic ethos in traditional Tongan culture.[36] But there is little doubt that whatever traces of liberal elements may be detected through such conceptual expressions, these have been almost completely dominated by what Hau'ofa has elsewhere called 'the basic authoritarian personality of Tonga'.[37]

Tonga's polytheistic religious belief system naturally complemented the sociopolitical hierarchy – indeed they comprised the two sides of the same coin. The standard view of the traditional system holds that every chief was possessed of some degree of supernatural power in the form of *mana* which was derived directly from the gods, and the higher the chiefly position, the greater the *mana*.[38] In addition, chiefs were surrounded by a system of taboos (*tapu*) and, again, the higher the chief, the more complex the taboos. But while commoners were required, on pain of death or at least a severe beating, to observe customary laws and taboos very closely, the obligations of chiefs were, depending on rank and circumstance, less strict. Following the pattern described above, it seems that the higher the chiefly rank, the greater the freedom to violate taboos without incurring supernatural wrath. It is also evident that murder, theft, and adultery were regarded as offences only when committed against a person of equal or superior rank, or if the stolen object was sacred.[39]

In all these respects, the Tu'i Tonga apparently enjoyed the greatest privileges. He was also distinguished from all other Tongan males in that he was not tattooed, nor did he undergo the otherwise common circumcision operation. The ceremonies surrounding special events in his life (and death), such as marriage and burial, were much more elaborate than those for people of lesser rank. Moreover, he was not addressed in the ordinary language of Tonga, but in a special honorific language.[40] This practice persists to the present day alongside another special language level for the nobility. Thus the three broad levels of the contemporary class system, that is, royalty, nobility, and commoners, correlate with three speech registers each containing a different, class-specific vocabulary.[41] The pre-Christian belief system described here clearly conforms to the type that Weber elaborated in his formulation of 'traditionalist authority': namely, that the cluster of norms associated with the system were, at least for the commoners, considered sacred and inviolable and that infractions 'would result in magical or religious evils'.[42]

Relations between chiefs and gods were mediated by priests, and this empowered the latter to the extent that they were second only to the chiefs themselves in terms of political influence.[43] Each chiefly lineage appears to have had its own deity with a priest presiding over rituals and the *fakahaeleanga* (sacred possessions of the god). The aid sought through the priest was sometimes accompanied by the offering of finger joints or even human sacrifice.[44] An aspect of religious belief that illustrates the degree of alienation between the chiefs and the common people within the social structure concerns the Tongan version of paradise (*pulotu*). Entry to *pulotu* was open only to the chiefly class, while it was believed that commoners turned into vermin after they died – hence the term *kainangaefonua* (eaters of the soil) was applied to the lower class. Furthermore, there were no moral conditions pertaining to eligibility for entry to *pulotu*, so chiefs gained automatic admittance regardless of their conduct during mortal life, while the exclusion of commoners, no matter how exemplary their behaviour, was apparently absolute.[45] Beliefs of this kind were clearly antithetical to Christian teachings, and the subsequent inculcation of the latter among the Tongan people necessarily produced a profound change in their entire way of thinking about the mechanisms of retribution and reward.

Associations linking the ruling strata with divine power and privilege have nonetheless continued to influence the way in which the contemporary royalty and nobility is viewed, and there remains a general belief that these higher classes are 'divinely pre-conditioned' as social and political leaders.[46] But this is hardly unique to Fiji, Tonga, or Western Samoa. As we have seen, the link between the Almighty and those in power in the terrestrial sphere is a common historic feature of conservative political doctrine in the West (as well as in other places, including Islamic and Confucian cultural areas). A general political problem with the ethos surrounding the ruling class in the present era concerns the apparent difficulty that many ministers and nobles have in accepting direct questioning, let alone the criticism that is normally part and parcel of a parliamentary system. Thus, while there are no constitutional impediments to freedom of speech – indeed such freedom is guaranteed by the constitution – there are very considerable social inhibitions. This is further reinforced by a degree of self-interest on the part of those who may be subject to criticism and who have so far resisted calls for accountability.[47] In summary, it is evident that the religious belief system was closely interwoven with and provided strong support for the traditional Tongan sociopolitical hierarchy and that its influence is manifest today in the cultural norms and values regulating interaction between the different strata. The impact of Christianity, however, was decisive for formal political developments as well as for diluting, at least to some extent, the ethos of the rigid class system with certain principles of equality and freedom.

European Contact and Christian Conversion

The decline in traditional religion accelerated with the eventual establishment of Christian missions in Tonga. There had been sporadic contact with Europeans (*papalangi*) since the seventeenth century and early visitors included Tasman and, later, Cook whose early impressions led him to call Tonga the 'Friendly Isles'. By the end of the eighteenth century, a few Europeans – including sailors, some escaped convicts from New South Wales, and missionaries – were effectively resident in the islands. Through trade and other means, Tongans were able to acquire European goods, including weapons with which local wars were prosecuted with increasing fatalities.[48] The petty wars of this period, however, retained the character of previous internal skirmishes in that they were concerned largely with the control of local resources and were not necessarily provoked by external pressures. In any event, the scale and intensity of these wars was as nothing compared with the later civil wars which exhibited all the characteristics of holy crusades. These wars, which were essentially over Christian conversion and political unification, were to finally draw the islands into a centralized state structure presided over by a monarch and a landed nobility.[49]

Initial attempts to establish Christian missions in the islands had met with dismal failure. The earliest missionaries, having arrived in Tonga-tapu under the sponsorship of the London Missionary Society in 1797 with high hopes of bringing salvation and civilization to the Tongan people, were forced to leave in despair after some had been killed and the rest forced to flee their initial base. The Wesleyans who followed in 1826 enjoyed greater success. Perhaps their most fortunate choice was to attach themselves to the paramount chief of Ha'apai, Taufa'ahau, who was later to become King George Tupou I. Christian conversion for leading chiefs in the ensuing period became very much a matter of political expediency. For example, Gailey's analysis points to the fact that

Taufa'ahau, who did not convert until 1831, manipulated both customary and European means of consolidating power, and did not allow the
missionaries to conduct a significant proselytizing effort until he was
convinced of its utility in assisting his own efforts at political consolidation.[50] Latukefu also writes that after some initial resistance, other
important chiefs who had suffered defeats in some of the ongoing power
struggles became disillusioned with what they perceived as the failure of
their own gods to assist them, and began to question the validity and
efficacy of the old ways. They also came to believe that 'the way to achieve
their ambitions of acquiring the wealth, knowledge, and power of the
white man was to adopt his religion, for he must have acquired all these
things from his superior and more powerful god'.[51] As for the lower
classes, they had much to gain, including souls and the prospect of an
afterlife, both of which had been denied them by the old religion.[52]

The subsequent spread of Christianity was relatively quick and less
than thirty years after the Wesleyans first established their base virtually
the whole of Tonga was brought within the fold, although not all as
Wesleyans. In the years following Taufa'ahau's conversion, wars continued between various factions, by now attracting the designation of
Christian and heathen. This was partially resolved by the conversion to
Catholicism of many remaining heathens on Tongatapu by a lately
arrived party of French Roman Catholic priests. By far the greatest
capacity for influence, however, undoubtedly lay with the Wesleyan
mission. This was partly due to its local development as a church which
assimilated the key characteristics of the Tongan social structure. It was,
in effect, 'a royal and chiefly church, with seats in the sanctuary alongside
its ministers for those who bore the titles of royalty, nobility or high local
rank'.[53] And when Taufa'ahau (using the title of King George[54]) issued a
code of laws for Tonga in 1838, the opening lines of the proclamation
clearly indicated the higher source of his authority: 'It is of the God of
Heaven and earth that I have been appointed to speak to you ...'.[55]

It is worth mentioning, however, that the introduction of the
European religion to Tonga (as elsewhere) was not simply a one-way
process of acculturation whereby Christianity in Tonga was implanted,
and remained, entirely European in form and content. It has been noted
that Christianity itself underwent some changes as a result of the process.
For example, many traditional melodies were worked into the church
music and Sunday feasts developed from pre-existing practices. It has
also been said that, today, the Tongan clergy of the Wesleyan-derived
Church of Tonga have internalized 'the histrionics of Tongan oratory so
thoroughly that their sermons [are] more pantomime and act than
spiritual guidance or homilies'.[56] Also, although the work of the
missionaries resulted in significant changes in traditional attitudes, there

were nonetheless contradictions inherent in the new religion, fusing as it did aspects of 'oppressive Hebraic tribalism and Christian individualistic ethics'. In the final analysis, the missionary 'ardour for success and the strength of chiefly dominance combined to produce a situation where Old Testament values were emphasized, reinforcing the local code of conduct and correspondingly suppressing the Christian egalitarian morality'.[57] A similar fondness for citing Old Testament sources of political morality in support of chiefly authority has been evident in Fiji as well as in Western Samoa. In the present political struggle for democracy in Tonga, however, it has been noted that many of the progressive clergy have been concerned to stress New Testament codes 'as the guiding principles of public and political behaviour'.[58]

To return to the earlier period, it is evident from the nature of the wars during this time that the concerns of warfare shifted under the impact of the new religious influence from traditional issues to a battle between the forces for centralization and those who opposed it. In the end, the latter were ultimately unsuccessful in maintaining the status quo and, by the closing decades of the century, the Christian chiefs and their retainers would become a new landed nobility while Taufa'ahau, as George Tupou I, assumed the position of sovereign.[59] The last battle of the era was fought and won in 1852 with Taufa'ahau emerging clearly as the victor. Hau'ofa writes that centralizing kingdoms are very often founded on the ashes of previously-independent aristocracies, and that Tonga was no exception. What Taufa'ahau achieved, then, 'was akin to the establishment of centralising kingdoms that contributed so much to the ultimate demise of feudalism in Europe'.[60] Having established himself as the most powerful Tongan of the time, Taufa'ahau was soon to impose formal constitutional political uniformity over the islands and develop the centralized kingdom which exists today. As a result, the old title of Tu'i Tonga also fell into disuse. The last Tu'i Tonga died in 1865 and no successor has ever been named. The Tu'i Ha'atakalaua title had already met with a similar fate when the last incumbent died in 1799.[61]

Constitutional Development

There is no doubt that the dominant Western powers of the nineteenth century regarded their own forms of government as the only appropriate model for any country aspiring to the status of a 'civilized' nation, and that those 'backward' nations which had not managed to develop the appropriate imitative institutions required both protection and political salvation – usually under the mantle of colonization. As Ferdon suggests, the sociopolitical system of 'traditional' Tonga hardly conformed to the Western ideal of civilized government, and the development of a 'constitutional monarchy' has therefore been seen as a vital factor in Tonga's relatively successful resistance to foreign control.[62] On the other hand, there was a great deal less in the way of strategic or economic value to be had in colonizing Tonga than there was, for example, in Fiji and Samoa and this must also count as a factor.

The constitution that was eventually promulgated or 'granted' to the people in 1875 by Tupou I was preceded by a series of edicts commencing with the Vava'u Code of 1838. This first code limited the arbitrary power of the local chiefs and established, at least in a formal sense, the rule of law. In addition, it sought to establish the supremacy of the monarch. Ledyard observes that in formulating the legal provisions of the code, the only assistance available was that of the Wesleyan missionaries and, as a result, it is permeated with 'both the influence of the Bible and of the typical, lower middle-class English thinking of the time'.[63] This was followed by the Second Vava'u Code of 1850 which elaborated many principles and practices established in the earlier code, further limited the power of the chiefs, touched briefly on land tenure, and defined the positions of the judges. The Emancipation Edict of 1862, as its title suggests, freed commoners from the effective serfdom they had endured for centuries. One missionary response was to herald the new edict as the 'Magna Carta of Tonga'.[64] It also contained a number of other measures, including a provision subjecting the monarch to the rule of law – an indication, according to one view, of how secure his position as undisputed ruler of Tonga had become.[65]

The constitution of 1875, which was strongly influenced by Hawaiian constitutional development and precepts of British constitutionalism, codified and expanded on the body of law established by the earlier codes. One important change brought about by the successive edicts, and more firmly enforced through the 1875 constitution, was the breakdown of local chiefly power. Most existing titled chiefships were not actually abolished, but were simply ignored by the new legal framework. Many chiefs became 'eiki si'i (petty chiefs) who, as Marcus tells us, were still able to pass on their titles and sit at the head of their kava circles, but found themselves effectively reduced to a status little higher than the bulk of the commoners around them. This resulted in one part of traditional Tongan society being more or less levelled rather than preserved in the new order.[66] This was a logical sequence to the previous codes and the Emancipation Edict which had done much to improve the lot of Tongan commoners and release them from the worst impositions of their servile status.

At the other end of the social spectrum, however, a select group of chiefs was chosen to become a new landed aristocracy or nobility. Thus Tupou I, although seemingly anxious to reduce the power of many chiefs in the old order and introduce a more egalitarian structure at the mass level, created an elite invested with enormous privilege at another level. So in what is widely referred to as a 'paradox and seeming blunder', the king appointed thirty chiefs as hereditary landed nobles (*nopeli*) as well as six ceremonial attendants with the traditional title of *matapule* who were also granted their own hereditary estates, thus 'carving out a permanent and constitutionally defined sector of traditional privilege in the new society'.[67] At the time, however, it seems that the formal creation of the noble class was necessary to dampen the opposition of the most powerful chiefs to the new order, and to gain their loyalty and support.[68] The new noble title holders, however, by no means encompassed the whole of the former chiefly aristocracy, and the great majority of the latter group were now officially untitled.[69] More generally, the new nobility reflected the influence of English feudal ideas. Powles notes that the Tongan noble title 'was created after the fashion of the English baronial; that is to say, although it is an honour or dignity held from the monarch, it is inalienable (except for treason), hereditary, and is permanently associated with estates'.[70] Powles goes on to point out the ways in which this deviated from pre-existing Tongan practices:

> In traditional times, adjustments would have occurred by way of the segmentation and re-alignment of groups. From time to time, succession would have deviated from the ideal of the blood line in order to accommodate the reality of contemporary power. Indeed the contrast between ancient and modern Tonga is exemplified by the fact that, while the Tupou dynasty may perhaps be dependent on some chiefly lines for the preservation of royal blood, the law of the state [now] places the supreme chief beyond the need to rely on support from other chiefs.[71]

With respect to the structure of power encoded in the constitution, it has been pointed out that certain desirable balancing elements common to both English and traditional Tongan law were largely omitted. For example, no formal provision was made for the reciprocity implicit in the relationships between chiefs and commoners in the earlier Tongan order and, while the powers of the higher chiefs were clearly spelled out and made enforceable, the document made no mention of chiefly obligations, let alone provisions for their enforcement. Furthermore, the lineages of the royal families and nobles were no longer dependent on the recognition and support of the people – they now held their positions by virtue of introduced concepts of legal succession enshrined in the constitution.[72]

The constitution, which survives to the present day with only a few amendments, is set out in three parts. The first, entitled 'Declaration of Rights', prescribes the general principles by which the monarch, judiciary, and government are to conduct themselves. The original declaration (which, interestingly, was one of the earliest examples of a constitutional bill of rights), outlawed slavery, punishment without trial, search without warrant, double jeopardy, retrospective laws, confiscation of property (except for public purposes), and protected freedom of worship, freedom of speech and press, provided for trial by jury, the writ of *habeas corpus*, and the taxpayer's right to vote.[73] The second part, concerning 'Form of Government', details the role and structure of the Privy Council (over which the monarch presides and which is the highest executive body although it has limited legislative functions), the cabinet (consisting of all ministers and the governors of Ha'apai and Vava'u, and presided over by the prime minister), and the Legislative Assembly (composed of all ministers, the representatives of the nobles, and the representatives of the people). It also sets out the method of ministerial appointment, the structure and role of the judiciary, and the law of succession to the throne, which was now to be based strictly on primogeniture. The third part, 'The Land', establishes the principles of inheritance pertaining to estates, deals with general laws of succession relating to property, and also contains a permanent prohibition on the sale of land to foreigners.[74]

The constitution locates the ultimate source of authority in the person of the monarch which is reflected in certain prerogatives reserved to him or her. For example, the prime minister, as well as all the other ministers, are appointed by the monarch who is not required to consult with any other person on the matter. This means that the ministers are directly responsible not to the parliament (or, by implication, to the people), but to the monarch.[75] The pre-eminent status and powers of the monarch, which are recognized emphatically by the constitution, have been summarized by Powles as follows:

1. It was the reigning Monarch who, in 1875, 'granted' the Constitution to the people of Tonga.
2. The sovereignty of the Monarch is declared in terms of the absolute authority ('*Pule*') to govern Tonga and its people (clauses 17, 31 and 41).
3. An important aspect of this authority is the Monarch's power over the Prime Minister and Ministers who are responsible to the Monarch for administering the government. The Monarch may dismiss and appoint at any time (clause 51).
4. All land is the property of the Monarch (clauses 44 and 104); and such estates will revert to the Monarch in the absence of an heir (clause 112).
5. The Constitution guarantees perpetual succession to the lineage of the Monarch (clause 32).

6.   The reigning Monarch cannot be impeached (clause 41).
7.   The Constitution which protects the Monarch cannot be changed without his consent (clauses 67 and 69).[76]

Unlike the Westminster system, on which Tonga's governmental structures are superficially based, the Tongan monarch therefore continues to enjoy a great deal of real power. As Powles notes, the formal constitutional niceties of sovereign privilege in Britain simply represent the remnants of a long-abandoned 'working' monarchy. To date almost none of the conventions which limit the formal sovereignty of the monarch, and which are normally associated with the theory of responsible government, have evolved in Tonga (even though the constitution does not necessarily constitute an absolute barrier to such development). Current governmental practice, then, is certainly contrary to the principles of democratic government, and clearly contributes to the lack of accountability complained of by the present pro-democracy movement.[77]

The Declaration of Rights, however, does suggest some desire to give effect to certain principles associated with more modern liberal values, and has been instrumental in securing the important right to freedom of speech in the contemporary struggle for reform. Even so, there remain considerable non-legal obstacles to exercising such rights because of the social inhibitions referred to previously. The clause guaranteeing equality before the law is phrased in unqualified liberal terms: 'There shall be but one law in Tonga, one for the Chiefs, and commoners, and Europeans and Tongese. No laws shall be enacted for any special class to the detriment of another class; but one law equally for all persons residing in this land'.[78] But there is no provision for enforcing the 'freedoms and rights' set out in the constitution. Moreover, the clause which declares the principle of equality before the law is embedded in a constitutional document which itself recognizes and entrenches traditional inequalities of privilege and status.[79]

Another important aspect of the 1875 constitution is the firm belief that its promulgation effectively secured Tonga against foreign domination and colonization. This is a common theme in the literature, and virtually all commentators affirm the apparent efficacy of the 1875 constitution in this respect. Gailey, for example, refers to developments in the latter part of the nineteenth century as being linked to 'efforts to stave off British annexation'.[80] Similarly, Latukefu describes the 1875 constitution as marking the culmination of a process by which Tupou I was able to bring to Tonga 'the type of legal and constitutional machinery which would enable her to gain recognition from the civilised nations and maintain her own independent and stable nation'.[81] Although Tupou I was on record as wanting some form of British protection during the time of his earlier difficulties with rival chiefs, this by no means signified a desire to come under foreign control. One indication of this was his steadfast refusal to sell any land to foreigners. He had also stated that: 'I verily wish to become a friend of Britain; in friendly alliance ... but it is not in my mind, nor in the mind of my people, that we should be subject to any other people or kingdom in this world'.[82] Niu argues, however, that the threat of annexation in 1875 was no greater than it had been in earlier periods and that the 'granting' of the constitution by Tupou I was inspired more by a desire to reach a compromise between the chiefs than for external reasons of state.[83] Whatever the reasons, it is nonetheless certain that the ability of Tupou I to bring the whole of the islands under central control and establish a national constitution was a significant factor in maintaining Tonga's formal independence throughout the period of colonial domination in the Pacific.

This independence, however, was qualified to a considerable extent by the later imposition of British protectorate status which the 1875 constitution was unable to guard against. This came about partly as a result of further internal complications in Tonga, at least some of which can be attributed to the Reverend Shirley Baker, originally a Wesleyan but later the instigator of the break-away Free Church of Tonga. Baker had been very close to Tupou I, and was the principal drafter of the 1875 constitution. His flirtations with German connections in the region as well as his political intrigues within the islands eventually led to his removal from Tonga under a British High Commission Order in Council on the grounds that he was a danger to 'the good order of the kingdom'.[84] The domestic difficulties in Tonga, which only increased with the passing of Tupou I and the succession of Tupou II, as well as Britain's desire to secure a sphere of influence in the Pacific against other foreign interests, eventually led to the establishment of British protectorate status and a 'Treaty of Friendship' for the islands in 1900. This was followed by a supplementary agreement five years later, the terms of which 'fell just short of annexation'.[85]

When read together, the 1900 Treaty and the Supplementary Agreement of 1905 effectively supplanted the constitution as the supreme law of Tonga, since the British government could now provide an ultimate sanction. This meant that Britain could lawfully, if indirectly, actually rule Tonga.[86] Tonga was thereby brought well within the British orbit of influence in the Pacific, especially since Tonga's foreign relations and internal finances (which had been particularly chaotic) were firmly under British direction.[87] Full independence was not regained until 1970, when Tonga's 'protected status' was revoked and Tonga resumed full responsibility for defence and external affairs. The treaty still exists, but it now simply expresses a desire for 'perpetual peace and friendship' between Tonga and Britain. Tonga remains a member of the Commonwealth.[88]

The constitutional system described here has been characterized as 'a masterful example of the integration of modern and traditional ideas of government'.[89] This depends, of course, from which perspective it is viewed. For its time, it certainly provided a much more liberal political framework than traditional Tongan structures allowed. Its 'modernity', however, has long since been eclipsed by the tide of events in the outside world, and it is often perceived by foreigners as maintaining an essentially feudal structure of power.[90] Also, as Powles points out, the Tongan constitution today is very much out of step with international opinion, and certainly with the standards set by the Trusteeship Council and Decolonization Committee of the United Nations 40 years ago: '[I]f Tonga had been a former colony seeking independence under UN supervision, the world body would not have permitted Tonga to become independent without a more representative electoral system'.[91] But while the constitution cannot now be regarded as 'modern', neither is it a document which reflects an authentic, pristine traditional order. Powles notes that there is little in Tongan law today that can be identified as being derived solely from traditional Tongan norms or customs. Rather, the statutory provisions that are regarded as 'legitimately Tongan' reflect a combination of traditional and introduced thinking.[92] At a more general level, Marcus points out that the body of Tongan tradition that is under challenge today is an amalgam of earlier Tongan culture with a particular version of *papalangi* culture. In short, it is a 'compromise culture' that is now being defended as *anga faka Tonga* (the Tongan way).[93]

The Reign of Queen Salote Tupou III

The daughter of Tupou II, Salote, was born in the year of the Protectorate and came to the throne on the death of her father just eighteen years later. For almost half a century she worked hard to consolidate the political system established by her great-great-grandfather, and the impression of Tongan political stability referred to earlier can be attributed largely to Salote's efforts. Her ability to strengthen the institution of monarchy has been attributed partly to her personal popularity, and partly to her political acumen. Marcus has described her reign in the following terms:

> By means of strong church organisation, important strategic marriages for herself and her children, and a popular image among the population as the protector of Tongan cultural identity, Queen Salote managed to neutralise the independent influences of local European and indigenous chiefly interests which were responsible for much of the unrest during Tupou II's reign.[94]

One of Salote's best known and most admired capacities related to her intimate knowledge of individual subjects and their family relations through their genealogies (*hohoko*). Marcus has pointed out that exclusive knowledge has always been a source of chiefly power in Polynesia, especially in relation to genealogical knowledge.[95] The genealogies themselves not only provide an intelligible chronology for the interpretation of important historical events, but also embody Tongan notions of rank, seniority, status, and power.[96] By placing all persons and groups within a grid of historic chiefly genealogies, Salote was eventually able to identify each and every one of her subjects – no mean feat when dealing with a population of around 40,000. Salote's cultivation of genealogical learning also involved the selection and training of particular nobles, thereby ensuring that the special knowledge would not be lost.[97]

When founding the Tongan Traditions Committee in 1952, a body dedicated to the preservation of genealogical and other traditional forms of knowledge (or knowledge of traditional forms), she declared to parliament that 'the customs of the people are its heritage'.[98] But the kind of heritage recalled through genealogical knowledge is one which can only be expressed in the idiom of chiefliness. As Herda points out, commoners of the pre-Christian era had no social or political reason to remember their ancestors. One implication of this is that genealogical credentials were important only to those who needed to establish legitimacy in a sphere of chiefly power and control in which commoners were, by definition, completely irrelevant. Herda goes on to argue that the 'traditional' Tongan past, being an exclusively chiefly domain, denies commoners a place in history because they have no means of access to their non-elite ancestors.[99]

Latukefu suggests that Salote's own impressive genealogy was an important factor in securing the intense loyalty and respect of her subjects. She was directly descended from two of the three major dynasties. Her connection to the Tu'i Kanokupolu line was through Tupou I while her mother was the great-grand-daughter of Laufilitonga, the last Tu'i Tonga. This was reinforced by her marriage to Viliami Tungi, heir to the third dynasty of the Tu'i Ha'atakalaua, who she also appointed to the premiership in 1923.[100] While Salote's own marriage was not simply a matter of uniting the highest lineages for politically instrumental purposes, there is no question that Salote cultivated what Marcus calls 'a politics of kinship and arranged marriages', by which means she 'upgraded the status of selected titleholders by linking them to the royal line or one of its collaterals'. As measures of contemporary status, the 'great' aristocratic lines provided the standard against which prestigious descent could be compared. Under Salote, therefore, 'the official chiefly system reached a pinnacle of mystification during recent times'.[101]

But Salote's command of the love and devotion of her subjects was not just a matter of her possessing impeccable genealogical connections, important as these were. From all accounts, her personal attributes as a generous, honest, and caring monarch did as much to consolidate the monarchy as any other single factor. She was devoted to many welfare measures, and took a special interest in women and education for girls. Public funds were used, not for personal benefit, but for the promotion of public goods in health, education, and other general facilities. Her knowledge of Tongan families and individuals extended to a personal interest in their problems. All this was repaid by an intense loyalty on the part of her subjects, probably unparalleled in any other part of the world. Her death in 1965 marked the end of an era which is widely regarded as Tonga's 'golden age'.

Another feature of Salote's reign was a conscious effort to insulate Tonga, socially and politically, from foreign influences. Given Tonga's geographic isolation, this was not especially difficult and, until the mid-1950s, the only physical means of contact with the outside world was a monthly call by a New Zealand banana boat.[102] Mass communication within Tonga was virtually non-existent before 1961 when a broadcasting service began. This was followed in 1964 by the founding of a weekly newspaper, the *Tonga Chronicle*.[103] But there remained a strong degree of 'official concern' over the social and cultural effects of developments in communications and, in recounting the methods of government control at that time, Fusimalohi says that a 'special effort was made to ensure the "purity" – particularly in cultural matters – of what went over the air waves.'[104] But while Salote guarded the mass of the Tongan people from the influences of alien cultures, it was a different matter when it came to the education of her children. Her son and successor, Taufa'ahau Tupou IV, completed his early education in Tonga but went on to attend school at Newington in Sydney. From there he entered the University of Sydney and completed the degrees of BA, LLB, thus becoming the first Tongan to graduate from a university.[105] He therefore came to the throne with a thorough grounding in Western education and a quite different approach to matters concerning development.

Transformations under Tupou IV

In contrast with his mother, who undoubtedly believed that 'modernization and progress should be subservient to the continued vitality of Tongan tradition', King Taufa'ahau Tupou IV has been described as a radical modernist who has brought to the throne 'the seeds of political instability and change'.[106] Writing in the late 1970s, Marcus argued that Tupou IV's approach over the years since his ascent to the throne was marked by a decline in attachments between the monarch and the nobility:

Whereas previous monarchs shared their glory with the nobility as a status group, either from the need for support or to support tradition, the present monarch and his legitimacy are clearly detached from the nobles, whose legally defined privilege remains secure, but whose prestige among the population wanes.[107]

On a similar theme, Powles notes that the very security afforded to nobles under the constitution with respect to land and their position in the legislature means that they have not been obliged to keep their traditional power alive by any other means, and it has therefore atrophied.[108] Hau'ofa suggests that it is often advantageous for any monarchy to play the aristocracy off against the common people, and vice-versa, and uses two examples to illustrate how this has occurred in Tonga.

Every year, Tonga celebrates Emancipation Day to mark the 1862 edict in much the same way that other nations celebrate independence or some other event to mark a national day. Hau'ofa points out that at this time, the commoners were liberated by the monarch, 'not from the shackles of any colonial regime, but from their alleged enslavement by their very own aristocracy'. In other words, they were liberated from control by a class drawn from their own people. Hau'ofa continues:

Little did people know then, or consciously know even today, that they were released from one form of bondage only to be herded into another albeit relatively benign form of subordination. But it worked, for the propagation of this belief in the royally decreed liberation, through annual celebrations, music and poetry, and through schools, has ensconced the monarchy firmly and centrally in the national psyche, and in the national affection.[109]

The second example concerns the way in which aristocratic representation in the parliament has acted to support the government. The nobles have consistently provided solid support for the government against proposals coming from the people's representatives. The latter are very much in the minority against the combined nobles' representatives and government ministers (who may be either nobles or commoners). One result of this has been that, at least until recently, people have directed much of their disaffection and frustration with the system of representation against the nobles and the ministry, rather than against the monarchy.[110] In concluding, Hau'ofa says that these two examples indicate the extent to which the status of the aristocracy has been weakened: 'it has been transformed from knighthood into pawnhood on the political chessboard'.[111]

To return to the social and economic transformations brought about in the time since Salote's demise, Tupou IV has certainly done much to bring Tonga in touch with 'modernization', if not through political reform, at least by opening Tonga to tourism and investment, encouraging the development of telecommunications, and supporting improvements in international transport facilities.[112] These benefits, however, do not yet extend throughout the islands. In an interesting comment on the isolation still experienced by outlying communities, a media report on the 1993 elections highlighted the surprise election of the only successful female candidate. The candidature of Mrs 'Ofa ki 'Okalani Fusitu'a, who was elected as a people's representative (PR) for the islands of Niuatoputapu and Niuafo'ou (which lie in the far north of the Tonga group), went almost unnoticed until her electoral success was announced. One of the factors accounting for this was poor communications: 'Niuatoputapu has a single radiophone with bad reception. The air service to Niuafo'ou has been cancelled since last October because of mango trees overgrown near the runway'.[113]

There is no doubt, however, that Tonga has experienced considerable change in the years since Salote's death and the accession of Tupou IV. Apart from infrastructure improvements and the growth of services, business, investment, trade, educational facilities, and increasing contact with the outside world,[114] there have also been substantial changes in political thinking on the part of a growing number of ordinary Tongans, though perhaps not in the way intended by Tupou IV. Campbell suggests that there was a certain inevitability that the forces created by Tupou IV through education and economic growth would, in the end, 'be discontented with a political system based on a social and economic pattern which had been superseded'.[115] It is also important to stress the significant role played by the new educated class of intellectuals in Tonga in the development of a much more critical outlook on politics and other social and economic phenomena over the last twenty years or so. Many of these people were educated overseas, but a growing number have attended, or been associated with, the Atenisi Institute, founded in Nuku'alofa by I. Futa Helu in the 1960s, whose guiding principle has been that 'criticism is at the very heart of education'.[116] Commenting more specifically on Tongan culture and tradition in this context, one graduate has said that:

> ... there are no *taboo* fields in education ... all issues are examinable ... all departments of culture are subjected to criticism. The same holds true for Tongan culture; 'Atenisi takes Tongan culture to be an object of *critical* examination, not a subject of *holistic* preservation. 'Atenisi cultivates both the social and intellectual environment of *doing things by questioning*. Reason, the question of why, is put in the place of traditions via authoritative discourse.[117]

Hau'ofa has also said of Atenisi's achievements that it has succeeded, 'where those who have tried to establish Marxist discourse elsewhere in our region have failed, in continuing to submit an entire society and its institutions to constant, microscopic scrutiny'. The result has been devastating for earlier established social, political, and religious pretensions, and has 'contributed immeasurably to the process of democratisation of the Tongan society'.[118] There is no doubt, then, that education imbued with a profound belief in the value of public (and political) criticism has played an important part in the rise of the pro-democracy movement and has assisted in bringing about a very different approach to the political prerogatives of the monarch and the nobility.

The Pro-Democracy Movement

The Tonga Pro-Democracy Movement (PDM) originated in the 1970s in a relatively haphazard manner, as a loose association involving mostly graduates of the University of the South Pacific and some civil servants.[119] Issues of concern during this period ranged over civil service salaries, irregularities in the conduct of elections, the number of seats in the legislature available to commoners, and inequities in the system of land distribution.[120] From the 1970s, one of the most active individuals in the movement has been 'Akilisi Pohiva, a former teacher from Ha'apai who was first elected to the Legislative Council as a people's representative (PR) in 1987. Before then he had studied at the University of the South Pacific and, on his return to Tonga, attended meetings and seminars at the Atenisi Institute. He had also been involved in various issues surrounding the conduct of politicians and in setting up a controversial current affairs radio program which critically scrutinized their activities. The radio program was banned by cabinet in 1982 for its controversial treatment of government activity. Pohiva himself, who had acquired a reputation as a radical activist and critic of government, was dismissed from his public service position in 1985 but later won an historic legal victory over the government when he took court action and was awarded damages and costs for unfair dismissal and denial of free speech.[121] Mr Justice Martin's remarks identified the political motivation behind Pohiva's dismissal:

> The reality of the situation is that Mr Pohiva was dismissed because he was the thorn in the side of government. He was held responsible for a series of radio programs which contained material critical of government. Cabinet was not satisfied with merely banning the program. They were determined to punish and if possible silence the person whom they believed to be responsible ... it was a blatant move to suppress criticism. It was a decision taken with malice and bad faith.[122]

Pohiva and several associates had also launched a broadsheet called *Kele'a* which raised political issues of public interest. In 1986, a whole edition of *Kele'a* was devoted to a critical exposé of overtime payments to parliamentarians and its revelations apparently produced widespread shock throughout the islands, especially when court action over the affair was initiated against all but three members of the Legislative Council.[123] The elections which followed in 1987 saw a marked increase in the number of candidates seeking election. A record 55 candidates stood for the PR's seats, and of eight sitting members, only three were re-elected.[124] Among the new members was Pohiva, who was elected as the third member for Tongatapu, even though he was yet to be vindicated by the court over his dismissal. This election was also the first one in which political and social issues took precedence over the more usual matters concerning local and kinship affiliations.[125]

The tone of debate in the new parliament differed markedly from previous years, much of it centering around the question of public accountability. This indicated that the issues were now matters of principle – 'of fairness and honesty in government' – and this meant raising questions concerning sales tax, remuneration received by parliamentarians, the sale of Tongan passports (see below), and general lack of accountability.[126] In the course of these developments, Hills reports that a number of PRs 'spoke in terms that were widely regarded as impolite and therefore un-Tongan, at least when used about nobles and ministers appointed by the Crown'.[127] This comment again highlights the points made earlier about the ethos which continues to surround the ruling elite, and how traditional beliefs have survived to the extent that ministers and nobles have difficulty in accepting criticism and direct questioning as legitimate forms of conduct in the political sphere. One of the highlights of the period came towards the end of the 1989 session when an ad hoc walkout of the legislature was staged by all PRs present in the chamber after the number one PR for Ha'apai, Teisino Fuko, lost a proposal for the establishment of a standing committee to prepare financial statements for the Privy Council. On returning to the chamber, they came armed with two proposals: one to reduce the number of nobles' representatives, and another to increase the number of parliamentary seats available to PRs.[128] Predictably, neither proposal succeeded in a chamber dominated by nine nobles' representatives and the king's twelve ministerial appointees, as against the nine PRs.

A major scandal over the sale of Tongan passports became the most prominent issue at this time. Many of them were sold to Hong Kong businessmen and mainland Chinese, with lesser sales to South Africans, Libyans, Thais, and Filipinos – including the notorious Imelda Marcos. The purpose of these sales had been to raise foreign exchange. Apart from the principle of selling Tongan nationality, however, Pohiva and others were concerned with where the money from these sales had gone. Pohiva's requests for information in parliament elicited little response and in late 1989 he undertook court action. Public support for Pohiva's campaign was evident in an unprecedented street protest over the issue, which attracted around two thousand people.[129] As a direct result, the government was later to convene an emergency session of parliament for the purpose of passing retrospective legislation to legalize the sale of 426 passports.[130]

At a broader level, the passport scandal can be seen as having driven home the importance of challenging 'the nobility's self-representation as the embodiment of Tongan tradition'.[131] In this respect, tradition is not viewed merely in relation to the sociopolitical hierarchy, but also in the way that social relationships are managed, for example, at the level of kinship obligations and duties. Gailey says that it is Tongan women who (in popular opinion) really manage to defend much of what is taken to be Tongan custom and morality at the grass-roots level, especially in terms of accountability and kinship. The passport scandal therefore had deeper implications for the way in which it impacted on customary notions of right and wrong actions. Gailey records the response of one Tongan woman:

> Look, my mother's sister married a palangi (foreigner), and they live here ... We don't think of them as half-castes – the children speak Tongan and live in the Tongan way. But according to the law, her children are not Tongan. So be it. But now look, here come these foreigners with no kin and, because they gave the king some money, they're Tongan. It just isn't our way.[132]

The more general issue of accountability has been assessed by Pohiva in terms of the contrast between the traditional sociopolitical structures of Tonga, and what is required for good government in the contemporary era. He says that under the traditional system, the issue of accountability was a non-issue: Tongan commoners simply presented their tributes to the chiefs and no explanation of how these were used was required, nor did they expect anything in return. Exploitation in this manner was considered a normal part of life. The constitution, however, guaranteed a new set of rights and freedoms under the rule of law. But today, where one should expect to see the rule of law prevail, there is instead 'the enforcement of conformity and compliance to the norms through the exercise of cultural and traditional means and practices'.[133]

The passport scandal and other issues of government accountability dominated public political debate in the period leading up to these elections. A feature of the campaign for these elections was an active effort on the part of conservative forces to rally support – a move which had never really been necessary in previous years because of the lack of 'issue campaigning' mentioned earlier, and which had only started to emerge in 1987. By 1990, however, the need for the conservatives to strengthen their hand was more pressing, and there was an attempt to enlist church support on a platform of 'church and state'.[134] In another unusual development, the king made several public comments during the campaign about the dangers of the demands for change getting out of control and the possibility of a coup d'état.[135] Pohiva, who was seen as the greatest threat to the conservative regime, was accused of being a revolutionary and a communist. This had the opposite of the intended effect, and he gained considerable mileage from the publicity which was reflected in his spectacular victory as the number one PR for Tongatapu, winning around 75 per cent of the votes.[136] The overall election result for the PRs was something of a landslide in favour of the reformists, especially in the Tongatapu and Ha'apai constituencies. In addition, one of the founders of *Kele'a*, 'Atunaisa Katoa, took the first seat for Vava'u.[137] The 1990 election results therefore served to strengthen the claims of the group which, although not organized formally in any way, let alone as a political party, was by now taking on some characteristics of a proper political opposition.[138]

Encouraged by these strong indicators of public support, the reformist lobby continued to press for change. The establishment of the Pro-Democracy Movement (PDM) as a formal body was eventually achieved in August 1992. According to its foundation chair, Father Selwyn 'Akau'ola, the purpose of the PDM was not to function as a political party, but to 'create an atmosphere where a dialogue by all interested parties could take place'.[139] In the period leading up to the 1993 elections, a major conference with the theme 'The Tongan Constitution and Democracy' was convened in Nuku'alofa (in November 1992) to promote this sort of dialogue. For four days, Tonga's political system received the full critical attention of a wide range of contributors, including some important church leaders. Around 400 participants, as well as a number of other observers crowded into adjoining rooms with closed circuit television, heard one Tongan church leader, the Reverend Siupeli Taliai of Tonga's Free Wesleyan Church, describe the 1875 constitution as 'ethically, criminally, and theologically barbaric'.[140] In his opening speech the Reverend Taliai elaborated:

> In our beloved Tonga today there is still structural injustice after a century of so-called constitutional rule. Political and economic power is concentrated in the hands of a tiny minority who are able to command financial rewards out of all proportion to their actual work. This is why the pursuit of justice always labours under the disadvantage of appearing subversive.[141]

Many of the arguments supporting reform drew from Christian teachings about equality as well as secular notions of human rights, and were voiced in direct opposition to notions endorsing the sanctity of chiefs and the monarchy, as well as to older Christian ideas about power which had allowed early missionaries to portray the monarch as god's anointed leader.[142] But to quote the Reverend Taliai again: 'The proclamation of the King as sacred in Clause 41 of the Constitution shows our heathen inclination, despite the fact that we are equal under the United Nations charter and in the face of God'.[143] Pohiva added his voice to the debate on the monarchy, saying that since all other monarchies with absolute power had failed, the lessons of history indicated that Tonga's present monarchical system was also destined to fail in its present form. He added, however, that 'the monarchy which surrenders power is bound to continue'.[144] This last remark is in accord with a widespread desire among pro-democracy supporters to see the monarchy retained, but with substantially reduced political power. In this respect, pro-democracy advocates have affirmed their belief in a genuine constitutional monarchy rather than a 'constitution under a monarchy'.[145] They believe that a system which elevates the monarch 'out of the legislature', and gives him or her 'the dignity and ceremony of a head of state such as Britain's Queen Elizabeth', would provide the most effective remedy to the present problems.[146] One commentator has stated succinctly a major problem facing reformists in Tonga. Powles points out that the monarch has so far governed with 'a relatively benign and gentle hand'. He continues, however, that it is now 'a question as to how to protect the interests of the people against the possibility of a less enlightened and more interventionist ruler'.[147]

A noteworthy aspect of this conference, as well as the movement for democracy in general, is the extent to which a plurality of religious denominations (and non-believers) have come together to support reform. Hau'ofa assesses the significance of this in the context of general democratic values, and in contrast with communities in other places which have resorted to religious fanaticism to promote their respective causes:

[The movement] is strongly interdenominational and is therefore ideologically pluralistic, which may act as a check against the kinds of religious political fanaticism that we have seen in Iran, Pakistan and closer to home ... in Fiji as exemplified by a powerful section of the Methodist Church. In Tonga also, one of the prominent leading personalities of the movement is a strong atheist critic of religious establishments, who has nevertheless been working closely with religious leaders on matters of national interest. Among the [movement's] supporters are members of the non-Christian Baha'i faith. Thus, although the movement is Christian in orientation, reflecting the strength of that religion in Tonga, and indeed our islands in the region, it is pluralistic in its inclusiveness of religious and sectarian doctrinal diversity, and of purely secular humanistic viewpoints. This accommodation of even seemingly irreconcilable ideological differences is a hallmark of the democratic culture.[148]

Apart from the substance of the matters discussed at the conference, which ranged over the full agenda of issues relating to the theme, the government's response indicated increasing unease and defensiveness. This became manifest in a series of attempts at repression, which included the refusal to permit any foreigners (including some of Tongan descent) to enter the country for the conference and instructions to the local government-owned radio station to prevent the broadcast of any convention speeches or other news.[149] In addition, it was reported that plain-clothes police were monitoring the conference 'under cover'. The report stated, however, that 'because of the closeness of Tongan society everybody knew who they were' and that although they were there 'to intimidate by taking the names of those in attendance', few took much notice.[150] Initially, Prime Minister Baron Vaea had indicated that the government would take some part in the convention, but evidently changed his mind by early November when it was announced that the government would in fact boycott the gathering.

These developments had followed on from a lively session of parliament before the convention. Referring to a report from the Tongan Department of Health, which indicated an increasing incidence of mental illness in the country, Crown Prince Tupouto'a remarked that some PRs were clearly unbalanced and may have personality disorders. Citing Hitler as an example, the prince informed the legislature: 'Personality disorders are characterised by the behaviour of a person who insists that he alone is right, and tries to win the rest of society to his way of thinking.' When one of the PRs attempted to interject, he was pointed out as an example of the kind the prince was speaking of.[151] This is not the first time that heated exchanges in the legislature had been reported. In an incident in the earlier life of the 1990–92 parliament, members had been instructed to go outside and 'cool off'. As the speaker, the Hon. Fusitu'a, followed Pohiva from the chamber, he apparently called out to the commoner: 'I'll kill you! What are you and how can a person like you challenge me?'[152] Once again, this incident shows the difficulty nobles have in engaging in open debate.

Another notable development on the conservative side of politics, just one month before the pro-democracy convention, was a meeting called by Prime Minister Vaea of cabinet ministers and the leaders of Christian churches. One of the issues discussed was the possible formation of a new political party to be called, somewhat perversely, the 'Christian Democratic Party'. More generally, the head of the government information unit, Eseta Fusitu'a (also an outspoken conservative and married to the Hon. Fusitu'a), announced: 'Both the Ministers and the church leaders reiterated their belief that Tupou I's well-proven method of Church and State combining to deal with the affairs of the nation, was still the best method for Tonga'.[153] In another report, however, it was suggested that most church leaders were in fact unhappy with the idea of a party which combined government and church members and that many were concerned that the government was simply trying to use the church to further its own agenda. An outspoken critic of the government and a strong pro-democracy supporter, the Catholic bishop Patelisio Finau, described the government's plan to form a political party using the churches as devious and manipulative.[154] It is also evident from the number of church leaders speaking at the pro-democracy convention that the establishment had not been able to swing the churches solidly behind their cause. If anything, the opposite had become the case.

In view of the government's attempts to institute a 'church and state' platform, thereby involving church leaders directly in the sphere of politics, it is ironic that some church leaders have had to defend their position of active support for democratic reforms. Bishop Finau, for example, was explicitly criticized for speaking out against injustices in the present political system. He had also clashed with both the king and Crown Prince Tupouto'a who accused him of being 'a marxist and an agent of the pope'.[155] On another occasion, the bishop stated that although he did not believe the church should become involved in formal party politics, it 'cannot unconditionally accept what the government says, but [has] to measure what the government does and help those without a voice'.[156] In a further comment on the problems posed by Tongan culture for reformist aspirations, the bishop argued that traditional attitudes to power were of the domineering kind with little or no recognition of consultation as a desirable practice. He added: 'This is not the way Christian power is meant to be and [so] there is a clash between our cultural way and Christian leadership'.[157]

Despite moves on both sides to institute more formal mechanisms of political organization, party organization was notably absent during the campaign for the 1993 elections, which started shortly after the conference. As before, each of the candidates ran as individuals, although a number were clearly identifiable as pro- or anti-democracy supporters, and the pro-democracy supporters ran more or less as a team in the Tongatapu constituency. A record number of 55 candidates contested the nine seats reserved for PRs, but pro-democracy supporters or sympathizers again proved the most successful, dominating the seats in Tongatapu, Ha'apai, and Vava'u. One report noted as significant the defeat of the outspoken pro-government member from Ha'apai, Viliami Afeaki.[158] The single PR returned for 'Eua, however, is a *matapule* and therefore predictably 'traditional' in his approach to politics. The other PR returned was the successful woman candidate from the Niuas mentioned earlier.[159] Although virtually nothing was known about her views on the pro-democracy cause at the time of her election, there was no doubting those of one of her unsuccessful opponents, the sitting PR for the Niuas, Siaki Kata. An article published in the lead-up to the election reported that Kata was a firm supporter of the status quo, believing that there were no benefits to be gained from changing the constitution or curbing the power of the monarch. On the contrary, Kata proclaimed: 'The people of the Niuas believe the King should have the power because he is a Christian and he knows what to do. In addition he was the first one to have the best education in Tonga'.[160]

Others who are sympathetic to the aims of the PDM are nonetheless reluctant to endorse change now, believing that the majority of Tongans are not yet ready for it. One of the PRs for Vava'u, for example, says that although he agrees that democracy is the best system of government, change in this direction cannot be rushed. Nor is Tonga ready for political party activity – consensus remains a more appropriate method in Tongan politics. The note of caution is not just because the people require higher levels of education before moving towards democracy, he also believes that the low level of economic development in Tonga makes it 'not yet fit for democracy'. In summary, this PR believed that change must come slowly and that people must first be educated to accept change, otherwise it may lead to violence.[161] Another informant (with no connection to the PDM), believed that Tonga was ready for change now. She admitted that, at first, she was frightened of political change, thinking that it might lead to violence. Now, feeling more secure about the situation, she wants full democracy as soon as possible. Furthermore, she said that there had been too much 'scraping and bowing to the king and nobles'.[162] Similar views were expressed by another informant (an active supporter of the PDM) who added that he was 'fed up' with the 'syrupy language of praise and homage to the monarchy and nobles'.[163] A supporter of the present system, however, offered the following reasons for retaining the status quo: first, the common one that democracy was unsuited to Tongan culture, but second, a more unusual one in that Tonga was 'too small', and that democracy was 'okay' only for bigger countries.[164] Pohiva himself, of course, believed that Tongan society had reached the point where it was more than ready for democracy, pointing out at the same time that the elite who opposed change were themselves already Westernized in terms of their lifestyle.[165]

The belief that a push for change toward democratization may lead to violence has been an underlying theme in some of the arguments emanating from the conservative side of politics in Tonga. We shall consider next the nature of the conservative response to the general elections of 1993, as well as some of the broader views about democracy and its relative value in the Tongan context.

The Conservative Reaction

Both local and overseas press reports heralded the 1993 election results as a significant triumph for the reformist cause. Pohiva certainly saw it in these terms, claiming that the results indicated a clear mandate for reform and conveyed an unambiguous message along these lines to the government.[166] But conservative spokespeople could not agree. Eseta Fusitu'a claimed that the result could as easily be interpreted as a victory for the pro-government camp because the actual votes cast – rather than the number of seats won – indicated a decline in support for the pro-democracy candidates since the last elections in the order of 6,000 votes.[167] If anything reflected an indisputable increase in support for the conservative side, however, this was manifest in the elections for the noble seats which took place a week before the election of PRs. Among the nine nobles elected were four new representatives, 'all of whom seem[ed] more conservative than the ones they replaced'.[168] But in view of the overall results, there is little doubt that the reform mood among the commoners in Tonga had been maintained throughout the period since the 1987 elections. This was despite concerted efforts by conservative elements to undermine the PDM and its aims before and during the campaign. Public opinion was not entirely behind the convention either. The following extract from a letter published in the *Tonga Chronicle* typified the feelings of the more conservative elements among the population:

> We are not happy about the plans for the convention and the stated reasons behind it because we really love and respect our King, the Royal Family, the Nobles of the Realm, and Ministers of the Crown, as well as Christianity ... the King rules the nobles and the people ... and his body is sacred ... We are frightened that this authority might be taken away.[169]

In the period immediately following the November convention, Radio Tonga was dominated by a premier's office program which dwelt at length on the evils of democracy. In what can only be described as an absurdity, the program actually pointed to the misfortunes of the modern Greeks – heirs to the original inventors of democracy – and made claims about the position of Greeks today as being confined to working in restaurants and related occupations.[170] The implication was that a democratic heritage should be regarded as a distinct disadvantage and, presumably, that the Tongan tradition of authoritarian rule was much to be preferred. A further inference of the program's message was that not all traditions are of equal value or intrinsic worth. This also supports nationalistic claims based on the relative merits of Tonga's own political traditions vis-à-vis those of the West.

In other efforts to belittle the pro-democracy conference, the Hon. Fusitu'a was reported as saying that many of those in attendance were just 'academics enjoying a bit of a holiday' and that 'the ripple' would fade quickly.[171] A few days before the elections, Police Minister 'Akau'ola spoke on Radio Tonga about the implications of the pro-democracy demands. He warned explicitly about the dangers of 'rebellion', stating that acts of this kind included promoting hatred of the monarch and government, conducting protest marches, and bringing in foreign doctrines.[172] He also reminded listeners that it was an offence to destabilize the state and challenge the authority of the king, and that the penalties for treason included the death sentence. The government-controlled station also replayed a speech given by Queen Salote calling on Tongans to uphold their traditions.[173] Shortly after the Hon. 'Akau'ola made his remarks, however, Prime Minister Vaea contradicted him to the extent of saying that the pro-democracy movement was free to air its opinions.[174] In another report, Helu wrote that Radio Tonga broadcasts during the three days before the elections consisted of an 'orchestra of denunciation', a bombardment of 'reactionary and antidemocratic propaganda', and 'inflated and terrorising rhetoric'.[175] Pohiva stated that at meetings with electors during the campaign, some nobles had claimed that the introduction of democratic reforms would lead to the removal of the king, that people would lose their land, and that Tongan customs and traditions generally would be affected for the worse.[176]

The government's stance, which amounted to unconditional support for the status quo, remained unchanged after the elections. Indeed, its position was explicitly re-affirmed in a statement issued by Prime Minister Vaea, who was reported as saying: 'Tongan people did not want democracy ... they liked having an elite leadership drawn from noble background ... [and] were quite happy living with their traditions and accepted the role of hierarchy.'[177] A further report quoted another government minister, the Hon. Ma'afu Tuku'i'aulahi, on his reaction to suggestions that the nobles' seats be either abolished or elected by the people. According to the Hon. Ma'afu, the best solution for Tonga to such proposals was to adopt Mao Tse-Tung's view of power, namely, that it 'comes out of the barrel of a gun'. He continued:

> We are a warring people and if you are talking about power, then we are talking about war ... It is absolutely unrealistic to think that you could talk your way in and take away the power of the nobles or the government without any violent confrontation, it is unheard of, it has never happened ... If you want power you have to fight for it.[178]

Oddly enough, ideas relating to this theme have also been used by pro-democracy supporters. One speaker at the November conference, prominent Tongan academic Epeli Hau'ofa of the University of the South Pacific, recalled that Taufa'ahau had not been heir to the Tu'i Kanokupolu title, but had achieved it through conquest, thereby earning recognition of his leadership ability. Hau'ofa went on to point out that Taufa'ahau's introduction of hereditary positions such as those created for the nobles had put an end to competition – an end which also heralded 'the beginning of weakness and the unfit'.[179] Rather than endorsing violent warfare as a means of legitimate competition, though, Hau'ofa's position undoubtedly reflects the characterization of modern democratic politics in terms of a competitive, but non-violent, struggle which has been expressed as the reversal of Clausewitz's famous dictum, that is, that politics is the prosecution of war by other means.[180]

Another general line of argument used by conservative opponents of the reform movement draws on relativist arguments concerning the merits, or demerits, of democracy. An interview with Eseta Fusitu'a on the subject of contemporary political developments in Tonga elicited the following views on the constitution and democracy:

> A constitution embraces the fundamental features of a country, when it does not, that country is in trouble. When you talk about this so-called democracy you are talking about a model associated with a western society. The Westminster model in India makes no provision for the multiple religions there, so the model remains but the society suffers.
> In Samoa, one of the original drafters (of the constitution), Jim Davidson, was conversant with Samoan society, so the constitution stipulated only Samoan matai (chiefs) could vote and only matai could be candidates. Put that Samoan model against the Australian model and they'll say 'bad, bad'. The 1991 constitutional change (giving adult Samoans universal suffrage but only permitting matais as candidates) is not entirely Westminster, but still reflects Samoa, and that's the way it should be. Our Tongan parliament was meant to reflect our multiple criteria for leadership – age, seniority and traditional leaders. If you look at that with palagi eyes we'll never understand each other.[181]

The latter point emphasizes the especially problematic view of a particular culture as something enclosed in a (falsely) abstracted horizon. Put simply, it denies the possibility that 'alien horizons' are open to understanding. It is for this reason that diverse thinkers have been sharply critical of the 'myth of the framework' – the myth which insinuates that 'we are forever enclosed in our own horizons, our own paradigms, [and] our own cultures'.[182] It calls attention also to the point that appeals to relativism are themselves dogmatic when they are directed to closing off the possibility of communication by denying a basis of shared understanding that is not tied to a particular culture.

Finally, it is worth recording here the views of Prince Fatafehi Tu'ipeiehake, younger brother of the king and prime minster of Tonga for over 25 years until his retirement in 1991. Responding to a question on whether he supported the theory that cabinet would be stronger if its members were elected by the people, the Prince indicated his opposition to the idea. His reason for supporting the present system? The belief that very few people had a sufficient or clear understanding of what goes on in the world beyond Tonga. 'Our local politicians are only good enough within Tonga, when we move out to the international arena ... the best approach for government [is] to call in only our capable people.'[183] And in answer to a further question on the best possible political system for Tonga:

> One thing that we should always remember is that no-one else knows what is best for us other than ourselves. We all talk about democracy but we do not know what it looks like. It has a different shape and a different colour for different countries ... Here it is different, people are just going about their daily lives, and when the breadfruit is in season they are very happy. I do not know what [you] would call that, carefree or what, but you can't talk to people like that about democracy.[184]

The clear implication of these remarks is that commoners have neither the political skills nor the wisdom, nor even the potential, to participate at a higher level of responsibility than that afforded by the present constitution. It follows that these qualities are believed to be the preserve of a ruling class which alone carries in its blood lines the requisite capacity to serve as governmental leaders. Nor is there any faith in the judgement of the common people to select leaders or choose between policy alternatives put forward by groups competing for power. Attitudes of this kind may be held sincerely, or may be prompted simply by a desire to maintain the status quo for self-interested motives. Either way, there is little reason to expect that people holding such perspectives on politics can be persuaded to reverse their views in the immediate future. And since the ruling class, which is evidently imbued with these views, holds all the power, the prospects for change do not seem imminent.

Conclusion

The PDM's activities may not yet have achieved anything in the way of tangible political reform, but they have certainly brought into the open many of the attitudes and perspectives characterizing both sides of the debate about political change in Tonga – a debate which is readily characterized in terms of tradition versus democracy. The reformist challenge, which has been carried forward in a framework of Western democratic norms and human rights principles, is clearly anathema to the present incumbents whose legitimacy and authority ostensibly derives from blood lines reaching back into the remote past, and through which flows the essence of Tongan tradition and cultural identity. It is in this sense, broadly speaking, that tradition and democracy are construed as opposing forces in a situation of changing political dynamics. One of the ironies is that the Tongan establishment, especially the younger and middle generation, is itself thoroughly Westernized in its lifestyle. Pohiva says that members of the royal family and the nobility mix with foreign friends in preference to other Tongans. Moreover, they spend a great deal of time overseas and also send their own children to English-speaking schools. This, he says, means that they have little respect for Tongan culture in actual practice, even though they tell other Tongans to stay within their own cultural milieu and not accept 'foreign ideas'.[185]

Quite apart from the practical institutional reforms that must accompany moves to greater democratization, the PDM clearly has a very difficult battle ahead in confronting fixed attitudes and challenging conventional wisdom about the legitimate source of political authority. At the same time the movement does not want to undermine the entire edifice of Tongan culture or tradition. That is not what the majority of Tongans would support either, for as James points out, attitudes towards chiefly leaders in Tonga, such as respect, deference, and love are part of the notion of '*ofa* (love or appreciation) which is central to Tongan culture.[186] Further, Hau'ofa says that most Tongans maintain a profound loyalty to their common heritage and to their identity as a single people who have 'travelled together' for 2,000 years or more. Part of this heritage is the aristocracy, which he sees as still having a positive role to play in a democratic Tonga.[187] Hau'ofa nonetheless supports the critical views about the establishment expressed by Pohiva, especially insofar as this elite do not actually live in a traditional manner themselves.[188]

The discussion has made clear the necessity for the movement to overcome deeply entrenched normative beliefs about the structure of traditional society and the values embodied in it, as against a system of government that is clearly Western and 'alien'. The development of democratic norms relating to a faith in the innate capacity of common people to exercise political judgement, as well as to perform the duties of political office, has been inhibited by the pervasive influence of a long-standing social system which does not recognize this capacity, let alone the political rights which are presumed to underscore it. As suggested in the foregoing discussion, the cluster of values which are at the core of this social system are expressed in the differential qualities deemed proper to two distinct classes of people. In Tonga, this system has been depicted as demanding a morality of *talangofua* (obedience), of *mateaki* (loyal) character, of '*ofa fonua* (love of the land) and of *angalelei* (good behaviour) on the part of the *tu'a* (commoner). For the upper strata, a quite different set of qualities is expected, including *to'a* (bravery), *fu'u* (prowess), *fie'eiki* (chiefliness) and *fiepule* (dominance). Thus the values embodied in the two sets of expectations have produced two opposed moralities, with one being completely subordinate to the other.[189] The moralities are nonetheless symbiotic or at least complementary – thus neither has any real meaning unless it is understood in opposition to the other, and the negation of one logically entails the negation of the other.

It is further suggested that the corpus of Tongan myths, the *talatapu'a,* function ideologically to fortify the oppressive elements of Tongan society. In illustrating this point, Kolo outlines the political dimensions of the *talatapu'a:*

> Many of the *talatapu'a* can be said to be aristocratic in nature; they deal with aristocratic figures and views. *Tu'a* are expected to believe that events told in these myths are actualities and historically true. In ceremonial speeches, we speak mythologically and symbolically, paying our utmost respect to the chiefly classes, the Kings and the Queens.[190]

This interpretation of the way in which myth is presented, and the function that it can serve, feeds back into the general idea that an historically situated notion of culture, expressed through the concept of a society's unique traditions, can serve as an ideological buttress to the power and privilege of traditional elites in a modern context. This is despite the fact that the conditions under which power configurations were originally developed and sustained, and under which the legitimating ideologies emerged and became assimilated as part of the culture, have undergone radical changes.[191]

Just as circumstances change, so too can attitudes – even those most ardently and passionately held. This is clearly evident in the revolution in thinking on the part of Tongan commoners which has taken place over the last few years. Helu maintains that the present situation would have been unthinkable twenty years ago. Given that Tonga had 'the most severely conservative culture this side of the equator', the extent and openness of the criticism now being directed at the highest established authorities represents an extraordinary turnaround in the way that people think.[192] Although the monarchy is still entrenched in an absolute form, Hau'ofa describes Tongan society in general as one which now has 'a vibrant democratic culture'.[193] But one of the few things that so far remains unchanged is the desire of the elite (like the desire of elites almost everywhere) to maintain power even in the face of compelling demands for reform. These demands reflect a global backlash against all forms of authoritarian rule and, although few have been as benign as Tonga's, the political system there has increasingly acquired the characteristics of an anachronism. As one commentator has put it, Tonga is at risk of becoming 'a country of primarily antiquarian interest'. He continues, however, that while Tonga's people do prize much of their history and value the elements of culture which make them distinctive, they would not wish to become an animated museum of anthropology.[194]

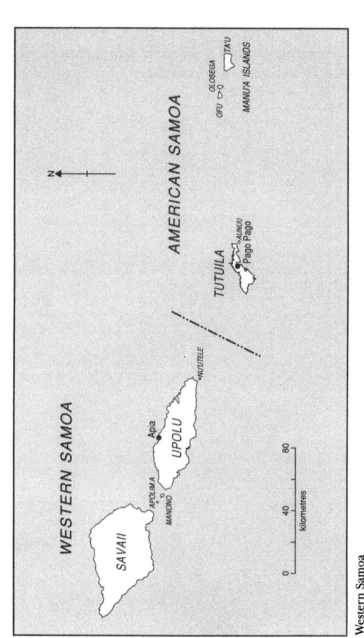

Western Samoa

CHAPTER 4

Preserving Tradition Through Democratization: The Introduction of Universal Suffrage in Western Samoa

Introduction

The islands comprising the modern state of Western Samoa consist of the two main land masses of Savai'i and Upolu and several smaller ones including Manono and Apolima. The total land area of Western Samoa is just under 3,000 square kilometres, making it considerably larger than American Samoa whose seven small islands (two of which are atolls) yield a land area of less than 200 square kilometres.[1] The present population is around 163,000. Like Fiji and Tonga, the earliest archaeological sites indicate that Samoa's first inhabitants belonged to the Lapita cultural complex with human habitation in the islands dating back at least two thousand years.[2]

In October 1990 the full adult citizenry of Western Samoan voted in a plebiscite to change an electoral system which, since independence in 1962, had restricted both candidature for parliamentary office and the franchise to bearers of traditional *matai* (chiefly) titles.[3] Western Samoa had adopted this restrictive system with the approval of the adult population of the time as demonstrated, ironically enough, via a plebiscite. Neither Western Samoa's former colonial trustee, New Zealand, nor the United Nations had been initially willing to accept *matai*-only suffrage. Both had been keen to see a more liberal system introduced in keeping with the democratic decolonizing spirit of the times. In the face of an overwhelming vote in favour of a constitution which made no provision for universal suffrage,[4] however, there could be little argument with the proposition that the people of Western Samoa stood firmly behind their chiefs and the concept of *fa'aSamoa*. Although the records of the Constitutional Convention at that time show support for a more liberal franchise among a number of high-ranking Samoans, majority Samoan opinion was nonetheless clearly in line with the belief that voting was a privilege to be enjoyed only by the *matai*, not just in the immediate future but 'until the end of the world'.[5]

While eligibility for candidature remains confined to the *matai*, the introduction of universal suffrage has nonetheless been hailed as 'a giant step in the process of democratizing Samoan politics and in legitimizing parliamentary rule'.[6] The major impetus for this measure of democratization, however, was driven not so much by a growth in support for democratic values per se, as by a desire to preserve important aspects of Samoan tradition. For some years it had been evident that the restriction of voting rights to chiefly title holders had distorted the *matai* system. There had been a proliferation of title holders whose main objective in securing *matai* status seemed to be to qualify as electors for the nation's parliament rather than to serve their families and communities in a traditional chiefly capacity. This development was seen by some as striking at the very foundations of the Samoan social system and, if left unchecked, held the prospect of destroying its distinctive characteristics. Attempts to curb the proliferation of titles by Western Samoa's Land and Titles Court had stemmed the tide only marginally and, in any case, had raised fresh problems concerning another important entitlement – the right of family groups to exercise autonomy in awarding titles. The only feasible solution, it seemed, was to extend the franchise to every adult citizen, thereby removing the incentive to become a '*matai palota*'.

In the debates on universal suffrage, the fact that the proposed reforms would bring Western Samoa more into line with widely accepted principles of democratic practice was almost beside the point. Indeed, it seemed more a matter of pride among Western Samoans, including many of those supporting reform, that their system was not modelled on foriegn political practices – democratic or otherwise. This kind of view, however, was expressed most emphatically by opponents of an extended franchise whose justifications for retaining the *matai*-only system of voting focussed almost exclusively on the importance of preserving Western Samoa's unique cultural heritage. This heritage was said to be embedded in the *matai* system itself which, together with a host of other interrelated cultural emblems and practices, is expressed in terms of a generalized conception of Samoa's social and political value system encapsulated in the term *fa'aSamoa*. Both sides of the debate, then, drew on traditionalist appeals. Reformists sought the introduction of a more democratic electoral system in order to preserve tradition, while those opposed founded their arguments in precisely the same ground.

There was some concern expressed on both sides, however, for establishing links between traditional Samoan political practice and democratic norms. This was evident in discussions about the position and function of *matai* which turned on a conception of traditional Samoan structures as inherently democratic in their own right, and in their own way. The essential features of *fa'aSamoa* which are held to be democratic relate most specifically to the method of selecting *matai*. Since all members of the extended kinship group (*'aiga*) are, in theory, eligible to be considered for a *matai* title, or to have a say in the award of titles, there is some basis for claiming that this process has a democratic character. Furthermore, it is claimed that open eligibility for *matai* status has produced a relatively egalitarian society in which there is no chiefly class as such – nor a distinct class of commoners. This is often contrasted favourably with the Tongan sociopolitical system.

In a general description of traditional sociopolitical organization, Davidson writes that 'Samoa contained no proletariat, none who could not take pride in their family connections, none who in youth could not look forward to the possibility of occupying a responsible position later in life'.[7] With respect to the more recent reforms, one opponent of universal suffrage proclaimed that:

> No Samoan is currently prevented from making his views known to his chief. All suli (heirs) have the right to dissent under the Samoan system. Why bring in a new system when the Samoan way is adequate? Plebiscite comes from plebeian which means commoner. There are no commoners in Samoa, only chiefs and their heirs.[8]

Whether or not Samoan sociopolitical structures can indeed be construed as democratic on the grounds outlined above, the emphasis on the inherently democratic nature of *fa'aSamoa* indicates that at least some importance is attributed to democratic principles. Nonetheless, these principles have been linked explicitly to Samoan tradition and thus contained firmly within the ambit of *fa'aSamoa*.

Given the preoccupation with *fa'aSamoa* reflected in most debates on contemporary political structures and values, the analysis focusses on how traditionalism is expressed through this concept as well as through notions of political legitimacy relating to the dynamics of *fa'amatai* (which refers more specifically to sociopolitical organization as embodied in the *matai* system). This is significant for how 'Western' democracy is perceived, and the extent to which its values are seen to be alien to Samoan traditions.

An important point to be noted at the outset is the apparent contradiction between the nationalistic expression of tradition through *fa'aSamoa* on the one hand, and resistance to nationalist centralizing tendencies on the other. More specifically, the concept of *fa'aSamoa* is construed in terms which imply a unitary cultural entity encompassing the whole of the Samoan people. The expression of traditionalist images

is therefore firmly embedded in a national context of cultural homogeneity very similar to Tonga and Fiji. Yet the political history of Samoa,
at least as it is depicted by many historians and commentators, reveals a
constant effort on the part of Samoans to resist the centralization of
political power in favour of a high level of local autonomy.

The Samoan Polity

Samoa's early sociopolitical system followed a hierarchical pattern which
is generally taken to be characteristic of traditional Polynesian
configurations, especially in the rigorous institutionalization of authority
structured around chiefly title-bearers. The homogeneity of cultural
practices and language within Samoa, and the network of kinship
groupings and allegiances which extended throughout the Samoan
islands, is also typical of Polynesian island groups which contrasted
markedly with Melanesian and Micronesian forms. On the homogeneity
of Samoan material and non-material culture, Gilson has written that:

> From Manu'a to the west end of Savai'i the people all acknowledged having a
> common identity as Samoans. With some local variations, they spoke the same
> Polynesian dialect; they dressed and housed themselves in similar ways; they
> built canoes to similar designs; they intermarried widely, recognized far-flung
> family and political relationships, and maintained these relationships by
> paying each other frequent visits ... they shared some of the same deities and
> creation myths ...[9]

Although both Samoa and Tonga have common Polynesian origins,
this does not mean that they share a common pattern of political
development. Many aspects of social, political, religious and economic
organization are comparable, and obviously reflect a similar cultural
heritage, but the two countries nonetheless show remarkable contrasts in
other ways.[10] This is especially evident in the lack of centralized political
authority in Samoa compared with what was achieved in Tonga, at least in
more recent times. It should not be inferred, however, that the early
sociopolitical organization of Tonga and Samoa were vastly different.
The distinctions evident today have been shaped very significantly by the
timing and nature of European contact. As Powles points out, the village-
based orientation of society in Western Samoa, as contrasted with the
'over-arching hereditary elite' model of Tongan society, is as much a
reflection of assessments made by early European explorers, traders, and
missionaries, as anything else. Furthermore, 'pacification' effectively
froze the two societies in the mould created for them.[11] The description
of Samoan sociopolitical organization that follows, and the implications
that flow from this, must therefore be understood in this light.

Any account of Samoan political structures must start at the localized level – that of the *nu'u*. While this is most commonly translated as 'village', Meleisea says that a better rendering of the term is 'polity', which more adequately connotes the status of the *nu'u* as a political unit.[12] The *nu'u* was (and is)[13] governed by a council of *matai* known as the *fono* which was the sole source of legitimate political authority within the *nu'u*.[14] Each *nu'u*, which usually was made up of between 200 and 500 people, comprised a territory controlled collectively by a number of corporate descent groups known as '*aiga* (which is often translated as 'family').[15] The '*aiga* itself has been described as a non-localized descent group headed by a *matai*.[16] In terms of its sociopolitical function, Krämer says that the '*aiga* was 'the pillar of Samoan political organization' and, because society comprised the sum of its '*aiga*, then Samoa was effectively a 'family state'.[17]

The relative status of each *nu'u*, as well the various '*aiga* and *matai*, were defined by means of a complex set of ceremonial speeches called *fa'alupega*. The *fa'alupega* contained a conventionalized history of the *nu'u* set out via the recitation of formalized greetings to the principal *matai* of the *nu'u*. Through the same mechanism, the *fa'alupega* provided a statement of the constitution of the village *fono*. Apart from establishing the internal hierarchy of the *nu'u*, the *fa'alupega* also demonstrated the autonomy of any given *nu'u* as a political entity.[18] This did not mean that political organization beyond the village level was non-existent. Without compromising the independence of individual *nu'u*, they often banded together in loose confederations of sub-districts and districts. This was achieved through the acknowledgement of common allegiances to particular high-ranking chiefs and demonstrated by gifts of food or services, or both. But none of this enjoined individual *nu'u* to accept political authority from outside their territorial boundaries. The sole legitimate source of this authority remained firmly within the *fono* of each *nu'u* and the *matai* who comprised it.[19]

The *matai* of each *nu'u* possessed the status of either *ali'i* or *tulafale* (orator), although in some *nu'u* there were special titles combining both types. These were known as *tulafale ali'i* (orator chiefs) and enjoyed a special status.[20] The higher-ranked *ali'i* were understood to possess some kind of supernatural authority which was transmitted genealogically through divine ancestors. It was generally believed that these high-ranking *ali'i pa'ia* (sacred chiefs) became *aitu* (spirits) after death, taking on either human, animal, or plant form.[21] This formed the basis of religious beliefs and practices, about which more will be said shortly.

In relation to the '*aiga* which selected them to serve as their *matai*, both *ali'i* and *tulafale* bore similar responsibilities. In the affairs of the village and the *fono*, however, their functions differed, although in a complementary fashion. The *ali'i* stood as the titular head of the *'aiga* and was the final authority. The *tulafale* acted more or less as an executive agent and performed various duties on behalf of the *ali'i*. In addition, the *tulafale*, as implied in the translation 'orator', was responsible for making formal speeches on behalf of the *ali'i*, and acted as the repository of the *'aiga*'s genealogical record, as well as of history and legends.[22] This implies that *ali'i* titleholders were superior in status to *tulafale*. But this did not hold as a general rule since, depending on the context of *nu'u* relationships and genealogical origins, *tulafale* titles sometimes out-ranked *ali'i* titles.[23] Another point to be noted is that the means by which *tulafale* legitimized their own ambitions was by acting on behalf of a higher ranking *ali'i*. Thus the greatest authority could, in practice, be exercised by those of lower rank. Some find the position of *ali'i* in this respect comparable to that of the Brahmans of India whose exalted sacred status does not necessarily attract the greatest measure of wealth or power.[24] This is also an aspect of the understanding within Samoan sociopolitical structures that *mamalu* (prestige) was not automatically synonymous with *pule* (power or the right to command), and is a factor in the frustration experienced by the first wave of Europeans who attempted to form alliances with the most prestigious chiefs.[25]

Another complicating factor is that titles could, depending on the individual qualities of particular incumbents, decline or rise in relative status within the wider hierarchy of titles. Titles could also emerge from the names of prominent individuals. Meleisea points out, for example, that some of the chiefs' names of the Tupua dynasty became titles.[26] It should also be noted that the *fa'alupega* did not set out a permanent, rigidly fixed hierarchy, either within or beyond the village level. As suggested above, different titles could vary in precedence, and this reflected the shifting balance of power. The dominant party for the time being was called the *malo* (now the word for government), and was especially powerful when it held one or more of the highest titles in Samoa. Although rivalry attended election to titles at all levels, bids for high titles at district level were most often accompanied by tensions between the various areas and parties. This meant that there were changing *fa'alupega* throughout Samoa, giving an impression of inherent instability.[27]

In the general framework of *fa'aSamoa* (or *fa'amatai*) a common inter-pretation of status attribution holds that individuals carried no particular status or rank by virtue of descent alone. Rank and status effectively belonged to the title rather than the person, and hierarchical status or relative ranking was determined almost exclusively by the status of the title itself. Another commonly held supposition is that an individual's genealogical connections to an *'aiga* could be traced unproblematically through either male or female lines in accordance with the principle of non-unilinear descent, with no determined order of precedence for either the male or female link.[28] Although titles were tied to particular 'aiga and therefore to notions of descent, Mead argued that the system generally reflected a disregard for primogeniture and direct descent, not to the extent that these were ignored entirely, but enough to allow aspirants with weaker 'blood claims' to titles to assert special ability or service to the 'aiga.[29] Similarly, in describing the ideal characteristics of fa'amatai in contemporary Samoa, one commentator says that the absence of rigid rules of succession like primogeniture means that all male and female descendants of a title are heirs with unqualified equal opportunity, thereby underscoring the 'unstated belief of Samoan culture that there are no commoners in social organization'.[30] This also implies that there are no bars to full female participation on a basis equal to males.

Ideal descriptions of sociopolitical structures, however, rarely coincide with reality. As in Western liberal democratic societies, the absence of formal bars to female participation in Samoa did not automatically produce tangible results in terms of female achievement of high status. As Franco points out, matai status was certainly possible for women, but apparently rarely attained. He cites the historic case of Salamasina, who succeeded in gaining the four paramount titles in all of Samoa in the sixteenth century, suggesting that her achievement may have provided a charter for female matai-ship. There were, however, very few other historic references to female chiefs.[31] In her 1928 study, Mead, although describing the nature of competition for titles as 'very democratic', observes nonetheless that the fact of being a woman presented serious obstacles to status achievement, and that at the time of writing, there was only one female matai in the Samoan islands: 'They seem to have been as rare as European queens and must be regarded as non-typical in every respect'.[32]

Despite the lack of realistic opportunities for equal participation (a situation hardly confined to Western Samoa, either past or present), the absence of strict rules concerning the passing on of titles has obviously contributed to making matai succession theoretically open to the full 'aiga membership. Ipso facto, all members are entitled to participate in the matai selection process. A 1962 title dispute reported in American Samoa (which like Western Samoa has maintained the matai system within its general legal framework), illustrates the extent to which matai status remains ostensibly open to all. In this particular contested case, 961 eligible individual members of the 'aiga expressed their choice of heir to the court. This meant that since there were 961 people competent to vote on a successor, there were theoretically 961 eligible to hold the title themselves. In commenting on the contemporary implications of this case, Holmes says that the main point which emerges is that such widespread eligibility for *matai* status means that virtually everyone has a stake in the traditional system, which has made Samoans 'less disposed to leave it for an uncertain destiny in the [European] world of status'.[33]

The elements of *fa'aSamoa* described above are those usually invoked to underscore claims about the essentially 'democratic' character of traditional Samoan structures and Samoan society's egalitarian or 'classless' character. Meleisea argues that another egalitarian aspect of *fa'aSamoa* was evident in the economic distribution of goods, at least in terms of the basic necessities. Historically, untitled people enjoyed about the same standard of consumption as the highest chief, and material inequalities were reflected only in the distribution of certain objects (like fine mats).[34] Furthermore, in the sphere of everyday life, only the highest-ranked *ali'i* were unlikely to take part in the daily work routine. Other *matai* usually laboured alongside the untitled, although they did act as work leaders.[35] As for domestic facilities, Meleisea's descriptions also stress the egalitarian nature of social arrangements:

> The largest houses of important title holders were built, not as personal chiefly dwellings but as meeting houses and for the entertainment of the *nu'u* and its guests. In house-building, rank determined how many tiers the stone house platform would have, but not the amenities of the house itself.[36]

Meleisea also goes on to point out that because of the economic structure of *fa'aSamoa,* there is no sense in which traditional Samoan society can be described as feudal. Early observers like Robert Louis Stevenson seemed well aware that appearances often masked a reality that was not necessarily comparable to anything in the European historical experience:

> To us, with our feudal ideas, Samoa has the first appearance of despotism. An elaborate courtliness marks the race alone of Polynesians; terms of ceremony fly thick as oaths on board a ship; commoners mylord each other when they meet ... And for the real noble a whole private dialect is set apart ... Men like us, full of memories of feudalism, hear of a man so addressed, so flattered, and we leap at once to the conclusion that he is hereditary and absolute. Hereditary he is; born of a great family, he must always be a man of mark; but his office is elective and (in a weak sense) is held on good behaviour ... Doubtless the Samoan chief, if he be popular, wields a great influence; but it is limited. Important matters are debated in a fono, or native parliament, with its feasting and parade, its endless speeches and polite genealogical allusions. Debated, I say – not decided; for even a small minority will often strike a clan or a province impotent. In the midst of these ineffective councils the chief sits usually silent: a kind of gagged audience for village orators ... the chiefs of Samoa are surfeited with honour, but the seat and extent of their actual

authority is hard to find ... The idea of a sovereign pervades the air. The name we have; the thing we are not sure of.[37]

Stevenson's description of the society he encountered in the late nineteenth century raises a number of other relevant points. In particular, the allusion to the concept of a sovereign which was not embodied in any actual individual, nor formalized as a permanent office with successive incumbents, points not only to the absence of a tangible, fixed, centralized authority in the islands, but also highlights certain European expectations about the nature of political authority and organization. The record of European exploration and colonial settlement generally reflects a concern with finding, or establishing, an overarching native authority, thereby making dealings very much easier. Preconceived notions of 'traditional authority' also led many Europeans to believe that centralized, hierarchical authority was, in any case, a natural feature of 'primitive' societies. But what was found in Samoa scarcely accorded with such expectations and baffled many early European visitors and settlers. The last two lines of Stevenson's astute observation captures precisely the ambiguity of Samoan political organization.

These points form the focus of Meleisea's thesis concerning what he describes as Samoa's 'unitary system of dispersed power'. Despite the high level of autonomy evidently enjoyed by individual *nu'u*, even among those of relatively low rank, Meleisea argues that oral traditions point to historic periods during which a single national authority was recognized throughout the Samoan islands. He further claims that although a centralized polity may not have materialized as a permanent feature of Samoan political structure, the *idea* of one certainly existed for many centuries, as evidenced by the existence of a national *fa'alupega*.[38] Meleisea elaborates:

There are *fa'alupega* for individual titles, for groups of titles (as in the case of orator groups), for the *nu'u* ... for districts and *for the nation*. The national *fa'alupega* of Samoa recognises firstly the local polities and districts through their principal orator groups, then the two most important groups not represented by the former, and finally the descent groups ... of Samoa through their highest ranking titles.[39]

Meleisea's argument cannot be taken as conclusive, however, as there is disagreement over the 'authenticity' of the national *fa'alupega* as a component of pre-contact tradition. So'o says that the national *fa'alupega* may have been a nineteenth century creation. Part of the evidence for this is that the *tama-a-'aiga* are included in the national *fa'alupega*, but the *tama-a-'aiga* were not a feature of Samoan society before the nineteenth century. Whatever ideas there may have been about a centralized point of authority around which district and village authorities revolved in a kind of loose confederation, there is no doubting the confusion surrounding European perceptions from the earliest period of contact. This confusion was to have an important influence on Western Samoa's colonial experience.

Samoa Before the Coming of Europeans

It is generally accepted that Samoa's 'modern' era of history and politics began in the sixteenth century with the emergence of Salamasina as a chief of the highest rank.[40] Tongans dominated the previous period but, after reaching the peak of their influence in the fourteenth century, appear to have been driven out by the sixteenth century.[41] Samoan oral traditions relating to earlier periods are not as detailed or coherent as those of Tonga, although they are consistent in relating the autochthonous origins of all Samoans and ascribing the descent of the most illustrious founding lineages to Tagaloa.[42] Nonetheless, oral traditions in the form of genealogies were, as in other parts of Polynesia, accorded special significance and those of high chiefs in particular were carefully preserved by committing them to the custody of a select class.[43]

Salamasina became *o le tupu o Samoa* (the paramount chief of all Samoa) when she gained all four of Samoa's highest titles – the *papa* titles (Tui Atua, Tui A'ana, Tamasoalii, and Gatoaitele). Although rank is considered to reside in the title rather than the person, Salamasina's genealogy as a descendant of great aristocratic families from Fiji, Tonga, and Samoa was clearly an important factor in her being awarded the titles in the first place. As Schoeffel remarks: 'The bestowal of the four titles upon [Salamasina] thus recognized her genealogical and titular paramountcy in the land ...'[44] This could have led to the establishment of a centralized polity under a single ongoing authority in the person of a *tafa'ifa* (the name, meaning 'one supported by four', given to one holding all four *papa* titles simultaneously).[45] But in subsequent developments (which are not clearly recorded) these titles seem to have dispersed again. This was a more logical development given the nature of Samoan sociopolitical structures, especially given that control over each title lay with different groups:

> On the death of a chief, his [or her] title returned to the people whose right it was to bestow it. When a Tafa'ifa died, the four *papa* and any other titles he [or she] may have held were 'scattered amongst the families' ... and efforts to gather them had to commence anew.[46]

Another factor is the intense status rivalry attending title bestowals, especially those of higher rank. Such rivalry usually worked against the accumulation of too many high titles by one person, although it hardly prevented attempts to do so. It is important to stress once again the extent to which status rivalry permeated the Samoan system. Freeman makes special mention of violent conflicts between rival contenders for the various *papa* titles which eventually caused the western islands of Samoa to divide into two major factions and which was a primary cause of frequent assassinations and large-scale warfare in which thousands lost their lives.[47] Nonetheless, the four *papa* were held at least once more by a single person, Malietoa Vainuupo, in the nineteenth century. On his death bed Malietoa Vainuupo declared his wish that he should be the last *tafa'ifa*.

By this stage, European influences were making their mark on Samoan society, especially as a result of European interest in establishing a centralized authority. In the meantime, two powerful orator groups known as *Tumua* and *Pule*, each representing two confederations of districts, had emerged. The Tumua group was made up of the *tulafale* of the Atua and A'ana districts who controlled the two *papa* titles of Tui Atua and Tui A'ana, as well as politically influential groups in Upolu who controlled the other two *papa*, Gatoaitele and Tamasoali'i.[48] The Pule comprised the *tulafale* of six important districts on Savai'i. In addition, a smaller confederation based on the islands of Manono and Apolima, called the *'aiga i le tai*, was linked to the *Pule* group. These groups controlled succession to the most important chiefly titles as well as acting as spokespeople for the titular rulers. Their political power and influence was further enhanced by their acknowledged authority in the sphere of genealogical, historical, and traditional knowledge.[49] The orator groups, which thrived in the dynamics of rivalry, were especially important in dealings with Europeans. These and other aspects of European contact, including the impact of Christianity, will be discussed shortly. It is necessary first to outline the nature of Samoa's religious belief system and its implications for the way traditional authority was (and is) understood.

We have seen that a fundamental aspect of Samoan chiefly authority and legitimacy, especially in relation to *ali'i*, is that such attributes were related directly to the *mana* believed to have been passed down by divine ancestors and meant, ultimately, descent from a deity. This was common throughout much of Polynesia and is certainly comparable to the Tongan belief system. Other features of Samoan religious beliefs common to most of Polynesia include the immanence of various gods in trees, plants, and inanimate objects.[50] In addition to a patron *aitu*, possessed by every individual person, as well as by each *nu'u* and district, there are references to 'national gods' believed to be the original deities responsible for creating the universe.[51]

Among the national gods the most important was undoubtedly Tagaloa who created the Samoan islands and from whom the most ancient human lineages, villages, and political institutions were traced.[52] The term *atua* was used to designate the various manifestations of Tagaloa, and was later applied to the Christian god.[53] The *ali'i*, to whom personal sanctity was attributed, enjoyed certain exclusive privileges and were entitled to special deference and respect. This was complemented by expectations that the public behaviour of *ali'i* should be circumscribed in order to protect their sanctity from defilement.[54] Both privileges and prohibitions were maintained by the application of supernatural sanctions but, as in Tonga, the degree to which these were invoked depended on rank. Furthermore, only the more senior *ali'i* possessed a pronounced aura of 'sacredness'.[55] With respect to crime and punishment, the rank of the offender viv-à-vis the victim was decisive in determining the extent of severity with which offences such as theft, rape, or assault were dealt with.[56] Again, this is directly comparable to the Tongan experience.

Despite the infusion of the religious belief system throughout social life, it seems that Samoan theology and its ritual manifestations were not rigidly organized through a set of distinct institutions. Accordingly, there was no powerful priesthood or set of religious offices set apart from the rest of society. Rather, the priesthood was drawn from among the *matai* and whatever power and authority the individual priests enjoyed derived directly from their *matai* rank.[57] The absence of separate institutions through which religious practices and beliefs might be expressed did not mean that the religious belief system was weak, nor that the priesthood was weak. George Turner of the London Missionary Society recorded his observations and general opinions about the system in the following terms: 'The constant dread of the gods, and the numerous and extravagant demands of a cunning and avaricious priesthood, made the heathenism of Samoa a hard task'.[58] Although statements of this kind probably exaggerated the evils of indigenous social and religious systems in order to fortify justifications for spreading Christian versions of the Truth, there is no doubting the powerful sanctions that the religious belief system reinforced in the sphere of chiefly power.

Even so, Samoa's belief system was transformed from 'heathenism' to Christianity with relative ease. It is generally agreed that the theologically based ideology supporting Samoan chiefly institutions in the pre-contact era was not greatly disturbed with wholesale Christian conversion. West notes that this contrasts markedly with Tahiti, and to a lesser extent with Fiji, where powerful priesthoods were destroyed. In the absence of a similar priesthood in Samoa, it was much easier for *matai* to simply take over Christian beliefs, which were then interpreted in terms of the existing social and political order.[59] Similarly, Gilson argues that the ideology linking chiefly legitimacy to sanctity was transformed with little loss of effective substance, 'the Samoans declaring, as if it had always pertained, that their chiefly institutions were given and are upheld by their Christian god'.[60] Gilson goes on to note that Christian pastors who engaged in converting the Samoans perfected their skills in playing upon the 'social and political susceptibilities of their congregations'. To the extent that this entailed accepting so much of the traditional order and mores, Gilson further asserts that Christianity has by no means acted as a revolutionary force and that public manifestations of religion, 'as measures of piety and of the efficacy of church affiliation, have become as characteristic of Samoan Christianity as they were of the system which the missions superseded'.[61]

This is not the whole story, however, and a number of important changes were brought about by Christianity. Meleisea argues that the religiously legitimated power of chiefs was weakened by some of the strongly egalitarian principles of Christian teaching.

> Overall, Christianity had a levelling effect in as much as it replaced the ideological justification for attributing great powers to a few great chiefs. It also re-defined chiefly power as a secular political authority by reducing the crucial distinction between ali'i and tulafale, which became more ceremonial than actual. Without the ideological justification of bloodlines which linked men and women to gods, the criteria of succession became more complicated in relation to the highest ranking titles. Greater numbers of individuals could lay claim to chiefly rank.[62]

On the other hand, Meleisea appears to agree with the views of such writers as West and Gilson where he states 'the idea that the high chiefly titles carried great prestige did not disappear with Christianity',[63] and that:

> Christianity became part of fa'aSamoa and was used, like the old religion, to legitimate its institutions ... [T]he system, which incorporated new practices, ideas and goods, was not perceived to have changed fundamentally ... the aiga, the nu'u, and the authority of the matai and the fono were still there.[64]

It would be pointless to attempt a reconstruction of Samoan history and sociopolitical development that showed a completely consistent picture regarding the impact of Christianity – or indeed the impact of other influences. But despite the apparent ambiguities and contradictions surrounding Christian conversion, there is no doubt that, as with Fiji and Tonga, there remains an association between divine power and chiefly authority in Samoa. This is exemplified in the very generalized portrayals of fa'aSamoa that are commonly written for simple consumption: 'A Matai ... is believed to have received that title from God – *o tofi mai le Atua.*'[65]

From Contact to Colonial Rule

The first European sighting of the Samoa group was by a Dutch expedition under the command of Jacob Roggeveen in 1722. Neither he, nor the French explorer Bougainville who sailed by the group forty years later, landed on any of the islands although some trading with Samoans took place over the sides of their respective vessels. The first recorded landing of Europeans was left to Bougainville's compatriot La Perouse, whose contact with the islanders resulted in a dozen of his party being killed. Although the British vessel HMS *Pandora* made brief contact in 1791 – and this again involved some violent encounters – it was not until John Williams of the London Missionary Society (LMS) landed on Savai'i in 1830 that substantial dealings between Europeans and Samoans began. In the meantime, some of the ubiquitous 'white drifters' of the Pacific, consisting largely of escaped convicts and lost or deserting seamen, had taken up residence in the islands. Their impact and influence, however, were fairly negligible. Despite this minimal contact with Europeans before 1830, the people of the Samoan islands had nonetheless learned something of developments in the outside world. Samoans returning from visits to Tahiti and Tonga had brought back stories of the European God and, according to one source, a Christian-inspired millenarian cult had been established on Upolu in the late 1820s.[66]

When Williams arrived in 1830, Malietoa Vainuupo held sway as the most influential of Samoan chiefs. Malietoa was keen to learn about the type of supernatural forces which appeared to support the skills and power in navigation and warfare observed among these *papalagi*.[67] Eight missionary teachers were left under his protection and, when Williams returned two years later, Christianization was well under way. Under Malietoa's lead, nearly all his people had renounced their heathen ways, apparently demonstrating their new commitment to the European God by eating their sacred *aitu*.[68] Malietoa had received the Europeans and embraced Christianity just as he secured a major victory in war over the A'ana and Atua districts and this factor, together with his traditional high status and his warm dealings with the missionaries, meant that he came to be treated 'as if he and his party were the national government and himself the "king" '.[69] This was a prelude to later developments. Given that the preferred form of government among many Europeans was one with a strict hierarchy and centralized legislature, and that this was thought to be the key to securing national stability, it is not surprising that much effort was expended in the latter half of the nineteenth century in attempting to construct an administrative pyramid linking villages at the base to wider district administrations, leading in turn to a pinnacle of authority in the form of a Samoan kingship based on the *tafa'ifa*.[70]

Although political life in Samoa was deeply influenced by pressures from external sources from the 1830s on, this did not undermine the local operation of *fa'amatai*. Nonetheless, efforts to establish a European notion of 'order', initially for the better regulation of shipping, trading, and other commercial activities around the ports of the island group, resulted in the drafting of codes controlling port activities. With the assistance of missionaries and the cooperation of village *fono* in the vicinity of Apia, minimum guidelines for conduct were established in the absence of any other European authority. The establishment of British and American consular offices, as well as a representative of the city of Hamburg, and the participation of European naval commanders in settling disputes (including disputes between Europeans and Samoans), further entrenched a role for European authority. On the question of authority, different camps of opinion emerged with settlers favouring a centralized, European-dominated model similar to Hawaii's which had enhanced settler interests there. The missionaries, however, favoured retaining a strong notion of Samoan sovereignty and a decentralized district-based model along the lines adopted in Rarotonga (Cook Islands). Opinion among missionary groups generally supported the view that attempts to institute a national government under a monarch would be fraught with all the difficulties that attended traditional struggles over high titles. Missionary opinion therefore differed quite markedly from that of other Europeans at the time, so it would be a mistake to generalize too broadly about 'European' pressure for centralization. Little attention was paid to such problems by Samoans themselves, their primary concerns for the time being remaining firmly focussed on their own internal political objectives.[71]

While Europeans devoted much of their effort to imposing order in the increasingly urbanized area around Apia, which now bustled with both Samoan and European activity, there were sporadic outbreaks of warfare between Samoans during the 1840s and 1850s. Davidson's analysis suggests that the inconclusive nature of these wars is evidence of European influence and mediation. The pursuit of titular political supremacy was no longer such an objective, given the high costs involved. More specifically, Davidson writes: 'Missionary teaching and the desire of the combatants to maintain their cash income had led to long breaks in the fighting and to the failure of the parties to pursue temporary gains to the limit'.[72] By the end of the 1850s, it seems that the idea of more 'modern' political institutions was coming into favour among many Samoans. At first this was limited to district and sub-district levels, but by the end of the 1860s, a number of *ali'i* and *tulafale* had instituted a form of confederation with government headquarters established at Mulinu'u at the eastern end of Apia harbour – where the present parliament is located. This experiment proved a failure since it did not enjoy the support of all the most powerful factions and was therefore unable to exert any real authority. Nonetheless, this period can be seen as one in which Western forms of government started to influence Samoan ideas about the benefits of political unity and security.[73]

By the 1850s Samoan political struggles had become a major factor in land alienation, since they distracted Samoan attention from the extent to which Europeans were claiming more and more land. Much of this took place through transactions which were poorly understood by most Samoans. A concerted land-grabbing exercise by European speculators in the period 1869–1872 inevitably weakened Samoan control over key resources and created confusion over the legality of certain transactions and conflict among rival European claimants. These were among the most significant factors leading to the creation of a renewed desire among Samoans for a confederation through which their collective interests could be represented. The various European groups, comprised mainly of British, American, and German nationals, were naturally keen to see a central authority established to make their own dealings easier.

A new Samoan government, incorporating a shared 'kingship' and two principal councils, was set up at Mulinu'u.[74] Far from settling problems of authority and disputed land transactions, however, the new government became the focus of further disputes. This was not a simple matter of Samoan interests versus those of Europeans – the interests involved were far more complicated as the various rifts and factionalization within 'national' groups during this period demonstrate. A battle fought in 1877, for example, was essentially between two Samoan groups, but had implications for the alignment of European interests which in turn were played off as circumstances shifted. By the end of the 1880s, after another spate of warfare in which settlers became targets for both of the major Samoan factions, German interests began to predominate, although not without resistance from Americans, the British, and some Samoan factions. In the last year of the nineteenth century, relative peace was eventually imposed. This was achieved through a number of new arrangements: first, by the withdrawal of British officials from all the Samoan islands (in exchange for concessions elsewhere, including treaty rights in Tonga); second, by the partitioning of the islands themselves with the eastern islands coming under American control; and third, by the assertion of unchallenged German authority in the western islands.[75]

Meleisea points out that just 70 years had elapsed between the time of the arrival of the first LMS missionaries and the dominance over Samoan affairs by 'a relative handful of foreigners'. He notes further that this has been compared by some historians with the 'success' of the Tongans in resisting such domination through the successful institutionalization of a central government, thereby implying Samoan failure to achieve a similar outcome. Meleisea goes on to argue, however, that this could have been achieved had the victor in the 1828–1830 war, Malietoa Vainuupo, pressed on, using the missionary presence as an additional lever, to establish a centralized monarchy.[76] Given the contingent nature of historical developments the alternative path proposed by Meleisea is plausible. And had it in fact come about, contemporary historians and commentators would no doubt be emphasizing the latent potentiality for such a system in the traditional Samoan polity, especially by reference to the position of *o le tupu o Samoa*. It follows, too, that the notion of what exactly constitutes the 'traditional' nature of the polity would now be much more in keeping with what is assumed for Tonga.

In the period immediately following the establishment of German control over Western Samoa, the new administration's major task was to forge a 'colonial relationship with a people who had never really accepted the premise of subjection as Europeans conceived it'.[77] Western Samoa's first governor, Dr Wilhelm Solf, in some ways resembled Fiji's Sir Arthur Gordon. He has been described as heavily paternalistic, but possessing at the same time a greater sensitivity towards Samoan culture than most of his German contemporaries. The official German perspective on their new South Seas colony (or at least that which predominated back in the fatherland), envisaged the islands as a source of revenue and an addition to German living space.[78] But Solf had quite different views:

> Samoa is so small and so remote that it has fortunately no commercial future … My congenial duty, therefore, is merely to guard it as it was – a little paradise – and do my best to keep the passing serpent out of our Garden of Eden.[79]

According to another commentator, Solf's vision of the ideal political arrangement for the Samoan Garden of Eden was based on a romanticized conception of an ancient Samoan 'parish' style of organization, the nurturing of which would eliminate the unstable influences of broader political structures (especially at the national level) and enable a return to a Golden Age in which national politics held no interest for Eden's inhabitants.[80] In this, he differed from Gordon in Fiji, who had sought to build up the system of indirect rule with both local bodies and a strong national component.[81] In contrast, Solf believed that direct rule, especially at the national and district levels, was crucial to harmonious government and that Samoans themselves would eventually have responsibility only for village level affairs. But initially, Solf inherited a political structure more or less 'crowned' by a titular Samoan leader,

Mata'afa, whose supporting party saw itself as a traditional *malo* and 'entitled to all the prerogatives of supremacy'. Furthermore, this party, together with many other Samoans, regarded the role of the Germans as one of 'friendly protectors' rather than as one of an administering authority.[82] These differing perceptions led inevitably to certain tensions, and Solf was never able to reconcile his aspirations with the reality of Samoan resistance to subordination. It is true that the power of certain key Samoan institutions such as *Tumua* and *Pule* were significantly reduced, but when New Zealand troops under the command of General Robert Logan landed in Apia harbour in 1914 and took control from the unresisting Germans, they found a Samoan community which, although relatively cooperative, was far from quiescent in its colonized status.

New Zealand's initial form of administration was essentially military, but Logan nonetheless wished to leave in place much of the German governmental structure. This accorded, in any case, with the Hague convention on laws and usages during war, and was also a convenient expedient in the absence of immediately viable alternatives. One of the most important institutions established under Solf's administration, in 1903, was the Land and Titles Commission, of which the present Land and Titles Court is a direct descendant.[83] Its primary function in Solf's day was to settle disputes relating to *matai* titles and land and, although its membership was European, Samoans were used as advisers and as clerks.[84] Its function today is much the same and it has become, moreover, a repository of legal norms and practices relating to the ill-defined area of Samoan 'custom and usage'.[85]

The war years and their aftermath brought more changes, especially in the economic sphere where Logan acted to liquidate German firms and repatriate most of Western Samoa's Chinese indentured labourers.[86] But the economic difficulties caused by these policies were as nothing compared with the havoc wrought by a major influenza epidemic in 1918 which wiped out almost 20 per cent of the Samoan population. The epidemic, introduced through the failure to quarantine a ship from Auckland, strengthened undercurrents of opposition to colonial authority and provoked an increase in Samoan unrest.[87] This was not the first time that Samoan groups had demonstrated resistance. There had been political eruptions under German rule, culminating in the formation of the opposition movement Mau a Pule under the leadership of Lauaki Namaluaulu Mamoe, an important *tulafale* and 'kingmaker' from Savai'i.[88] Although the leading figures in this movement were exiled to Saipan in 1909, and remained there until permitted to return by the New Zealand authorities, the Mau was later to gather strength and purpose in the struggle for independence. The most notorious event of the New Zealand colonial period was 'Black Saturday' – 29 December 1929 –

when a prominent Mau leader, Tupua Tamasese Leolofi III and ten other Samoans were killed by New Zealand police during a Mau protest march. Two other high-ranking Mau leaders, Tuimaleali'ifano and Faumuina, and about fifty other Samoans were wounded.[89]

After 1919, New Zealand had continued administering Western Samoa as a League of Nations mandate on behalf of Great Britain and, from 1946 until independence on 1 January 1962, as a United Nations (UN) trust territory. The negotiations over trusteeship prompted further agitation and, only a month after the trusteeship agreement had been completed, Western Samoans petitioned the UN for self-government for the whole of Samoa. The petitioners cited the Tongan precedent as proof that self-government under a protective power was a viable option. Comments of the following kind, however, typified perceptions on the other side.

> Tonga is not ... a strictly parallel case. Tonga enjoys long-established political unity, whereas in Samoa the traditions of factions are still strong and there is little national sentiment. Tonga possesses a nucleus of well-educated Tongans able to assume key administrative posts ... it is very much to be doubted whether self-government can prudently be given to the Samoans at once.[90]

In the meantime, conflict between the Mau and the New Zealand authorities continued. But by the mid-thirties a newly-elected New Zealand Labour government, imbued with a relatively strong anti-colonial ethic, adopted a much more liberal and conciliatory approach to Samoan political activism and abandoned many unpopular laws and policies. After trusteeship status came into effect, the Samoa Amendment Act was passed in 1947, giving Western Samoa a significant measure of self-government. This allowed for much more direct Samoan participation in government and accorded with the requirements of trusteeship which, unlike the old terms for mandated territories, contained specific provision for 'orderly political advancement'.[91] Much was to be achieved in this direction under the guidance of the liberal-minded high commissioner, G. R. Powles, who arrived in 1949 determined to make progress in self-government his guiding principle.[92]

It was the creation of the Legislative Assembly in 1948 and the moves towards independence in the 1950s that first provoked real consideration of suffrage. The first three sets of elections for the Legislative Assembly, conducted in 1948, 1951, and 1954, were on the basis of *matai*-only suffrage. This early practice was reinforced by a constitutional convention in 1954 where the matter was debated at some length. Although the records of the debates show that some *matai* favoured universal suffrage, mainstream Samoan thinking at the time was clearly conservative. This was often expressed in terms replete with biblical references. One speaker addressing the subject of suffrage, for example, found certain cultural similarities between Samoa and ancient Israel (such as the practice of circumcision and the value placed on virginity), and then went on to refer to the judges and prophets of Israel as *matai* from among whom the head of government was appointed. He further urged his fellow *matai* to 'establish and form our own Government on our own traditions and customs'.[93] Another, drawing a further salutary lesson from the Bible (although the logic of the reference is not clear), argued that

> the recognition of the matai system can never be abolished because we all feel it is our inheritance of birthright from God. For instance, when we refer back to what God gave Israel the authority was exercised generally by non-titled persons. That was the time that Israel was in a very desperate position.[94]

Radical nationalism and cultural conservatism often go hand in hand. Indeed, the latter is usually an important ingredient in the ideology of most national liberation movements. Davidson notes that the dominant tone of Samoan thinking on such matters as suffrage was characterized by 'a desire for cautious advance and for maintaining a firm link with the past'. And when a Samoan politician ventured outside the mainstream of Samoan thought, it was usually only to say that, while universal suffrage may be a desirable long-term goal, it was unlikely to come about in the foreseeable future.[95] But some Samoans held quite different views. Boyd reports that a number of vocal protagonists of universal suffrage were active in the 1950s. Some were members of the Samoan Democratic Party – a short-lived organization formed by unsuccessful candidates after the 1951 elections. They pointed to the example of American Samoa, where a bicameral legislature with universal suffrage and secret ballot elections for the lower house had been introduced in 1952.[96] Support for a similar system in Western Samoa, however, was limited and the recommendations of the Convention were that 'for the time being in the Samoan constituencies only Samoan matais should have the vote or be nominated as candidates'.[97] The following years brought no change in majority Samoan opinion and, in the face of international criticism which viewed *matai*-only suffrage as stifling participation and initiative, leading *matai* spokespeople continued to defend the system as an essential part of their culture and heritage and a 'natural' Samoan institution.[98]

Although New Zealand favoured a broader basis for suffrage, and did not agree that this would damage Samoan traditions, the proposals for *matai*-only suffrage were accepted.[99] In reporting to the United Nations in 1960, New Zealand indicated its view that change could not be forced:

The concepts of secret voting and majority decisions are alien to Samoan custom, under which decisions of all kinds are made by discussion which continues until·unanimous agreement is reached ... The Administering Authority, while it continues to point out the desirability of working towards a more liberal suffrage, does not intend to force such a suffrage upon the people ... against their wishes.[100]

In May 1960, an ordinance creating a Constitutional Convention was enacted. This had been preceded by a working committee which produced a draft constitution for consideration by the Convention. During the debates in both bodies, the question of suffrage was, of course, one of the most important items. The draft constitution did not make provision for universal suffrage, and when it came to be debated by the Convention, one Samoan delegate, the liberal-minded Paitomaleifi (who had also moved, unsuccessfully, to have capital punishment abolished), moved to introduce universal suffrage in the final version of the constitution (although his amendment still included provision for *matai*-only candidature). Despite arguments which sought to demonstrate that universal suffrage would do no harm to the 'dignified customs and traditions of Samoa', the amendment was lost on the voices of a clear majority. In relating these events, Davidson points out that some members who had not (publicly) supported the amendment indicated later, in private, that they would have in a secret ballot.[101]

Matai-only suffrage was not entrenched in the constitution. It was envisaged that the electoral regulations would continue to provide for *matai*-only suffrage and, indeed, this was the case until 1990. As mentioned earlier, approval of the constitution itself, along with the proposal for independence, was put to a UN-sponsored plebiscite in which all adults, *matai* and non-*matai* alike, were eligible to vote. This had been at the insistence of the UN despite the usual objections that it was contrary to Samoan custom.[102] But voters were not asked to approve of any particular provision of the constitution, just the constitution as a whole. The two questions asked were:

1.   Do you agree with the constitution adopted by the Constitutional Convention on 28 October 1960?
2.   Do you agree that on 1 January 1962 Western Samoa should become an independent state on the basis of that constitution?[103]

With an overwhelming 'yes' vote of about 80 per cent for both questions, the last obstacle to Western Samoa's long-awaited independence and the end of colonial rule was cleared. But it was not to mark the end of debate over suffrage. Furthermore, by not entrenching *matai*-only suffrage in the constitution, the way was left open to future change by a simple act of parliament. One commentator sees this merely as a concession to 'the possibility of evolutionary change',[104] but another views it as revealing a manifest intention that change should take place in the future, arguing that although the political and social desirability of limited suffrage was recognized at the time of independence, it was not intended to remain in place indefinitely.[105] It is clear, at least, that the framers of the constitution were not of one mind on the issue and that even at this relatively early stage some *matai* held much more liberal views. The major point of agreement among the delegates that was never in question, and which has been voiced consistently by Samoan leaders of all kinds throughout both the colonial and independence periods, was on the value of *fa'aSamoa* understood as a unique Samoan social and political order based on the authority of the *matai*. Most of the arguments both for and against universal suffrage have revolved around this rather than around substantive questions concerning the values or desirability of democracy.

Politics and Law after Independence: The First Twenty Years

The extent to which the nationalistic expression of *fa'aSamoa* was entrenched in the political psyche of the newly independent state of Western Samoa is evident through its enshrinement in the constitution:

> WHEREAS the Leaders of Western Samoa have declared that Western Samoa should be an Independent State based on Christian principles and Samoan custom and tradition.[106]

This explicit constitutional recognition of 'Samoan custom and tradition' ensures the prominence of *fa'aSamoa* in legal and political contexts as a matter of principle, and other sections establish custom and usage as a source of law in relation to *matai* titles and customary land. But at the same time the constitution provides no definition of 'Samoan custom and tradition'. This has been left, largely by default, to the Land and Titles Act 1981 which provides a loose working definition. Powles summarizes the relevant parts of the Act as follows:

> 'the customs and usages of Western Samoa accepted as being in force at the relevant time' – and includes ... principles accepted 'by the people of Western Samoa in general' and the customs and usages accepted as being in force 'in respect of a particular place or matter.'[107]

At the heart of issues concerning custom and tradition is, of course, the *matai* system or *fa'amatai*. Although the constitution makes no specific mention of chiefly authority, it does refer, in articles 100 and 101, to the holding of *matai* titles and customary land in accordance with custom. According to Powles, this 'appears to encompass the necessary attributes of the traditional authority of chiefs in relation to such matters'.[108] Another important area of legislation in which *matai* are concerned relates to the authority of village *fono*. This has an important bearing on some of the more recent political developments in Western Samoa as they relate to custom and tradition. These will be discussed in more detail later. For the moment, it is sufficient to note that the government decided, in 1990 (and at the same time that the question of universal suffrage was acted on), to give formal statutory support to the village *fono* for the first time by incorporating it into the structure of local government and the administration of justice. As Powles states: 'The Village Fono Act 1990 purports to "validate and empower" the village council in the exercise of its "power and authority in accordance with the custom and usage" of the village'. He adds that the view held by many *matai* is that their authority in the village is unquestionable to the extent that it needs no validation by the national parliament.[109] As we shall see later in the discussion, however, the passage of the Village Fono Act seems to have given encouragement to some *matai* or *fono*, or both, to assert their authority much more aggressively.

The Land and Titles Court, established in its present form by the Land and Titles Act of 1981 (when it became independent from the Justice Department), enjoys exclusive jurisdiction in two important areas, namely, in disputes between Samoans over customary land, and in disputes over the allocation of *matai* titles.[110] Given that the concerns which finally prompted the move to universal suffrage were related to the proliferation of *matai* titles, and the problems which have attended this practice over the years since independence, the Land and Titles Court has been at the centre of much debate. Indeed, the court has played a leading role in shaping critical attitudes towards what had been happening to the *matai* system since titles started proliferating so rapidly. In one of its reports to parliament in the early 1980s the Court showed no hesitation in critically assessing these developments and their implications.

> The proliferation resulting from the splitting and creation of new titles has implications which go far beyond the mere multiplication of title holders which fill the *Savali* every month. The matai system which has taken all our years of existence to evolve to suit the needs of a basically agrarian society which draws its physical, social and spiritual strength from its family, land and people is fast crumbling down under the modern pressures of democracy. Thus the matai which was originally elected to be the custodian of family tradition, land and people has now become a pawn in the politician's game.
>   As more are appointed for political, for identification and for prestige purposes [than] they are to assume genuine guardianship roles in their extended families, the matai registry is glutted with title holders that have no

matai responsibilities ... Clearly the Samoans have to sit back and reflect on measures to halt the reckless abuse of the system and to introduce responsible and intelligent changes ... For voting purposes there are other ways other than wrecking the matai system ... In an effort to curb the disregard of the traditional values of our people inherrent [sic] in our matai system, it might serve to remember the historical decision passed by the High Court of American Samoa in relation to the Mauga title.

Should we assume the power to split a matai title, it must follow that we should assume the responsibility to split communal lands, 'ava cup title, taupou title, Honorific salutation, traditional food tray, traditional shares in a pig or sacred fish, and in all other prerogative traditionally inherent in the matai. Should the splitting continue, Samoa and its culture and custom will eventually disappear. This Court will not allow such to happen to the Samoan people.[111]

Although the practice of title-splitting was not a new phenomenon in Western Samoa, and is sometimes endorsed by the Court as a means of resolving factional problems within an *'aiga*,[112] the contemporary surge in title proliferation started only during the 1960s after representative institutions were introduced. It should also be noted, however, that in the colonial period, the missionaries as well as the New Zealand administration are said to have encouraged the practice in order to increase their influence (which was usually calculated on the basis of *matai* rather than population).[113] Referring to developments in the 1950s, Meleisea argues title proliferation then indicated an increasing lack of consensus about what constitutes Samoan tradition.[114] But by far the largest increase has taken place since independence. Powles reports that between 1961 and 1979, the number of *matai* rose by about 6,600 which, in percentage terms, represented an increase from 3.9 per cent of the population to 7.2 per cent.[115] Eligibility for voting, however, has not been the sole reason for this increase. Powles notes both some broader reasons behind the trend as well as the concerns that it has generated:

The vigour of Samoan chiefship has promoted its expansion over the last 25 years to the point where a large proportion of public servants and businessmen have taken titles, reflecting the desire to gain additional advantages by using non-traditional achievement to acquire traditional privileges ... The same vigour has led to the proliferation of chiefly titles by means of the splitting of titles between persons important to the group, and the resurrection of old title names... Thus the process by which chiefship has successfully invaded areas previously non-traditional has tended to spread and weaken chiefly authority.[116]

Reviewing the situation again in 1983, Powles found that the trend had continued, and that it had done so for much the same reasons (and with the same consequences) that he had identified earlier:

Chiefship [in Western Samoa] exhibits greater adaptability and strength than elsewhere in the Pacific, but the pre-occupation of the Samoan people with status rivalry in all spheres of life has brought about profound change in the traditional system. On the one hand, chiefs have used their rank to secure national political advancement and commercial success, while untitled politicians, public servants and businessmen have sought chiefly titles to enhance their prospects. With the creation and splitting of titles, the system has been 'watered down' – and after the removal of some 2,500 titles conferred 'contrary to custom', there remain over 11,000 registered *matai*, or a ratio of one in every five adults as opposed to one in nine in 1961.[117]

In 1976 a committee chaired by Tupua Tamasese Leolofi IV was appointed by parliament to consider the existing law, practices and procedures relating to the election of members of parliament. The nine terms of reference focussed on a variety of issues, including suffrage, the distinction between the territorial constituencies and individual voters' seats, and electoral abuses (including corruption).[118] This report is worth considering in some detail because although its major recommendations were not adopted, it specifically raised some important issues relating to tradition and democracy, and also set out a strong argument in favour of democratic reforms. It differed from a number of other reports in that it did not restrict its critical comments simply to the adverse effects of the electoral system, but elaborated explicitly on the nature and value of democratic government (while at the same time acknowledging the importance of tradition).

One of the first difficulties experienced by the committee was in eliciting the views of non-*matai*. 'In carrying out its work, the Committee had high hopes that comments and evidence would be received from everyone – man or woman – holding a matai title or otherwise, but most of those who gave evidence were matai.'[119] The committee noted that part of the problem may have been due to indifference on the part of some non-*matai*, but they also believed that many non-*matai*, especially in the more remote villages 'still hold a sense of fear and are thus reluctant to speak on any matter which [is] included in the authority of the matai'.[120] The opinions of *matai* on the question of suffrage, however, were not so difficult to gather, and the committee reported that this body of opinion remained very firm in supporting the continuation of *matai*-only suffrage because 'to act otherwise might tend to affect the matai system as well as the Samoan customs'.[121] But referring to problems experienced in adducing the genuine views of the people, the committee also reported that:

In the customs and traditions of Samoa, there are specific matai of a village or a district who speak for the community. At the meetings of the Committee with each district visited, the Committee noted the presentation to them of the views of such district by someone who acted as spokesman for that district. In this manner, it may be assumed that the opinion of that district was unanimous, but the Committee was desirous to hear the personal views of each and every person on this matter. It is understood that although a district was said to be unanimous in one opinion, there is a great number of people who hold a different view which could not be made known in such a meeting. This opinion is established in some of the districts visited by the Committee where the individual views expressed individually after the meetings were quite different from those publicly expressed in the presence of a big gathering.[122]

The report went on to consider the relationships between Samoan custom, elections, democracy, and the *matai* system. In relation to custom, it was recognized that traditions and cultures are not static, but are subject to change from a range of external influences that cannot always be resisted. Elections were part of an introduced system brought in to facilitate the operation of parliamentary government, but adapted to customs and traditions by restricting the suffrage to *matai*. The report then noted that democracy entailed the right of all the people to exercise control or *pule* over the government and that suffrage restricted to *matai* was incompatible with this principle. With respect to opinions expressed by *matai*, the Committee stated that it was 'well aware of the stubborn argument by the matais that the "pule" or power should remain with them to make any decision',[123] but nonetheless concluded that:

... the dignity and honour of the matai cannot be taken away from our customs and traditions, but in the democratic principles of parliamentary Government at the present time, all the people have the 'pule' or the power to govern. It is vitally important therefore that each and every person qualified must voice his or her opinion. This will not affect the matai in any way. There will be problems if the matai continues to withold that authority instead of making it available to the people generally from whom some good useful thoughts may come.

The Committee also firmly believes that there is no longer a close association between the matai and members of his family under which it can be said that the vote of the matai is the vote by his whole family. But, the Government is for all the people, and it is therefore vitally necessary for every person who has reached the age of 21 years to vote.[124]

The Committee also examined a proposal, supported by a majority of *matai* giving evidence before the committee, that the Western democratic system of conducting elections for parliament be abandoned altogether because of its corrupting effect on the *matai* system. An alternative to elections was sought in the revival of customary practices which, in effect, required that district-wide meetings of *matai* be convened in order to reach unanimous agreement on a representative for each district. Alternatively, it was proposed that each village in a district could take turns in providing a representative. If unanimous agreement could not be reached (through either of these methods), it was further proposed that the government should appoint the member for that district. In response, the Committee noted that the record of elections in past years demonstrated a marked shift away from traditional methods of choosing representatives. Whereas in 1961, 21 constituencies had returned members unopposed, more or less through a consensus reached in the manner described above, only twelve did so in 1973, and this was further reduced to six in the 1976 elections. The Committee therefore found that the country had largely failed to abide by its own customs and traditions, even though the option of selecting members in the traditional manner was still available despite provisions for elections. In an article published two years before the Committee was established, a similar trend had been noted in relation to applications before the Land and Titles Court. Although the Court encouraged the settlement of title disputes by means of traditional negotiations within the 'aiga, and most families did indeed attempt this, Samoans were looking increasingly to the Court to resolve disputes that were, by tradition, the exclusive concern of the 'aiga. In the period since 1935, there had been an approximate six-fold increase in both land and title disputes before the Court.[125]

In relation to proposals for reverting to more traditional methods of selecting representatives, the Committee's report emphasized again a real concern about the lack of opportunity afforded to non-*matai* to express their views, and the way in which this was concealed by the myth of unanimity in traditional decision-making: 'A person who has been agreed to unanimously by the matai of a district is not the true representative of that district because there are included in the same district those who are not matai and who should have a voice in that election'. And once more the democratic nature of elective parliamentary representation was stressed as an important aspect of Western Samoa's government: 'It is not possible to abolish the existing form of elections by secret ballot because it is an integral part of the Parliamentary System in all Governments including Western Samoa'.[126] Concerning the nature of consensus and unanimity, it is worth noting Powles' comments about the real nature of *fono* decisions. He says that to describe traditional decision-making in the *fono* as 'unanimous' implies a degree of consensus which would seldom have existed in fact. Rather, there was consensus only on the obligation to abide by a decision once it was reached. Unanimity was therefore a public goal, and its public expression was essential for the purpose of making the decision binding.[127] It is also worth mentioning the exclusive nature of *fono* discussions. These are exclusive in the sense that non-titled people are not merely barred from participation (although they can sit outside and listen), but the language of the *fono* itself is inaccessible. It is framed in a 'restricted code' to which only *matai* have complete access.[128]

The Committee also considered the practice of creating *matai* through title-splitting. It is evident from this section of the Committee's report that although it favoured democratic reforms, it nonetheless supported very strongly the retention of customs and traditions as integral to the Samoan way of life. The practice of title-splitting for electoral advantage was condemned as one which undermined the 'dignified status of these titles' and affected 'their rank in the social life of the country'. In addition, the Committee stated its firm belief that universal suffrage was necessary not only to curb the proliferation of *matai*, but other undesirable practices such as bribery (on the grounds that it would be virtually impossible to bribe all the additional people admitted to voting rights under a system of universal suffrage).[129] On the question of suffrage then, the recommendations were as follows:

> (a) It is now proper to grant the right to vote to all those people who have reached the age of 21 years to vote for members of Parliament, but only when a person holds a matai title that he or she may be eligible to become a candidate for the elections ...
> (b) That laws relating to the election of matai be reviewed and revised to forbid the making of any more inferior matai as well as to avoid the increase of the number of matai in the country unnecessarily [sic].[130]

These recommendations were not acted on by the government, despite the very strong wording of the report and the high status of its chair and membership. But this was hardly the end of the matter. In 1979, the problem of title proliferation and undesirable effects on the *matai* system again became the focus of a parliamentary enquiry. In keeping with the romantic style always adopted in matters relating to *fa'aSamoa*, the new report described its area of concern in the following terms: 'The subject matter of this investigation ... can be regarded as priceless pearls in the lives of the Samoan people ... we have been entrusted with the task of "custodians of our heritage and caretakers of the future"'.[131] The committee heard numerous complaints from witnesses about the practice of title-splitting. One example concerned a village in which over 200 *matai* were made on one day, followed by over 400 on the following day.[132] The committee found that the multiplication of *matai* of a family or a village was 'contrary to the customs', arguing, among other things, that there were insufficient lands in either bush or village sites to justify the increasing number.[133] Other witnesses, however, argued that the government had no business interfering in the bestowal of titles and that it should remain at the discretion of the village or family concerned. 'If for example 50 matais have been made in the family, and is holding the family together and no dissension is evident, then why interfere?'[134] The committee left the matter of universal suffrage unresolved and its strongest suggestion for coping with the problems was for the registrar of the Land and Titles Court to continue to deregister titles where appropriate, even though they recognized that this was an enormously difficult task which generated a great deal of ill-feeling.[135]

In 1982, a challenge to the constitutional validity of sections 16 and 19 of the Electoral Act 1963, which dealt with the question of suffrage, was mounted in what is known as the *Olomalu* case. In the Supreme Court, St John CJ held that the provisions of the Electoral Act dealing with the registration of *matai* as voters, and those dealing with the separate individual voters' roll, were inconsistent with article 15 of the constitution which covers 'freedom from discriminatory legislation' (and which is the last of thirteen articles comprising 'fundamental rights').[136] This decision was challenged, successfully, by the attorney-general in the Court of Appeal. The reasoning in both courts involved a variety of issues too complex to deal with here.[137] Of particular importance to the general concerns of this study, however, is the interaction between custom (and customary law), and the rational–legal provisions of a modern constitution, which were touched on during the hearings. In responding to a point made by the attorney-general in the Supreme Court, which proposed that the validity of sections 16 and 19 were supported strongly by 'the unique nature of Samoan culture', St John CJ found that although specific areas of custom had been preserved explicitly by the constitution (notably by article 100 relating to the *matai* system), this was not generally so.[138] In further elaborating, His Honour identified one of the major difficulties faced in attempting to reconcile custom with constitutional law in countries such as Western Samoa.

> Indeed the notion of national government and custom are not easily reconcilable ... The framers had to cater for both facets. They left Samoan culture where it had always been, on the land and in the family organisation, but they super-imposed on that culture a national government ...[139]

Bayne argues that the analysis of the relationship between custom and the issue of suffrage could have been taken further. He draws attention to Davidson's observation, made fifteen years earlier in relation to the propensity of villages and families to create additional numbers of *matai* in order to bolster their influence at elections, that 'like all conservatives, [the Samoans] run the risk of retaining the form of traditional institutions when their spirit and purpose have disappeared and, in so doing, of failing to satisfy contemporary demands'.[140] Since the abuse of *matai* titles had continued in precisely this way to the time of the Supreme Court hearing, Bayne says, 'a judge could well have taken judicial notice of these matters'.[141] But even if His Honour had done so, there is no reason to expect that it would have made any difference to the outcome of the Court of Appeal's decision. As another commentator has pointed out, this Court's concluding remarks appeared to have excluded, at least in the foreseeable future, any judicial role in overseeing the 'progressive attainment of the standards required by article 15'.[142] These remarks are revealing, not only for the limited role envisaged for the judiciary in such matters, but also for the light they shed on interpretations and ambiguities concerning the 'democratic' nature of the *matai* system.

> We recognise the argument that in an indirect way the matai system is democratic. At the same time ... there may be room for doubt whether all those adult citizens who are not qualified for the individual voter's roll do have a really effective voice in the territorial constituencies ... These, however, are questions not of law, but of social and political policy: questions which, on our interpretation of the Constitution are to be decided by Parliament, not by the courts.[143]

The Rise of Political Parties and Party Politics

Politics in the independence period had, in the meantime, been affected by the development of political parties. Several small parties emerged before, and just after, independence, but these were short-lived due largely to the fact that they had been formed (often by Europeans and part-Europeans) for fairly limited and immediate purposes.[144] As for Samoans, it has been suggested that the momentum created by the Mau, and the unity of purpose that was evident in the independence period, may have been effective in delaying the formation of Samoan political parties. After this, however, Samoan leaders began manoeuvring for political ascendancy in the national sphere, especially the leading chiefs known as *tama-a-'aiga* (which means, literally, 'sons of the families', and refers to heirs to the four *papa* titles).[145] On independence, two *tama-a-'aiga*, Tupua Tamasese Mea'ole and Malietoa Tanumafili II, had been chosen to hold joint office as head of state. But other *tama-a-'aiga* were by no means obliged to remain aloof from politics, and some chose to pursue careers as parliamentarians. Indeed, it seemed during the first fourteen years of Western Samoa's independence that the office of prime minister would also be dominated exclusively by *tama-a-'aiga*.

Western Samoa's first prime minister was Mata'afa Faumuina Fiame Mulinu'u II, one of the *tama-a-'aiga*. Mata'afa remained in office until 1970 when another *tama-a-'aiga*, Tupua Tamasese Leolofi IV (who had succeeded to the Tupua Tamasese title on the death of Mea'ole), won the support of parliament for the prime ministership. Mata'afa regained office after the 1973 elections and continued until his death in 1975, after which the head of state appointed Tupua Tamasese to the prime ministership. Writing after the 1973 elections, one commentator suggested that the rationale behind choosing a *tama-a-'aiga* as prime minister was embedded in the traditionalist view that he or she is the 'appointed ruler' – an essentially ascriptive role which carries with it the obligation of promoting the 'honour system' implicit in *fa'aSamoa*.[146] But changes in strictly traditionalist attitudes had been foreshadowed by Tupua Tamasese himself three years earlier. Although he prefaced his remarks with the statement that his country 'faces the modern world with a fairly unshakeable faith in the validity of her own way of doing things', Tupua Tamasese also acknowledged the blend of both indigenous and foreign aspects of politics in Western Samoa. Most significantly, he alluded to the probability that a non-*tama-a-'aiga* would be elected to office in his own lifetime.[147]

Tupua Tamasese did not have long to wait. At the first session after the 1976 elections, he was beaten for office by a non-*tama-a-'aiga*, Tupuola Efi. This represented a break in the practice, which had held since independence, that the office of prime minister be held by a *tama-a-'aiga*. The implications of this have been set out by So'o:

> If the ardent traditionalists were uneasy about Tupuola's appointment as PM, the other non-*Tama-a-Aiga* title holders aspiring for this office accepted it as a blessing in disguise. Since Tupuola Efi's appointment in 1976, the non-*Tama-a-Aiga* title holders have held the office of PM up to the present (1992). Thus, the office that once seemed reserved only for the *Tama-a-Aiga* title holders, is now open to any MP, regardless of what title he/she holds.[148]

The rise of Western Samoa's present-day political parties was concurrent with the emergence of non-*tama-a-'aiga* as contenders for the prime ministership, and these were to bring further challenges to Samoan political traditions. Following the 1976 elections, Tupuola Efi's opponents in parliament began to consolidate as an opposition faction. After the 1979 elections, Tupuola succeeded in retaining the prime ministership by just one vote, while his parliamentary opponents organized themselves formally as the Human Rights Protection Party (HRPP). In 1982, the HRPP won a majority of the seats and formed a new government, initially under the leadership of Va'ai Kolone but later under Tofilau Eti Alesana (both also non-*tama-a-'aiga*). On this occasion, incidentally, only two members were returned unopposed through the process described previously as the traditional method of reaching a consensus on the question of district or constituency representation. From this time on, party competition along the lines of Western political practices was to dominate virtually all such processes.

By the time of the 1985 elections, Tupuola and his supporters had also organized themselves as the Christian Democratic Party (CDP). The HRPP, however, was by far the most successful party, winning 31 out of the 47 seats. But it did not survive its term intact. A split in the HRPP saw eleven HRPP members, including Va'ai Kolone, defect to form a coalition with the CDP, and Tofilau's budget was defeated in December 1985. In the 1988 elections, the coalition won by a single seat, but a defection by one member to the HRPP enabled Tofilau to resume the prime ministership. The coalition was renamed the Samoan National Development Party (SNDP), with Tupuola Efi as leader and Va'ai Kolone as deputy leader.[149] The HRPP and the SNDP have now become consolidated as the two major parties in Western Samoa.

Political parties to this time emerged within parliament in a fashion similar to that which marked the rise of parliamentary political parties in Great Britain in the eighteenth century. But they did not do so simply in imitation of Western parliamentary practices, but also in response to the dynamics created by the parliamentary system within Western Samoa itself. These dynamics, which were underscored by the exigencies of competitive politics (in a partially democratic system), in the end required a break with the traditional style of choosing representatives. This traditional style, however, although apparently consensual at the level of appearances, was itself a fiercely competitive process in many respects, with the final public consensus masking any number of divisions within the group. It has been remarked that party politics in Western Samoa retains certain characteristics of the 'fluid, age-old politics' of the country, and that many Samoans would view the conduct of contemporary party leaders 'as a continuation of the jockeying between traditional Samoan leaders'.[150] So while the development of Western Samoa's party system can be viewed as a further approach to Western norms, it nonetheless resonates with aspects of earlier Samoan practices. This depiction of change stresses continuities rather than ruptures, and tends to downplay the influence of any external factors, including international pressures for democratization. But Western Samoa's final move to universal suffrage was prompted less by concerns about the values of democracy or by the desirability to conform to any external standards of democratic practice, than by pressures for change from within Western Samoa, including those created by competitive party politics.

The Introduction of Universal Suffrage

Following the 1985 elections, it was reported that Tofilau Eti was keen to press ahead with a referendum on the question of universal suffrage.[151] Tupuola Efi had also been on record as supporting a wider franchise.[152]

If this was so, however, nothing was to come of it at this time. In the meantime, reports from the Land and Titles Court indicated that the *matai* system was still engaged in an exercise of virtual self-destruction. In her 1986 report, the Registrar had complained that the system was 'fast crumbling' under pressure and that the *matai* registry was becoming glutted.[153] Again, in 1988, the report of the Land and Titles Court stressed the urgency of the problem. In the two years since 1986, the number of *matai* had grown from 20,808 to 24,574 with almost 2,000 petitions still waiting to be heard. It was calculated, on the average time taken to decide a case, that it would take about 25 years for one Bench to clear the backlog. On the issue of newly created titles (as opposed to those which were simply split), it was noted that these lacked 'family trees', but it was difficult for the Court to dispute large village groups which tended to boycott attempts by the Court to discredit such new appointments.[154]

In June 1990, the government under Tofilau Eti decided it was time to act, announcing that it now fully supported universal suffrage and that it would conduct a plebiscite in October 1990 to gauge public opinion on the issue. The government's principal argument in support of universal suffrage was that the move would help preserve Samoan custom and tradition in general, and the *matai* system in particular, from the corrosive effects of title proliferation. In addition, it was thought that universal suffrage would discourage politicians from engaging in bribery and other corrupt practices during elections (although it had often been argued that this 'bribery' was really part of *fa'aSamoa*).[155] Both arguments were clearly based on the concerns which had been expressed publicly over several decades.[156] On the other side, arguments against universal suffrage also reiterated the views put forward on previous occasions.

The referendum, itself conducted under universal suffrage, resulted in an affirmative vote on universal suffrage of 19,392 with 17,464 against (and 2,742 informal). The government moved immediately to amend the 1963 Electoral Act to allow for the replacement of the *matai* voters' roll by a single electoral roll for both *matai* as well as for all adult citizens previously excluded.[157] *Matai*-only eligibility for candidature remained in place, so to the extent that the change represented a move to demo-cratization, it was only a partial one. Nonetheless, the stage was now set for a very different type of campaign for the 1991 elections. One of the major differences made by the introduction of universal suffrage was that it allowed, for the first time, the majority of women to exercise voting power. This had been denied under the *matai*-only system in which men predominated. The HRPP was well aware of the potential power of their votes and indeed, following the success of the plebiscite, the government had introduced very swiftly two initiatives relating directly to women. The first was the establishment of a Women's Department, and the second was the proclamation of a new public holiday on Women's Day.[158]

Although it is not possible to gauge the extent to which the effective enfranchisement of women influenced the election result, it is more than likely that the HRPP's return to power in April 1991, with an initial majority of ten seats, was assisted by the women's vote. In addressing the nation on election night, victorious Prime Minister Tofilau Eti made special mention of what he thought were major factors in his success. These included the general popularity of universal suffrage and the formation of the Women's Department.[159] Some critics of universal suffrage, reflecting on the events of 1990–91, credit the HRPP's victory largely to these same factors, although their interpretation of the motives and principles involved is quite different. Aiono Fana'afi Le Tagaloa, Professor of Samoan Studies at the National University of Samoa, wife of conservative opposition MP Le Tagaloa Pita, ardent opponent of universal suffrage, and equally ardent supporter of *fa'amatai*, has said that the bill for universal suffrage was, among other things, a 'bait for women' and a political ploy on the part of the HRPP to retain power.[160] This view is supported by her husband who has also labelled it as an unprincipled action taken by a government which, realizing that it had insufficient time to create more *matai* before the next elections to bolster its support, had rushed the legislation through in order to avoid electoral defeat.[161] Whatever the motives, what does come through clearly is this: the notion that the *matai* system, and the limited franchise before 1990, provided equally for the expression of a women's voice in politics is unsustainable.

Le Tagaloa Pita is the founder of one of Western Samoa's newest political organizations, the Matai Forum, which in 1993 proposed taking legal action in the Supreme Court against the HRPP government over the manner in which universal suffrage was introduced. The essence of Le Tagaloa's argument is that resolutions of the Constitutional Convention have the force of law, and that any change can only be legally (and morally) effected either through an amendment to the constitution itself, or by convening another proper Constitutional Convention. He adds that: 'I regard the constitution as a source, a charter for the *fa'amatai* ... the Convention embodied *fa'amatai*. The system and its values, which had been inculcated in the mind of our society and embodied in the resolutions of the Convention, have been cheated'.[162] But there is no doubt in Le Tagaloa's mind that democracy itself is a good thing, and that it is already at the heart of *fa'amatai*: the official slogan of the Matai Forum is *'Temokrasi Samoa fa'amatai'* which translates literally as 'Samoan democracy is the *fa'amatai*'.

Another aspect of the 1991 elections that bears mention is the defeat of Tupua Tamasese Tupuola Efi in the ballot for his seat by just 27 votes.[163] In an analysis of the new trends which saw a *tama-a-'aiga* lose to a much lower-ranked political newcomer, one commentator observed that:

> Universal suffrage has brought him down from the top of the mountain where chiefs abide and look at things differently, to canoe level where the untitled and most of the women reside. Traditionally, chiefs will think twice about dumping and deserting their paramount chief. Not so with young voters under universal suffrage, many of whom are well educated and looking at things logically and without fear, with individual freedom and human rights ideas in their minds.

But it was noted also that Tui'atua Tupua Tamasese, as the more humble Tupuola Efi in the 1970s, had himself challenged the assumed paramountcy of the *tama-a-'aiga* in politics and opened the way for broader participation.

> When he defeated his first cousin and incumbent Prime Minister Tupua Tamasese Leolofiaana IV in 1976, he opened the floodgate to what we call *tagata lautele*, everybody or the common person. He became the first person to lead the country without a Tama Aiga title... It can be said that universal suffrage is a part of that freedom and development. It is a healthy development in the political life of the country, and Tupua Tamasese, a Tama Aiga now, has played a big part in that.[164]

In a further post-mortem on the defeat of Tupua Tamasese Efi, which also reflects on the changes being wrought by the interaction of *fa'aSamoa* with introduced concepts and practices, and some of the dilemmas raised by this, the same writer noted that:

> The defeat of the Tama Aiga, Tuiatua Tupua Tamasese, is not the same as the defeat of Tufuga Efi or Tupuola Efi. This is the Tuiatua Tupua Tamasese being battered about in the free for all arena of modern politics where public figures are made accountable for their actions. In our modern parliamentary system, a system laid down by the founders of our Constitution, the traditional and customary umbrella of the *faleupolu*, the orators, is not there to protect the orators' chiefs, or Tama Aiga, from the sun. Under the laws of Independent Samoa, everybody stands under the hot sun of accountability ...
> ... Many people have nothing against Tufuga Efi or Tupuola Efi becoming a politician, but they get worried when a holder of a Tama Aiga title enters politics, and is bruised in it. For they believe deeply in things Samoan, our culture, customs and traditions. For the Tama Aiga, our paramount chiefs, are the mountaintops of that faa-Samoa.[165]

Fa'aSamoa and Fa'amatai

Throughout most of this discussion, the Samoan 'traditional system' has been understood as referring generally to *fa'aSamoa,* but more particularly to *fa'amatai*. According to some, the latter is far more meaningful than the former, especially within Samoa, and this issue is worth exploring in a little more detail. Aiono Fana'afi, for example, maintains that the term *fa'aSamoa* is used more by *palagi* than by Samoans (at least among themselves). She adds that as a concept, *fa'aSamoa* lacks real substance whereas *fa'amatai*, which is to be understood as 'an ideal social system', resonates in a meaningful way with actual social experience.[166] With respect to the democratic nature of *fa'amatai*, Le Tagaloa Pita argues that it is comparable to the system by which the president is elected in the United States, because the *matai* effectively comprise an electoral college. He asserts, then, that to all intents and purposes the system was already at least as democratic as the United States before the introduction of universal suffrage. In further support of this position, Le Tagaloa goes on to stress the consensual aspect of the Western Samoan system: '*matai* is a political office and a *matai* has to be accepted unanimously by the heirs'. One person one vote, on the other hand, 'is a farce – it doesn't produce democracy'. Furthermore, 'it has made a mockery of the system' in Western Samoa because although the people can now all vote, they can't all stand. 'This is not democracy.' The government 'should have gone all the way, or not at all'. As it stands, 'it is a mutilated system'.[167]

Supporters of universal suffrage, although obviously differing in their approach to the question, nonetheless support *fa'amatai* in terms similar to those expressed above. The registrar of the Land and Titles Court, for example, despite her criticisms of developments in the *matai* system before the move to universal suffrage, nonetheless claims that *fa'amatai* is an important, living, dynamic tradition. Furthermore, it has retained its flexibility, and therefore its vitality, by *not* being entrenched in the constitution. In addition, she agrees that *matai*-making is indeed a democratic process and one that has not necessarily been carried out simply to create more voting support (although she says foreign influences have produced distortions). *Matai*-making on an increased scale, she says, has also been done for the purpose of family identity (where the title functions as a family name) or for prestige (especially if a person is working for the government). Titles may also be pursued by those wanting a greater say in family or village affairs, and also by those wanting to share the burden of social obligations.[168]

Another view of the issues, put forward by a senior *matai* from a village near Apia who supported the introduction of universal suffrage, reveals both similarities and differences with those views set out above. Leota Siaki says, first, that the HRPP has been very progressive in terms of democracy, although it could not have acted sooner than it did. Western Samoa needed 'a new, educated generation to grow up before universal suffrage could be accepted' and further changes to the system will depend on more education still. On the question of the strength of tradition, he said that one should not 'count on customs being wiped out as they are still very strong at the village level'. This refers specifically to *fa'amatai* which, 'if erased would be very bad' especially in terms of 'saving the land': 'Full democracy would mean loss of land, so it is very important to maintain the *matai* system to prevent loss of land, otherwise we could end up like the Maoris or Hawaiians. Only the *matai* system can control and safeguard land'. On the introduction of universal suffrage and its effect on *fa'amatai*, Leota believes that this move has weakened the system to some extent, but that people needed to be given more rights. Western Samoa 'needed to join the world more', that independence had not meant 'cutting the modern world off, it meant joining it, but as a free country'. On the democratic nature of the *matai* system, he says that he did not believe it to be democratic, but its justification lay in its protective capacity both in terms of land as well as its function in preventing 'social collapse' through external influences. Western Samoa as a whole, however, was much more democratic and accountable than Tonga. Finally, he stresses the importance of the *matai* system in maintaining law and order in the villages, which meant it need not be imposed by the national government.[169]

This last point raises several issues concerning *fa'amatai* and its allegedly democratic and egalitarian character. The first issue concerns the increase of suicide among young men aged between fifteen and 29 which became evident in the 1970s and 1980s. In the search for sustainable hypotheses to explain this phenomenon, some researchers looked primarily at cultural and structural factors embedded in the *matai* system. Macpherson and Macpherson propose, first, that 'in a society as authoritarian as Samoa, altruistic suicides are to be expected', and that these are committed by individuals who, having violated some norm or proscription, cannot subsequently bear the feelings of shame that are generated by their action: as a Samoan saying goes: '*sili le oti i lo le ma:* death is better than shame'.[170] The second hypothesis suggests that Western Samoa's gerontocratic social system means that youths, who have become well aware of opportunities outside the traditional system but are unable to take advantage of them, together with a sense that they lack means of either challenging the existing power structure or escaping it, probably feel a declining commitment to social norms and a heightened sense of disillusionment about their prospects. In other words, 'young untitled people become alienated from central values but are forced to continue to live by them'.[171] The first hypothesis explains the 'normal' level of suicide to be expected in such a society, while the second explains the anomic increase.[172]

These factors have been highlighted by another commentator on the issue who, noting that Western Samoa has one of the highest rates of suicide in the world, says that the appalling statistics demonstrate a remarkable gap between leaders and led. Quoting the Director of the YMCA (which carried out a national suicide awareness campaign in 1981), the article says that the suicide rate is influenced not just by the number of powerholders, but also by how power is exercised.[173] Another researcher, who supports the basic findings of Macpherson and Macpherson, has contributed further comments òn the nature of *fa'amatai* and its essentially oppressive character, especially within the *'aiga*. These observations also contrast very strongly with the idealized versions of *fa'amatai* invoked in support of its egalitarian and democratic nature. Norton says that Samoan chiefship is peculiarly oppressive, a characteristic which derives not simply from its patriarchal nature, but from the way in which status rivalry among *matai* and among *'aiga* 'give to domestic authority a taut and often violently impetuous quality unique in Polynesia'. Norton argues that 'the unrelenting haughty severity' with which *matai* are inclined to assert their authority in everyday life derives, paradoxically, not from 'power well-secured but from the uncertainties and ambiguities of the *matai*'s position among his peers'. Norton goes on to analyze the authoritarian nature of *fa'amatai* in terms of its localized context.

> Chiefly authority is weakest at the levels of its widest territorial span, and most oppressive at the domestic hearth. Authority which in other Polynesian societies is exercised in more distant relations over more numerous subjects is in Samoa asserted most forcefully within the intimate relations of the extended family ... The very uncertainties of an *'aiga* chief's status among his peers in the village intensifies his concern to assert power and prerogative. In this he is strongly supported by other senior members of his *'aiga*. The incessant external jealousy and rivalry gives the *'aiga* a most oppressive quality for its young members. The tyranny is endurable when there is an honourable course of service to follow in pursuit of reputation and perhaps eventually the chiefship itself, but it can be unbearably claustrophobic and demeaning when such roles are lost ...[174]

Support for the interpretation of *fa'amatai* as authoritarian and oppressive is also found in more general analyses which note that certain aspects of the system have become subject to new pressures. Meleisea, for example, writes that since independence there has been growing dissatisfaction with the way in which various principles of *fa'aSamoa* have been invoked selectively in order to justify certain actions. For example, some *matai* have referred to 'their traditional rank and status as justification to deprive others of the opportunities offered by the new system

either through political, social, economic or other avenues'.[175] These
remarks, as well as the analyses cited above, support Nakata's view that
Western Samoa's prevalent neo-traditionalist ideology reinforces a
political commitment to maintaining *fa'amatai* and the status quo of its
power structure and relations.[176] Analyses directed to the more specific
issue of suffrage follow a similar theme. On *matai*-only suffrage, some of
the more obvious problems relate to the fact that it creates government
of *matai*, by *matai*, and for *matai* – 'a strange contrast with democratic
principles'. Furthermore, this is seen as a legacy of New Zealand's error
in catering to 'pseudo-nationalistic' interests when allowing *matai* to gain
so much political control at independence.[177] Far from revealing an 'ideal
social system' or a democratic egalitarian society, then, these critical
analyses point to a thoroughgoing authoritarianism embedded in the
fabric of *fa'amatai*. The last substantive issue to be discussed in this
chapter, namely the Village Fono Act, highlights some of the more
specific problems that have emerged in this context.

The Village Fono Act of 1990

In September 1993 a Western Samoan villager was shot dead in front of
his family, after having his house and other property destroyed. This was
apparently done under the authority of *fa'amatai*. The slain man, Nu'utai
Mafulu Matautia (himself a *matai*), had recently returned to Lona village
on the main island of Upolu from New Zealand, where he had lived and
worked for twenty years, to set up a shop and small bus service. Following
some disputes with *matai* in the village, including a refusal by Matautia to
pay fines imposed by the *fono*, a ban had been placed on his shop and bus
service. The acrimony was further aggravated by the fact that Matautia
had recently played for a rival village in a national village cricket competition in which Lona village was knocked out by the rival village, which
then went on to win the competition. The dispute escalated in late September when Matautia banned a villager from crossing his property to
ring the bell for the evening curfew. In the final confrontation, a large
crowd of villagers gathered and, after burning Matautia's property, two
young untitled men apparently shot him dead on the instructions of
some senior *matai*, the fatal shot being delivered at close range between
Matautia's eyes, just outside the *fono*. His body was then dumped before
a gathering of *matai*. The killing was later described by Western Samoa's
Police Commissioner as justice in 'an old barbaric Samoan way'.[178]

In the immediate aftermath, a Samoan lawyer practising in New
Zealand was reported as saying that the *matai* who had ordered the
killing would probably argue that their action was legal under the Village

Fono Act of 1990 which validated the power and authority of the *fono* 'in accordance with custom and usage' and set no limits to its operation. The same report noted that:

> As a result, the Act has been used to justify brutality toward those who violate custom, including punishments such as 'saisai', in which offenders are trussed up like pigs and cooked.
> Men without matai titles are required by custom to be totally obedient to the chiefs, or as one chief put it: 'You must obey everything! Obey completely! Even though your chief be in error'.[179]

Three weeks later, a *matai* from the Apia area was banished from his home village by its *fono* for a period of one hundred years. His offence was to assist in the campaign of a candidate from another village in a local by-election. Again, this action was justified under the Village Fono Act.[180]

The question of the Village Fono Act takes us back to 1990 when it was enacted. This was the year in which the government had also moved to introduce universal suffrage. In order to 'soften the blow' to Samoan tradition that this move entailed, the government had raised the possibility of 'compensatory measures'. One was the creation of an upper house (which did not go ahead), but another was the formal empowerment of the village *fono* through the Village Fono Act.[181] This legislation had also been prompted by challenges to *fa'amatai* through court cases where it had been argued, successfully in a number of cases, that the imposition of certain aspects of traditional authority (such as the right of the *fono* to banish offenders as well as to control commerce) violated individual rights guaranteed in the constitution. Many *matai* naturally saw these developments as an encroachment by the courts on their own traditional area of jurisdiction.[182] The Village Fono Act, however, bolstered the authority of the *fono* by recognizing in formal law a wide range of traditional powers, sanctions and punishment. Some of these were specified, such as the imposition of fines, but the general recognition of traditional authority was framed so as to allow virtually unlimited scope for the imposition of punishment:

> The Act allowed every village *fono* to exercise any power or authority in accordance with the customs and usage of that village (S.3.2). It established that past and future exercise of power and authority by every village *fono* with respect to the affairs of its village which is in accordance with custom and usage is validated and empowered (S.3.2).[183]

In the wake of the execution in Lona village, much attention has naturally been focussed on the 1990 act. While some *matai*, and others, no doubt believe that the *fono* was justified in its actions, and had the necessary authority to act as it saw fit within its traditional capacity, others do not. One senior *matai* from the same district (but not the same village) in which the incident took place, who is also an MP and former justice minister, called for the arrest of the prime minister himself on the grounds that since he was responsible for the Village Fono Act, he was also responsible for the execution. Ulualofiaga Talamaiveo Niko said that he had warned in 1990 that the new law would allow the *fono* 'to revert back to the old traditional punishments, with people being burnt and baked in an oven', and that the whole thing had been on the verge of exploding. 'A lot of chiefs went around saying they had the authority to burn, to do this, to do that. A lot of people now say they have the power to do anything.'[184]

These developments are clearly at odds with the process of democratization that seemed to be gaining in strength with the introduction of universal suffrage. At the time of writing, the outcome of the case involving the Lona village execution, and the fate of the Village Fono Act itself, have yet to be determined. Some believe that the act will almost certainly be repealed.[185] But under the present circumstances, broad participation in the new democratic processes opened up by universal suffrage will be very difficult if village *fono* can use their authority, and their ability to impose severe punitive measures, to dictate local political matters and direct support to particular candidates.[186] This had already been evident in the 1991 elections, as described by So'o:

> The irony about universal suffrage, which supposedly champions the ideals of individual right [sic] and freedom of choice, was that after the elections some voters suspected of voting for candidates other than those agreed to by the ... *fono* were punished. At Tupua Tamasese Efi's constituency ... a prominent campaigner for Moananu Salale, from the village of Lufilufi which bestowed the title 'Tupua', was expelled (*faatulai*) from the village. At Savaia, a village in the constituency of Lefaga and Faleseela, where the HRPP candidate lost to a SNDP candidate, the members of a family who were taken by the SNDP candidate's vehicle to vote for him, were punished. They were asked to provide ten pigs and 100 taros, and when the exact amount was not supplied, they too were expelled from the village. The village council had made a decision before the elections that everyone was to vote for their HRPP candidate, Taula Ierome.[187]

Conclusion

A notion of Samoan culture expressed generally in the term *fa'aSamoa*, but often more specifically as *fa'amatai* is deeply implicated in major political issues in Western Samoa. Both *fa'aSamoa* and *fa'amatai* are conceived as the products of a body of tradition that is uniquely Samoan and, to this extent, they serve as important cultural symbols of national differentiation. Although the general idea of *fa'aSamoa* existed before the coming of Europeans, and was understood as differentiating Samoan ways from those of, say, Fiji and Tonga, *fa'aSamoa* has served increasingly as a standard against which certain Western social and political practices are set. In the dynamics of subordination created by European colonization of Samoa, this was a natural development. Thus the nationalist aspects of traditionalism in Western Samoa, expressed as *fa'aSamoa*, can be seen as having evolved initially in a defensive mode, 'as Samoans tried to resist external domination and to assert their own worth and dignity'.[188] The ideology supporting resistance to foreign domination, however, has not disappeared with independence and the nationalistic expression of *fa'aSamoa* has continued to serve important purposes. As with most expressions of nationalism, it functions not only as a means by which externality, or the 'alien', is defined or constructed, but as a very powerful internal reference point for political legitimation. Further-more, it is in the domestic sphere that *fa'aSamoa* shades into *fa'amatai*, the latter denoting a much more explicit conception of internal political legitimacy.

The politics of universal suffrage in Western Samoa can best be understood in this context, especially with respect to arguments concerning the legitimacy (or otherwise) of certain political forms, institutions, or practices vis-à-vis *fa'amatai*. This also has implications for the relationship between aspects of 'tradition' and certain interpreta-tions of democracy. First, it is evident that the main cluster of arguments employed by opponents of universal suffrage proceed from the premise that alien forms of politics are contrary to traditional (and therefore more legitimate) political norms and rules. Second, it is asserted that universal suffrage in terms of 'democratization' is quite unnecessary because the traditional system of *fa'amatai* is itself inherently democratic, though different in form to Western versions of democracy. Further-more, the introduction of universal suffrage represents a real danger to *fa'amatai* because it is essentially contrary to the principles on which *fa'amatai* is based, namely, the unquestioned political authority of *matai*.

These issues are different in character from those related to the breakdown of the *matai* system under its own weight, this being the major factor in the move to universal suffrage – apart from the political advantages which may have accrued to the HRPP in the process. With respect to this particular issue, the question of democracy, in terms of its values, practices, or institutional forms, was really quite irrelevant. 'Democratization' (or at least partial democratization) in the form of universal suffrage was an exercise undertaken in the name of tradition and directed ultimately towards its preservation. Many aspects of Samoan politics are paradoxical, and contain any number of ambiguities and contradictions. But the story of universal suffrage and the logic of both resistance to and support for its introduction does reveal at least one consistent principle of political rhetoric in Western Samoa, and that is the value assigned to Samoan tradition as the ultimate standard and point of reference for acceptable political norms and practices.

CHAPTER 5

Conclusion:
Tradition Versus the West

European contact and imperial expansion in the South Pacific has left the countries in the region with a significant array of social, political, and economic legacies. Western religious beliefs, Western political and educational institutions, and integration into the global economy have been received with varying degrees of enthusiasm. With few exceptions, Christianity has probably had the greatest success in becoming established as a central element in the lives of Pacific Islanders – if we take church attendance and other external indicators of devotion as appropriate indicators. At the other end of the spectrum, and especially in the three countries considered here, Western democratic practices have been received with a great deal less ardour – at least among some significant sectors – despite the importance that elites in all three countries attach to the word 'democracy' as a regime legitimator. So although virtually all agree in a general sense that democracy is good (and that there ought to be more of it – in other countries), very different approaches to its institutionalization and values have been espoused by political leaders. External indicators, such as the adoption of constitutions, parliaments, electoral procedures, and so forth therefore cannot be accepted as proof positive of the unqualified acceptance of democracy and its values as the basis of the political system.

The case studies show that each country has a unique body of culture or tradition (however defined); that each has had very different experiences with imperialism and European contact generally; and that each has developed different approaches and responses to politics since independence. At the same time, a number of common threads run through their varying cultural, historical, and political experiences. First, each country, including Tonga, was forced to adopt certain political institutions at the behest of one or other of the colonial powers and to discard a number of traditional practices. In Fiji, the extent to which existing structures were altered or subsumed varied according to the region. Under British colonial rule, especially in its indirect form, some regionally-based practices were identified as more authoritative (and more desirable) than others and were thus given precedence in the new order. In addition, a large non-indigenous population was introduced, which gave rise to the dynamics of a plural society as well as providing a foil for the assertion of what is 'authentic' in terms of political legitimacy. These factors have been particularly important for the way in which representative (but undemocratic) institutions have taken shape.

In Tonga, although formal colonization never took place, British imperialist influences were nonetheless decisive for the kind of political institutions that were adopted in the nineteenth century and which remain in place today. As with Fiji, many existing loci of power, especially in relation to lower-level chiefs, were subsumed in the process. The result has been the entrenchment of a monarchy and aristocracy which, while reflecting some aspects of pre-contact structures, also reflects significant European influences. In Western Samoa too, although colonization argu-ably had less impact on local modes of organization, and local chiefs from all parts of the islands retained much of their authority, it resulted nonetheless in new national political institutions being grafted onto what was an essentially village-based system of political organization, thereby altering the political dynamics irrevocably.

The contemporary national political institutions of each country, therefore, stand as monuments to the pervasive influence of Western imperialism, both in direct as well as more subtle forms. This influence, however, cannot be construed as a force aimed primarily at destroying all traditional practices. Indeed, colonial powers were often concerned, albeit in a paternalistic manner, to protect and maintain what they believed to be traditional political practices and institutions, especially those relating to chiefly power. In the process, nonetheless, a great deal of the flexibility that characterizes a dynamic tradition was lost and much of what remains today, especially where it has been codified, has become rigid. Furthermore, Fiji, Tonga and Western Samoa all now provide for the retention of their highest chiefly figures as heads of state, as well as for the recognition of chiefly status in a number of other ways (for example, with respect to control of land). It has been pointed out, however, that 'the nature of statehood alters the powers and duties associated with leadership in ways that are both significant and subtle'.[1]

Although it is generally recognized by indigenous political elites that contemporary national political institutions, as well as certain subsidiary political arrangements, are very much a product of foreign imperialist influences, these same institutions are frequently defended, if not as the embodiment of pristine traditional practices, then at least as something which comes close to giving legitimate expression to indigenous cultural values. The fact that they are not fully democratic in a Western sense is answered by an appeal incorporating similar grounds. This leads us back to some of the points raised about democracy in chapter 1.

Much of the discussion has shown that ambivalent attitudes to democracy have been particularly evident in many of the debates concerning the inherent value of indigenous institutions and practices, encapsulated broadly in the term 'tradition'. While there is no necessary or logical imperative that demands the placing of this concept in opposition to a notion of modernity or 'Westernity', these debates show the explicit construction of such an antithesis. The contrast has been sharpened, and perhaps receives its clearest articulation, where the focus turns on the issue of political rule. Of course, this does not apply just to Fiji, Tonga, and Western Samoa. It is now ubiquitous in the Pacific as well as in many other parts of the world. Nor should this be taken to imply that the non-Western world is primarily responsible for constructing the antithesis in these terms. As we have seen, much of the responsibility for this quite obviously rests with the old imperial powers as well as with earlier schools of thought emanating from the Western academy. Even latter-day academics (and not just anthropologists) have often continued to valorize the 'authentic' or 'pristine' wherever it can be found (or thought to have been found), and to contrast this with practices arising from cultural hybridization. Moreover, valorization in this way implies the superiority of the original, the authentic, or the true tradition over and above anything contaminated by external (especially Western) influences.

Ideas of this kind have been given further impetus by a new age of 'white liberal guilt' and 'political correctness' in which it has become unfashionable, in some circles, for Westerners to offer critiques of indigenous representations of their traditions. This is especially problematic where Fourth World indigenous peoples are seeking to redress some of their very real grievances concerning the treatment of their ancestors as well as the marginal socio-economic position that present generations occupy. Reluctance to engage in political critiques of indigenous traditions and cultural practices is also motivated, no doubt, by fear of being branded eurocentric at best, or racist at worst. This is part of the reason behind the hermeneutic trend to privilege the 'insider' perspective as well as the extreme relativist position discussed earlier. At the same time, it is simply not polite to point out that some non-Western political elites exhibit those same tendencies themselves. Racist and ethnocentric attitudes, however, are hardly the exclusive preserve of Caucasians. Nonetheless, criticism by Westerners of non-Western political elites is often construed as an act of Western cultural chauvinism. In the sphere of regional politics, Australian politicians have often been caught in this dilemma. The furore created in late 1993 by Australian Prime Minister Keating's implied remark that his Malaysian counterpart, Mahathir, was acting in a 'recalcitrant' manner in his approach to Asia–Pacific Economic Cooperation (APEC) exemplifies this problem.[2]

In the Pacific, the problem posed for external critique has been highlighted by an article that asks a pertinent question: Why can't Pacific Islanders face up to criticism? Among the issues raised were the implications of a remark by Cook Islands Prime Minister, Geoffrey Henry, warning Australia and New Zealand against indulging in critical assessments of political developments in the region, including Fiji's racist constitution. Henry was reported as believing that

> the preservation of their good relations with island states depended on their 'great caution' in making 'value judgements'. A 'cultural renaissance' was sweeping the Pacific with imposed western values, like constitutions, under reevaluation by a more educated generation.[3]

Taking issue with Henry's remark, the report pointed out that this amounted to a claim for special treatment, effectively placing the island nations beyond rebuke. It also drew attention to the element of political opportunism inherent in claims to 'insider' immunity from external critique, noting that in objecting to criticism, Henry 'opted for Pacific Way expediency, confident that nowadays it is rarely expedient for big countries to be seen bullying far smaller ones, even justifiably'.[4]

Just as the tradition-versus-modern (Western) dichotomy is based on some very misleading assumptions, so too is the insider-versus-outsider dichotomy. Furthermore, the promotion of a dichotomy in these terms can serve an obvious instrumental purpose for the benefit of indigenous elites. To gain a more fruitful perspective on the insider–outsider debate, and some of its political consequences, it is therefore pertinent, first, to ask what these elites are actually defending against external critique and who do they speak *for*? This becomes clearer when we note that appeals to immunity from external criticism are made in the context of elite defence of certain national political institutions. In the case studies, conservative political elites in Fiji and Tonga have defended undemocratic political institutions which clearly sustain their own positions of privilege. They have not simply defended these institutions from external critique – indeed such critique has been a relatively minor thorn in their sides, especially in the case of Tonga. By far the greater impetus for democratic reform has come from within the countries concerned. In Fiji, it has come from Fiji Indians as well as dissident Fijians. In Tonga, the groundswell of support for the PDM has been generated almost entirely by internal developments, and the critique of existing political arrangements emanates largely from among Tongans themselves.

The situation in Western Samoa is different in a number of respects – political institutions there have already been further democratized, although limitations remain in relation to eligibility for candidature. Also, the move to universal suffrage came about not so much in response to a new enthusiasm for democratic values among the general Samoan population, as from certain political advantages anticipated by the ruling HRPP. In other words, the pressure for democratization came from above rather than from below. Even so, the demand for greater opportunities for political participation within Western Samoa has undoubtedly been a key element in the creation of so many more *matai*, leading in turn to the pressures that eventually saw the introduction of universal suffrage. Moreover, speculation about the new opportunities created for women's participation, and hence strong support among Western Samoan women for the reforms, is not without foundation.

The point in drawing attention to the internal forces seeking democratic changes, especially those coming from below, is that conservative elite defence of existing political institutions (including much of the rhetoric about the superior value of traditional ways) is often directed against the values and practices of Western democratic politics, but its major target is the internal challenges. These challenges may be inspired by external factors and influences, but the major proponents for change in the three countries we have considered here have been drawn largely from the respective citizenries. With reference again to Keith-Reid's article on 'facing up to criticism', he notes that some of the remarks made by Australian Foreign Minister, Gareth Evans, about the Fiji coup have been interpreted as unreasonable and harsh criticism. He points out, however, that 'a substantial part of the Fiji population, possibly 50 percent, possibly more than 50 percent, would agree that [the] remarks were reasonable and fair'.[5] And for one Tongan academic, writing in the Atenisi tradition,

> the insider-outsider distinction which asserts that only a Tongan, for example, can understand tala-e-fonua, not an 'ignorant' outsider, is itself a political statement and not an intellectual one. Politically, this assertion may work, serving a specific subjective demand, but it does not hold any worth on the objective level … [For the outsider] the disadvantages do not render observation impossible. Observation is, in fact, made possible by the existence of both universal and unique phenomena in all human societies …[6]

Several other implications of the insider–outsider dimension should be mentioned. The first arises directly out of the problem posed for traditionalists by internal critiques of the existing order. The critics clearly cannot be branded as unwelcome interlopers in the same way as European democratic critics (although they are often just as unwanted). Nor can the protective armour of inviolable sovereignty be assumed: internal critics cannot be told that what goes on inside the borders of their own countries is none of their business. Finally, they cannot be told, as many Western critics have, that 'you simply don't understand our traditions because you are a Westerner and are not a part of them'. Conservative elite supporters of 'traditional' institutions must therefore turn to other arguments. Foremost among these is the notion that internal critics are traitors to their own cultures and traditions.

The depiction of internal critics who appeal to democratic norms in arguing for reform as treasonous is sometimes linked to the notion that these critics are themselves 'too Westernized' or 'out of touch' with the realities of their own culture or traditional ways. This device attempts to externalize even an indigenous critic, thereby rendering his or her criticism illegitimate on much the same grounds as other external critics. Put another way, an internal critic may be branded as 'inauthentic', ostensibly on the grounds that she or he has received a Western education, but in fact on the grounds that she or he is criticizing rather than defending 'tradition'. It is hard to imagine that an indigenous *defender* of tradition would be invalidated for being Western-educated, at least in these terms. The following comment by a conservative Samoan opponent of universal suffrage (who is herself Western-educated) not only illustrates the ironies of some of these points, but also contrasts Western democracy unfavourably with the organic development of the Samoan *matai* system while invoking the 'democracy as indigenous' argument:

> The accusation of undemocratic [that is] levelled at the [*matai*-only] electors roll tends to be one-sided in both physical direction and cultural philosophy and attitude, coming as it has from westerners and western-educated Samoans who seem unable and unwilling to see that the *fa'amatai* culture of the Samoan is a perfect and logical manifestation of the will and authority of the people. In that respect, the *fa'amatai* is a truly democratic system ... perhaps more democratic than the much vaunted democracy of the west that has remained an ideal. That ideal may inspire and instil hope, it is true; but, in reality, it has not been developed as the *fa'matai*, the ideal social organisation most appropriate and relevant to the Samoan people and their culture in the past, present, and future centuries.[7]

A further important aspect of the insider–outsider debate is that it concerns not only people, but concepts too. Some values, such as consensus, harmony and community-oriented ways are all construed as inherent elements of the Pacific Way. Conversely, images of disputation, discord, dissensus and individualism are depicted as typically Western, if not uniquely so. In this context Western democracy, which purportedly encapsulates the latter concepts and, by implication, none of the former, is construed as an external, alien form of political rule unsuited to South Pacific societies. The contrasting images of 'the Pacific Way' on the one hand, and the values that are said to characterize Western democracy on the other, could be unpacked – or deconstructed – at great length. But one or two points here must suffice.

First, the depictions of both 'the West' and 'the Pacific' are of course grossly generalized and over-homogenized, and miss many subtle, and not-so-subtle, elements of both 'Pacific' and 'Western' ways. This has been remarked on in chapter 1, but it is necessary to emphasize once again that the West itself, like the Pacific, is made up of extremely heterogeneous components. Furthermore, we have seen in some of the earlier discussion that the history of political thought in the West contains many elements that are directly comparable to contemporary expressions of conservatism or traditionalism in the Pacific. Among these was an abiding reverence for the past. Of these historic aspects of Western thought, one writer has noted that one of the most remarkable aspects of Western ideology was in fact its 'leech-like addiction to the past'.[8] Neither conservatism nor traditionalism, then, can be attributed as uniquely characteristic of South Pacific island societies (or of any other non-Western societies). Similarly, the propensity for innovation and change is hardly restricted to the West. To deny these points is to endorse the 'fatal impact' thesis and its connotation that pre-contact societies were inherently static and lacking internal dynamics.

A second point is that the 'consensus' which is said (most often and most loudly by conservative elites), to characterize the Pacific Way is quite misleading. For example, the institution that is often invoked to exemplify the consensus style in Western Samoa is the *fono*. A closer inspection of practices in the *fono*, however, would reveal that the 'consensus' is, on many occasions, *not* reached in an atmosphere of free and frank discussion where the contribution of each participant enjoys equal weight. As for the Tongan *fono*, scarcely anyone would deny that it was, traditionally, an occasion when chiefs simply issued orders and those below were obliged to receive them without question or dissent. Furthermore, the whole ideal of consensus is a key feature of authoritarian rule. This is not to say that consensus does not feature in the practices and principles of Western democracy, nor that it has no place in such a system. While dissent is considered inevitable and indeed so crucial to the continuing vitality of a democratic political system that it receives institutional protection, consensus is nonetheless required about the very institutions which provide this protection (although these also remain subject to change through democratic procedures). The institutional protection of the right to dissent, as well as a host of other rights, is one of the central elements of constitutionalism. In other words, there is a high degree of consensus about the right to dissent in various ways and about the institutions that protect such rights.

To return to the notion of 'democracy as alien', Larmour, among others, identifies this as a major theme in the 'foreign flower' debate, that is, democracy is seen as 'something introduced from outside rather than grown from below'.[9] Robertson has noted some of the implications of this construction in drawing attention to the contradictions between the existence of popular movements for democratization on the one hand, and the 'prevalent and disturbing view that democracy and accompanying notions of freedom and human rights are foreign to non-Western societies, unrelated to their cultures and their histories'. He identifies one of the most salient points about this contradiction, and that is that it 'appears to ignore completely struggles for independence in so many former colonies, struggles that were often against suppression and the anti-democratic and non-representative institutions of colonialism'.[10] Said, too, has drawn attention to 'the grand narratives of emancipation and enlightenment [that] mobilized people in the colonial world to rise up and throw off imperial subjection'.[11] The general point is that, as a response to colonialism, many non-Western countries themselves developed a tradition of democratic resistance and this is as much a part of their history as any other component.

While there is a certain validity in invoking memories of resistance to colonial oppression to counter the anti-democratic tendencies of contemporary elites, it does not do to romanticize these movements, nor to place them all in the same conceptual basket as movements driven by a desire for democracy. Self-determination can indeed be a democratic concept, but it is not necessarily so. On the contrary, it may function as a useful banner under which all kinds of unpleasant ideologies and patently anti-democratic activities can be justified. The push for 'ethnic cleansing' in former Yugoslavia stands out as a prime example, while in Fiji, 'self-determination' for Fijians has been used to counter Fiji Indian claims to equal political status. A leading exponent of traditionalism in Fiji says that the coup 'was a turning point when self-determination was reintroduced by revolutionary means'.[12] By this he clearly does not mean self-determination for Fiji Indians. He describes the relationship between indigenous Fijians and Fiji Indians as a 'host and guest relationship' which is cast in terms of traditional Fijian understandings of a person as 'either a *taukei* (indigenous or owner) or *vulagi* (visitor or foreigner)'. He then asserts that this host and guest relationship has been 'challenged and upset by the introduction of the human rights concept in which all are considered equal'.[13] Ironically, this commentator has also adopted a position within the 'democracy as indigenous' camp, as we shall see shortly.

With respect to the identification of self-determination with 'democratic' demands for independence from a colonial ruler, it must be stressed that this does not automatically render the movements democratic. Larmour has pointed out that although democracy is often contrasted with colonial rule, the latter was itself resisted by some quite undemocratic movements. By way of example, he notes that one of the central strands of Western Samoa's Mau movement 'was the restoration of chiefly, rather than popular, authority against colonial paternalism'.[14] In addition, attempts to invoke memories of resistance to colonial rule among members of the eastern Fijian chiefly establishment is to invoke virtually nothing, except perhaps the memory that these Fijians (or at least their immediate forebears) actually resisted 'liberation' from colonialism. The major proponents of independence were Fiji Indians and, in the end, the British themselves. Today, however, the notion of sovereignty for South Pacific states is held up not only as an icon of freedom from colonialism, but as a symbol denoting immunity from certain kinds of external interference.

It has been noted at several points that the idea of sovereignty is often deployed in defence of external criticism. This has been an important theme not only in defensive postures against the incursions of external critique, but also with respect to understandings of democracy *as* sovereignty. This has been put clearly by one of Tonga's leading conservative figures, the Hon. Fusitu'a. In response to a question about whether he considered the present political system in Tonga to be democratic, he replied, first, in the relativist fashion, that Tonga was the best of democracies – for Tongans. He then added that a country that decides *for itself* how to run its affairs *is* a democracy.[15] The definition of democracy in these terms is therefore linked directly to a notion of sovereignty. This also provides additional grounding for the relativist stance, thus accommodating mutual reinforcement of democracy as sovereignty with democracy as relative. In addition, this can be used to feed into the notion of democracy as indigenous – a position that has two distinct aspects worth considering.

In the first instance, the notion of democracy as a pre-existing feature of indigenous society has often been put forward in defence of existing institutional arrangements. This claim has been made most explicitly in Western Samoa, but it has also featured in some of the justifications surrounding the Fiji coup and the promulgation of the 1990 constitution. Goldsmith sets out the general form in which the 'democracy as indigenous' view is usually promoted: 'Democracy is an "indigenous" notion and already exists in its own way in most Pacific societies, but the

Western, or introduced, forms of democracy are irrelevant or incompatible with it'.[16] This position can be contrasted with the idea of democracy as alien, a theme which has been much more pervasive in arguments for retaining the status quo in all three of the countries discussed here. Again, Goldsmith summarizes the general form that this second notion usually takes: 'Democracy is an alien notion, subversive of traditional institutions, a danger to the organic harmony of hierarchical systems of authority'.[17] In this second formulation, democracy is of course understood as 'Western', while in the first form it is not. Furthermore, the first form arguably requires the relativization of the concept of democracy in a way that renders it incompatible with some of its important principles and values.

The problem of relativism has been discussed at some length in chapter 1, and there is no need to repeat it here. Nonetheless, it is important to emphasize that exercises in relativistic interpretations of democracy very often serve an instrumental purpose. In the case of Fiji, for example, the conservative political elite has revised the concept of democracy in order to meet certain conditions dictated by their own interests. This revision necessarily entails the lapse to relativism made explicit in the claims, put forward by Rabuka and Ravuvu, that what is democratic in a European society is not necessarily democratic in Fiji. Similarly, the Hon. Fusituʻa's defence of 'Tongan democracy' is clearly entwined with the defence of a system of privilege of which he is a major beneficiary. As indicated above, however, these arguments are also related closely to the 'democracy as alien' mode of argument. Goldsmith describes the two forms as variants that, at least potentially, represent two sides of the same coin, an analogy that suggests 'that they can flip from one side to the other both in rhetoric and in realpolitik'.[18] It was noted earlier that one exponent of the 'democracy as alien' position has also, at times, adopted the 'democracy as indigenous' perspective. Ravuvu has therefore 'flipped the coin' to the indigenous version of democracy when arguing for recognition of some Pacific ways as compatible with democratic values:

> ... democracy is long established in some Pacific communities. In our experience in the Pacific democracy based on consultation and consensus has long been established among most Pacific island communities. To us it is very important to see that the human being comes before any other thing. Before a decision is taken you have to talk it over with almost every member of your community before you come to an agreement. That was done publicly, so we can look at one another and see who really are the dissenters, so we can be very careful about them. Today we have to go to the poll to do that secretly.[19]

Questions about aspects of Ravuvu's claims also deserve raising in relation to the idea of consensus. For example, what is to be implied by his apparent approval of a system whereby dissenters are readily identifiable – as opposed to a system in which people can, at least in one important respect, express dissent without fear of recrimination? It is doubtful, too, that the widespread consultation alluded to by Ravuvu actually took place in situations where chiefly hierarchies and social stratification were firmly entrenched. Certainly this cannot be said to characterize Tonga where communication between chiefly leaders and commoners was (and remains) strongly circumscribed by a range of prohibitions and inhibitions on the part of both chiefs and commoners. It has been remarked, for example, that in Tonga, as well as in other Polynesian societies, 'isolation from speaking' between chiefs and commoners (or at least non-chiefs) is an ingrained feature of the sociopolitical system.[20]

A further point that needs to be emphasized concerns the whole issue of 'alien' or introduced concepts and practices in the South Pacific, and some of the hypocrisy that attends discussions of this issue. We have seen that some legacies of imperialism in the region have been accepted wholeheartedly. This has broader implications for the way in which elements of both 'tradition' and 'Western ways' are selectively praised or condemned, honoured or repudiated, depending on the particular issue at stake, for it is one of the keys to understanding a system of thought to ask about the selectivity of its interpretation of tradition.[21] With respect to Fiji, Tonga and Western Samoa, this is best illustrated by reference to religious practices and to political institutions. Amongst the indigenous people of all three places, the beliefs and practices of the wholly Western religion of Christianity have become very widespread. Indeed, a much higher percentage of indigenous people in these countries, and Pacific Islanders generally, can probably be described as 'practising Christians' than is the case in most Western nations at least in terms of participation. The practice of Christianity in the three countries, as well as in the Pacific generally, is also one example of a tradition that is clearly post-contact but that is nonetheless widely endorsed as having significant intrinsic merit.

On the other hand, many of the Western values that support the practice of democratic politics have been rejected by some traditionalist elements in these polities on the explicit grounds that they are alien and therefore contrary to 'our way of life'. It is further suggested that democracy as a form of government lacks legitimacy vis-à-vis those traditional forms of political authority which are manifest in the chiefly systems. This argument can be countered in a number of ways. First, and most simply, it can be countered by pointing to the hypocrisy or inconsistency implicit in its major premise, for the great majority of Fijians have been more than happy to adopt such Western institutions as Christianity. The fact that democratic institutions are both 'alien' and 'Western', then, is not in itself a sufficient argument against democracy, for its rejection is based on a premise that is regarded as acceptable in terms of other introduced practices.[22]

A second counter to the argument is the demonstration that the political framework which is represented by the chiefly elite as 'traditional', and therefore legitimate, is in fact a neo-traditional/colonial transformation incorporating, incidentally, such Western concepts as 'nation', 'sovereignty', and the like.[23] As pointed out earlier, this demonstration is in itself unremarkable. Furthermore, tradition as a dynamic concept cannot be other than variable if it is to satisfy the changing requirements of any group. This is implicit in the notion of a 'living tradition'.[24] But there is very little that is dynamic about an 'invented tradition'. Indeed, as Jolly notes, invented traditions 'are characteristically invariant, employing fixed ritual routines or stereotypic symbols'.[25] Most importantly, the usual purpose of an invented tradition is, as Hanson suggests, 'to legitimate or sanctify some current reality or aspiration'.[26] The case studies have shown that the chiefly elites, especially in Fiji and Tonga, have not hesitated to use invented tradition both to sanctify their own dominance and to exclude others from a meaningful share of political power.

In short, the rhetoric suggests that democracy as a form of government is both inappropriate and illegitimate in the South Pacific because it is Western and because it is not a part of 'our tradition'. Claims like this also prompt other questions. We should ask, for example, which Fijian 'tradition' supports the political order now in place in Fiji and what gives this order its legitimacy? The short answer is to be found in the story of the eastern chiefly establishment's rise to prominence under colonial rule – a process that also involved the incorporation of many elements of Western conservative practices. In more general terms, Durutalo has pointed out that Pacific island cultures have long been in the business of integrating Western values (such as Christianity), and that 'the difficulty of these cultures to eclectically accept innovations from the outside should not be exaggerated'.[27] From the Fijian context, we should also consider again the statement issued in June 1987 by Ganilau's Council of Advisers:

> ... democracy and its ideas of liberty and equality are not appropriate to the situation in Fiji ... they are contrary to the Fijian way of life where liberty exists only within one's own social rank and equality is constrained by a fully developed social hierarchy.[28]

The sentiments underpinning this statement, to which the Tonga elite also subscribe, are virtually identical to some central aspects of early

English conservative thought, and this brings us back to another important point. Those liberal-democratic institutions which developed in Britain (and which indigenous elites now reject), arose in almost precisely the same type of 'fully developed social hierarchy' where, for example, status was largely ascriptive and political power was contingent upon a high status within that social hierarchy. Liberal-democratic political ideas nonetheless succeeded in displacing the 'descending thesis of government' implied by the hierarchy (although over a longer period of time).[29] It cannot therefore be argued that the existence of a social hierarchy as described by indigenous elites is really valid as a condition for rejecting as inappropriate (or impossible) the introduction of democratic institutions.

Another question concerns interpretation. First, it is obvious that 'tradition' does not speak for itself. It must be both activated and articulated by a (putatively) authoritative and legitimate voice. At the same time, any other voice raised in opposition is denied legitimacy and authority. Further, the selection and interpretation of certain aspects of tradition, rather than the wholesale promotion of all that is reputedly traditional, implies a purposive motive which we are entitled to call instrumental. Finally, it is worth noting that although a 'tradition', a 'custom', or a 'folk-way' may very well reflect the popular character of a practice, it does not exclude the 'indubitable truth' that 'a folk-way may be the way of the folk in power'.[30]

In considering Fiji, Tonga and Western Samoa, we can also see that the concept of tradition has reached the level of awareness at which it can be treated critically or reflexively. But this is the same general level of consciousness at which it can be appealed to in those normative terms which promote the importance of tradition. In the national politics of all three countries, this kind of appeal has a strong political motivation and has been clearly instrumental in terms of legitimating chiefly authority. It is an ideological or doctrinal rendering of tradition that operates to demand conformity with its precepts and prescriptions and which is aimed at conserving a particular political order. In addition, its ideological purity depends, at least implicitly, on the construction of the same dichotomy between 'traditional' and 'Western' that has been so roundly condemned in anti-colonial literature but which has now been inverted in a form which pervades the rhetoric of those who denounced it in the first place. This unquestionably produces the same false essentialism which has seduced past generations of scholars into believing that there are determinate characteristics of Western and non-Western 'minds'.[31]

The Orientalist critique that did so much to expose the bases of these misconceptions is therefore in danger of being appropriated for the purpose of promoting an inverted dichotomy of the same misguided proportions, but this time in the service of autocratic indigenous elites. In this process, the elevation of tradition is not concerned merely with asserting the worth of indigenous material culture or aesthetics. Rather, it moves inexorably to encompass a powerful notion of political identity – a notion that inevitably carries with it a certain normative orientation with respect to a 'correct' locus of political authority. In turn, this can generate the construction of yet another master narrative about the proper point of convergence for one's political/cultural loyalty. Culture in this sense functions as a source of identity which, in Said's words can be 'a rather combative one' in that it is often asserted aggressively, in a xenophobic process differentiating 'us' from 'them'. Said, in the process of distinguishing this sense of culture from the material and aesthetic aspects, continues:

> In this ... sense culture is a sort of theatre where various political and ideological causes engage one another. Far from being the placid realm of Apollonian gentility, culture can even be a battleground on which causes expose themselves to the light of day and contend with one another, making it apparent that, for instance, American, French, or Indian students who are taught to read *their* national classics before they read others are expected to appreciate and belong loyally, often uncritically, to their nations and their traditions while denigrating or fighting against others.[32]

It is also useful to consider traditionalism in terms of a self-contained discourse that functions to unify a particular field of thought in such a way as to exclude alternative modes of thinking – or at least to delegitimate them. The particular function of traditionalist discourse in the contexts dealt with in this study is to present a simple unitary view of an 'authentic', pre-contact past (it must be pre-contact to ensure its pristine quality, and it must be depicted as authentic to ensure its validity). This view is then used to identify the 'legitimate' locus of political power (namely, in a chiefly system) which in turn ascribes legitimate political power and authority to a particular class of people (namely, chiefs). This logically entails the exclusion of alternative sources of authority and legitimacy and makes especially problematic the task of mounting an effective political opposition, which in turn undermines efforts to develop more effective democratic political practices and institutions.

Traditionalism is a method of idealizing the past, and of judging and moulding the present by the assumed standards of a past era. The selective nature of representations of the past, and the apparent ease with which these selections can be made by those who command the requisite symbolic resources, make it especially flexible in fashioning contemporary political agendas.[33] Although often camouflaged by a variety of romanticized images, traditionalism can operate at the crudest level of instrumental propaganda in seeking to legitimate some current state of affairs. And in those cases where political power is seen as the god-given right of an exclusive group who occupy the apex of the 'natural order', then the invention of a tradition which supports this order can readily be justified in its own terms. Orwell's observation on the nature of propaganda and historical revisionism is therefore a fitting conclusion to this discussion.

> The primary aim of propaganda is, of course, to influence contemporary opinion, but those who rewrite history do probably believe with part of their minds that they are actually thrusting facts into the past ... More probably they feel that their own version was what happened in the sight of God, and that one is justified in re-arranging the records accordingly.[34]

Notes

Introduction

1 Asesela Ravuvu, 'Culture and Traditions: Implications for Modern Nation Building' in Ron Crocombe, Uentaba Neemia, Asesela Ravuvu, and Werner Vom Busch (eds), *Culture and Democracy in the South Pacific* (Suva, Institute of Pacific Studies, University of the South Pacific, 1992), p. 57.
2 Rowan Callick, 'Forward to the Past?', *Australian Left Review*, no. 131, August 1991, p. 22.
3 Ron Crocombe, *The Pacific Way: An Emerging Identity* (Suva, Lotu Pasifika, 1976), p. 1.
4 Ibid., p. 13.
5 Bernard Narokobi, *The Melanesian Way* (rev. edn, Boroko and Suva, Institute of Papua New Guinea Studies and Institute of Pacific Studies, 1983), p. 9.
6 Isikeli Mataitoga, 'Westminster Style Democracy and Cultural Diversity: A Critique of the Fijian Experience' in Crocombe et al. (eds), *Culture and Democracy*, p. 93.
7 Paul Nursey-Bray, 'Consensus and Community: African One-Party Democracy' in Graeme Duncan (ed.), *Democratic Theory and Practice* (Cambridge, Cambridge University Press, 1983), p. 97.
8 James Clifford, *The Predicament of Culture: Twentieth-Century Ethnography, Literature, and Art* (Cambridge, Mass., Harvard University Press, 1988), pp. 177–178.
9 Senghor quoted in Manning Marable, *African and Caribbean Politics: From Kwame Nkrumah to the Grenada Revolution* (London, Verso, 1987), p. 45.
10 Ibid., pp. 45–46.
11 Edward Said, *Culture and Imperialism* (London, Vintage, 1993), p. 276.
12 James Carrier, 'Occidentalism: The World Turned Upside Down', *American Anthropologist*, vol. 19, no. 2, May 1992, p. 197.
13 Roger M. Keesing, 'Creating the Past: Custom and Identity in the Contemporary Pacific', *The Contemporary Pacific*, vol. 1, nos 1 and 2, Spring and Fall, 1989, pp. 22–23.
14 It should be noted in passing that it is all too easy to confuse substantive differences for those which are simply idiomatic. This point was made many years ago by Robin Horton in 'African Traditional Thought and Western Science', *Africa*, vol. 37, no. 1, January 1967, p. 50.

176

15 Keesing, 'Creating the Past', p. 28.
16 See Stephanie Lawson, 'Conceptual Issues in the Comparative Study of Regime Change and Democratization', *Comparative Politics*, vol. 25, no. 2, January 1993, pp. 183–205.
17 Michael C. Howard, *Fiji: Race and Politics in an Island State* (Vancouver, UBC Press, 1991), p. 7.
18 Uentabo Neemia, 'Decolonization and Democracy in the South Pacific' in Crocombe et al. (eds), *Culture and Democracy*, p. 3.
19 Alan Ward, 'The Crisis of our Times: Ethnic Resurgence and the Liberal Ideal', *Journal of Pacific History*, vol. 27, no. 1, June 1992, p. 90.
20 Epeli Hau'ofa, 'The New South Pacific Society: Integration and Independence' in Antony Hooper, Steve Britton, Ron Crocombe, Judith Huntsman, and Cluny Macpherson (eds), *Class and Culture in the South Pacific* (Auckland and Suva, Centre for Pacific Studies of the University of Auckland and Institute of Pacific Studies of the University of the South Pacific, 1987), p. 7.
21 Ibid., p. 12.
22 See Roger M. Keesing, 'Class, Culture, Custom', (paper presented to workshop on the Global Anthropology of Oceania, University of Lund, Sweden, October 1991), p. 9.
23 Robert T. Robertson with Akosita Tamanisau, 'Pacific Overview: Not So New World Order' in David Robie (ed.), *Tu Galala: Social Change in the Pacific* (Wellington and Annandale, Bridget Williams Books and Pluto Press, 1992), p. 30.
24 Ashley Montagu, *Man's Most Dangerous Myth: The Fallacy of Race* (4th edn, Cleveland, World Publishing Company, 1964), p. 244.
25 Ward, 'The Crisis of our Times', p. 88.
26 I. F. Helu, 'Cultural Survival', (Opening Address at the University of the South Pacific Cultural Program Week, Suva, 27 April 1991), p. 4.
27 F. O. Kolo, 'Historiography: The Myth of Indigenous Authenticity' in Phyllis Herda, Jennifer Terrell and Neil Gunson (eds), *Tongan Culture and History* (Department of Pacific and Southeast Asian History, Australian National University, 1990), pp. 2–3.
28 Ibid., p. 7.
29 Donald P. Spence, 'Saying Goodbye to Historical Truth', *Philosophy of the Social Sciences*, vol. 21, no. 2, June 1992, p. 246.

1   Tradition and Democracy

1 See Raymond Williams, *Keywords: A Vocabulary of Culture and Society* (London, Fontana, 1976), p. 268.
2 Edward Shils, *Tradition* (London, Faber & Faber, 1981), p. 12.
3 Martin Krygier, 'Law as Tradition', *Law and Philosophy*, vol. 5, 1986, pp. 240, 244–245. These points have been explicated by me in slightly different contexts in 'The Tyranny of Tradition: Chiefs and Politics in Contemporary Fiji' (paper presented at a symposium on 'Chiefs Today', Association for Social Anthropology in Oceania, Kona, Hawaii, 24–28 March 1993); and Stephanie Lawson, 'The Authentic State: History and Tradition in the Ideology of Ethnonationalism' (paper presented at the conference 'The State in Transition', La Trobe University, Melbourne, 6–8 August 1993).
4 Stephen Horigan, *Nature and Culture in Western Discourses* (London, Routledge, 1988), p. 15.

5 This point is especially relevant to the idea of 'ethno-occidentalism' which
   concerns 'essentialist renderings of the West by members of alien societies';
   see James Carrier, 'Occidentalism: The World Turned Upside-Down',
   American Ethnologist, vol. 19, no. 2, 1992, pp. 195–212.
6 See Graham Maddox, 'Constitution' in Terence Ball, James Farr and Russell
   L. Hanson (eds), *Political Innovation and Conceptual Change* (Cambridge,
   Cambridge University Press, 1989), p. 53.
7 T. A. Sinclair, *A History of Greek Political Thought* (London, Routledge and
   Kegan Paul, 1951), p. 40.
8 See, for example, Alan Ward, 'The Crisis of our Times: Ethnic Resurgence
   and the Liberal Ideal', *Journal of Pacific History*, vol. 27, no. 1, June 1992,
   p. 90. See also Roger M. Keesing, 'Creating the Past: Custom and Identity in
   the Contemporary Pacific', *The Contemporary Pacific*, vol. I, nos. 1 and 2,
   Spring and Fall, 1989; Alain Babadzan, '*Kastom* and Nation Building in the
   Pacific' in Remo Guidieri, Francesco Pellizi, and Stanley J. Tambiah (eds),
   *Ethnicities and Nations: Processes of Interethnic Relations in Latin America,
   Southeast Asia, and the Pacific* (Austin, University of Texas Press, 1988), pp.
   199–228; and Stephanie Lawson, 'The Myth of Cultural Homogeneity and
   its Implications for Chiefly Power and Politics in Fiji', *Comparative Studies in
   Society and History*, vol. 32, no. 4, October 1990.
9 See especially Eric Hobsbawm and Terence Ranger (eds), *The Invention of
   Tradition* (Cambridge, Cambridge University Press, 1983).
10 For example, Cotton has noted attempts in Singapore 'to reinvent
   Confucianism for a population never especially familiar with it'. See James
   Cotton, 'The Limits to Liberalization in Industrializing Asia: Three Views of
   the State', *Pacific Affairs*, vol. 64, no. 3, Fall 1991, p. 320. For a more extensive
   analysis see Stephanie Lawson, 'Institutionalizing Peaceful Conflict: The
   Challenge of Democratization in Asia', *Australian Journal of International
   Affairs*, vol. 47, no. 1, 1993, pp. 15–30.
11 J. H. Plumb, *The Death of the Past* (London, Macmillan, 1969), pp. 30–31.
12 Billie Melman, 'Claiming the Nation's Past: The Invention of an Anglo-
   Saxon Tradition', *Journal of Contemporary History*, vol. 26, nos 3 and 4,
   September 1991, p. 575.
13 See Max Weber, 'The Social Psychology of the World Religions' in H. H.
   Gerth and C. Wright Mills (eds), *From Max Weber: Essays in Sociology* (London,
   Routledge and Kegan Paul, 1948), esp. pp. 56–57, 296.
14 Michael Walzer, *The Revolution of the Saints: A Study in the Origins of Radical
   Politics* (New York, Atheneum, 1974), p. 8.
15 For a general discussion of feudalism see Walter Ullmann, *Medieval Political
   Thought* (Harmondsworth, Peregrine, 1975).
16 J. G. A. Pocock, *The Machiavellian Moment: Florentine Political Thought and the
   Atlantic Republican Tradition* (Princeton, Princeton University Press, 1975),
   p. 338.
17 Ibid., p. 50.
18 J. J. Smolicz, 'Tradition, Core Values and Intercultural Development in
   Plural Societies', *Ethnic and Racial Studies*, vol. 11, no. 4, November 1988,
   p. 387.
19 H. T. Wilson, *Tradition and Innovation: The Idea of Civilization as Culture and its
   Significance* (London, Routledge and Kegan Paul, 1984), p. 100.
20 Ibid., p. 100.
21 Edward Said, *Orientalism* (New York, Vintage Books, 1978). But as Clifford
   points out, an oppositional critique of 'Orientalism' can scarcely avoid

falling into 'Occidentalism': see Clifford, *The Predicament of Culture*, p. 258. Carrier ('Occidentalism: The World Turned Upside Down', *American Anthropologist*, vol. 19, no. 2, May 1992 p. 8) describes 'Occidentalism' in terms of an 'essentialist rendering of the West by Westerners', but there is no reason to suppose that an equally essentialist view of the West cannot also be constructed by non-Westerners.

22 See James Carrier, 'Introduction' in James Carrier (ed.), *History and Tradition in Melanesian Anthropology* (Berkeley, University of California Press, 1992), p. 1.

23 Ibid., p. 3.

24 Ibid., p. 5.

25 Ibid., p. 7.

26 Babadzan, '*Kastom* and Nation Building', p. 207.

27 Carl J. Friedrich, *Tradition and Authority* (New York, Praeger, 1972), p. 13.

28 Karl R. Popper, *Conjectures and Refutations; The Growth of Scientific Knowledge* (4th edn, London, Routledge and Kegan Paul, 1972), p. 131.

29 I. C. Jarvie, 'Explaining Cargo Cults' in Bryan R. Wilson (ed.), *Rationality* (Oxford, Basil Blackwell, 1970).

30 Graham McDonald and Philip Pettit, *Semantics and Social Science* (London, Routledge and Kegan Paul, 1981), p. 38. I might add that a local news program in the New England area in 1991 showed the congregation of a country church praying for rain on behalf of the farmers of the district. We can hardly claim, therefore, that the character of the Hopi activities described above differs significantly from that of some elements of the so-called 'modern (Western) society' that inhabits the northern slopes and plains of New South Wales, Australia. The difference is largely one of idiom.

31 Contemporary literature on Third World development – or underdevelopment – is replete with critiques of modernization theory; but for a conservative account which deals most explicitly with the notion of tradition and the 'rationalism' of modernization theory see Shils, *Tradition*.

32 Shils, *Tradition*, p. 5.

33 Michael Oakeshott, *Rationalism in Politics* (London, Methuen, 1962), p. 1. Cf. Friedrich A. Hayek, *Law, Legislation and Liberty: A New Statement of the Liberal Principles of Justice and Political Economy*, vol. 1: *Rules and Order* (Chicago, University of Chicago Press, 1973), especially pp. 8–34.

34 Oakeshott, *Rationalism in Politics*, p. 4.

35 See Georges Balandier, *Political Anthropology* (transl. A.M. Sheridan Smith: New York, Pantheon, 1970), p. 172.

36 Michael Freeman, *Edmund Burke and the Critique of Political Radicalism* (Oxford, Basil Blackwell, 1980), p. 29.

37 Popper, *Conjectures and Refutations*, pp. 130–131.

38 Ibid., p. 122.

39 Ibid., p. 122.

40 William Connolly, 'Appearance and Reality in Politics' in Michael T. Gibbons, *Interpreting Politics* (Oxford, Basil Blackwell, 1987), p. 155.

41 Bronwen Douglas, 'Ritual and Politics in the Inaugural Meeting of High Chiefs from New Caledonia and the Loyalty Islands', *Social Analysis*, no. 18, December 1985, p. 60.

42 Robert Eccleshall, *Order and Reason in Politics: Theories of Absolute and Limited Monarchy in Early Modern England* (Oxford, Oxford University Press, 1978), pp. 77–78.

43 Lévi-Strauss quoted in Antony Hooper, 'Introduction' in Antony Hooper and Judith Huntsman (eds), *Transformations of Polynesian Culture* (Auckland, The Polynesian Society, 1985), p. 7.

44 Ibid., p. 78.

45 Pocock, *The Machiavellian Moment*, p. 334.

46 Walter Ullmann, *Medieval Political Thought* (Harmondsworth, Peregrine, 1975), p. 226.

47 Ibid., pp. 225–226.

48 George H. Sabine, *A History of Political Thought* (London, George G. Harrap, 1948), pp. 334–335.

49 Asesela D. Ravuvu, *The Fijian Ethos* (Suva, Institute of Pacific Studies, University of the South Pacific, 1987), p. 321.

50 Tomasi Vakatora quoted in Shelley Ann Sayes, 'Changing Paths of the Land: Early Political Hierarchies in Cakaudrove, Fiji', *Journal of Pacific History*, vol. 19, no. 1, 1984, p. 3.

51 See Feleti E. Ngan-Woo, *Fa'a Samoa: The World of the Samoans* (Wellington, Office of the Race Relations Conciliator, 1985), p. 35.

52 Emiliana Afeaki, 'Tonga: The Last Pacific Kingdom' in Ron Crocombe and Ahmed Ali (eds) *Politics in Polynesia* (Suva, Institute of Pacific Studies, University of the South Pacific, 1983), p. 57.

53 Robert Nisbet, *Conservatism* (Milton Keynes, Open University Press, 1986), p. 27. In these theoretical schemes, incidentally, there is no necessary opposition between nature and culture as there is in so many other Western metaphysical constructs; see Horigan, *Nature and Culture in Western Discourses*, p. 2.

54 Bernard Narakobi, *The Melanesian Way* (rev. edn, Boroko, University of Papua New Guinea, 1983), pp. 9, 13.

55 Ati George Sokomanu, 'Government in Vanuatu: The Place of Culture and Tradition' in Ron Crocombe, et al. (eds), *Culture and Democracy in the South Pacific* (Suva, Institute of Pacific Studies, University of the South Pacific, 1992), p. 55. Emphasis in original.

56 Asesela Ravuvu, *The Facade of Democracy: Fijian Struggles for Political Control 1830–1987* (Suva, Reader Publishing House, 1991), p. 92.

57 Malama Meleisea, *Change and Adaptations in Western Samoa* (Christchurch, Macmillan Brown Centre for Pacific Studies, 1988), p. 5.

58 George E. Marcus, 'Contemporary Tonga: The Background of Social and Cultural Change' in Noel Rutherford (ed.), *A History of Tonga* (Melbourne, Oxford University Press, 1977), pp. 210–211.

59 Friedrich, *Tradition and Authority*, p. 114.

60 S. N. Eisenstadt, 'Post-Traditional Societies and the Continuity and Reconstruction of Tradition', *Daedalus*, vol. 102, no. 1, Winter 1973, p. 22.

61 Elizabeth Colson, *Tradition and Contract: The Problem of Order* (London, Heinemann, 1975), p. 75.

62 Ibid., pp. 83–84. Cf. Martha Kaplan, 'Luve Ni Wai as the British Saw It: Constructions of Custom and Disorder in Colonial Fiji', *Ethnohistory*, vol. 36, no. 4, Fall, 1989, pp. 349–371. Kaplan notes that for Fiji's first Governor, Sir Arthur Gordon, the chiefly system had a moral resonance as an ordering system.

63 Published as *Mankind*, vol. 13, no. 4, August 1982 (guest editors Roger M. Keesing and Robert Tonkinson).

64 Hobsbawm and Ranger (eds), *The Invention of Tradition*.

65 Ibid., p. 250.

66 Ibid., p. 254. For a critical discussion on the attempted transformation of custom to legal creed in a Melanesian context, see Jonathan Aleck, 'Traditional Law and Legal Traditions in Papua New Guinea: A Reappraisal of the Relationship Between Law and Custom' (paper presented to the 49th Annual Conference of the Australasian Law Teachers' Association, Canberra, September 1990).

67 For example, Keesing, 'Creating the Past'; Lawson, 'The Myth of Cultural Homogeneity'; and Stephanie Lawson. *The Failure of Democratic Politics in Fiji* (Oxford, Clarendon Press, 1991).

68 Margaret Jolly, 'Specters of Inauthenticity', *The Contemporary Pacific*, vol. 1, no. 1 Spring 1992, p. 49.

69 Ibid., p. 49.

70 Keesing, 'Creating the Past', p. 37. A similar point is made by Goldsmith in his excursion into the problematic nature of dealing with such prior notions as 'invention'. See Michael Goldsmith, 'The Tradition of Invention' in Michael Goldsmith and Keith Barber (eds), *Sites: Social Anthropology and the Politics of Interpretation* (Palmerston North, Department of Social Anthropology, Massey University, 1992), esp. p. 33.

71 Ibid., p. 37.

72 Robbins Burling, *The Passage of Power: Studies in Political Succession* (New York, Academic Press, 1974), p. 9.

73 Ernest Gellner, 'Concepts and Society' in Bryan R. Wilson (ed.), *Rationality* (Oxford, Basil Blackwell, 1970), p. 42. Judgements about what is 'best' and 'worst' are obviously problematic and are ultimately coloured by the vantage point of the observer, whether an 'insider' or an 'outsider'. But, again, a surrender to relativism means that nothing can be said at all. For a critical discussion on the postmodernist promotion of culture-centric analysis and its relativistic implications see Jonathan Friedman, 'Beyond Otherness or: The Spectacularization of Anthropology', *Telos*, No. 71, Spring 1987, pp. 161–170. Issues of this kind have a number of implications for ethical relativism and so the importance of maintaining a sharp edge to our critical faculties, lest we become 'anthro-apologists', must be emphasized.

74 Jolly, 'Specters of Inauthenticity', pp. 63–64. Cf. 'Introduction' in Elizabeth Tonkin, Maryon McDonald and Malcolm Chapman (eds), *History and Ethnicity* (London, Routledge, 1989), pp. 9–11, where it is suggested that oppositions between fact and fiction, history and myth, reality and symbol, etc., have just about reached the end of their useful analytic life.

75 Nicholas Thomas, *Entangled Objects: Exchange, Material Culture, and Colonialism in the Pacific* (Cambridge, Mass., Harvard University Press, 1991), p. 202.

76 Carrier, 'Introduction', p. 12.

77 The impact of tourism on perceptions of cultural tradition is an important area of concern, although it cannot be considered here in the detail it deserves. As a matter of interest, however, it is worth noting some comments made in an anthropological essay which describes, among other things, the way in which a hotel development project in Papua New Guinea is likely to impact on the local Chambri people. Apart from working as maids and caretakers, the Chambri 'will also be paid to present themselves as professional primitives'. One of the ironies is that 'these images [of the primitive] ... may well, in one transformation or another, reflect what Margaret Mead (and even we) once wrote about them'. See Deborah Gewertz and Frederick Errington, 'We Think Therefore They Are? On

Occidentalizing the World', *Anthropological Quarterly*, vol. 64, no. 2, April 1991, p. 89.

78 Quoted in David Weisbrot, 'Custom, Pluralism, and Realism in Vanuatu: Legal Development and the Role of Customary Law', *Pacific Studies*, vol. 13, no. 1, November 1989, pp. 86–87.

79 Margaret Jolly, 'Custom and the Way of the Land: Past and Present in Vanuatu and Fiji', *Oceania*, vol. 62, no. 4, June 1992, p. 330.

80 See, for example Bronwen Douglas, 'Rank, Power, Authority: A Reassessment of Traditional Leadership in South Pacific Societies', *Journal of Pacific History*, vol. xiv, part I, 1979, p. 2n, where it is specified that 'traditional' refers to 'pre-European contact'.

81 Carrier, 'Introduction', p. 14.

82 Edmund Leach, 'Concluding Remarks' in Hooper and Huntsman (eds), *Transformations of Polynesian Culture*, p. 219.

83 See Alan Moorehead, *The Fatal Impact: The Invasion of the Pacific 1767–1840* (rev. edn, Sydney, Mead and Beckett, 1987). As Linnekin notes, this thesis implies also that change and innovation in Pacific societies originated only after European contact. See Jocelyn Linnekin, 'On the Theory and Politics of Cultural Construction in the Pacific', *Oceania*, vol. 62, no. 4, June 1992, p. 253.

84 Richard Mulgan, 'Peoples of the South Pacific and Their Rights' in Ramesh Thakur (ed.), *The South Pacific: Problems, Issues and Prospects* (Houndmills, Macmillan, 1991), p. 117.

85 Cf. Aleck, 'Traditional Law and Legal Traditions', p. 51: 'For the purposes of contrasting law and custom in Papua New Guinea, Western law (that is to say, the introduced and adopted Anglo-Australian common law) is typically understood and represented in dichotomous formulations as the complete inversion of virtually all features by which Melanesian custom is generally characterized.' See also Roger Keesing, 'Theories of Culture Revisited', *Canberra Anthropology*, vol. 13, no. 2, 1990, p. 14: '[Reified culture] provides an ideal rhetorical instrument for claims to identity, phrased in opposition to modernity, Westernization, or neo-colonialism.' Manifestations of this phenomenon are also clearly evident in anti-Western Islamic fundamentalism where contemporary conditions of degradation are viewed as corruptions of an 'original cultural essence' which can only be retrieved by 'a return to the pristine beginnings which reside in the early years of Islam'. See Aziz Al-Azmeh, 'The Discourse of Cultural Authenticity: Islamist Revivalism and Enlightenment Universalism' in Eliot Deutsch (ed.), *Culture and Modernity: East-West Philosophic Perspectives* (Honolulu, University of Hawaii Press, 1991), p. 471.

86 Stephanie Lawson, 'Conceptual Issues in the Comparative Study of Regime Change and Democratization', *Comparative Politics*, vol. 25, no. 2, 1993, pp. 183–205.

87 Al-Azmeh, 'The Discourse of Cultural Authenticity', p. 482.

88 Cf. H. B. Acton, 'Tradition and Some Other Forms of Order', *Proceedings of the Aristotelian Society*, vol. LIII, 1952–53, p. 1, where he says: 'The supporters of tradition have believed in a "natural" order of society to which men should piously conform.' But what Acton is referring to is really traditionalism in the sense described earlier.

89 *Fiji Times* editorial quoted in Peter Larmour, 'A Foreign Flower? Democracy in the South Pacific', *Pacific Studies*, vol. 17, no. 1, March 1994, p. 45.

90 Alastair Davidson, 'European Democracy and the Pacific Way', (paper presented to the conference of the Pacific Islands Political Studies Association, Rarotonga, Cook Islands, December 1993), p. 5.

91 Ibid., pp. 4-6.

92 A term borrowed from Michael Goldsmith, 'The Great Pacific Democracy Debate' (paper presented to the conference of the Pacific Islands Political Studies Association, Rarotonga, Cook Islands, December 1993). Larmour, in 'A Foreign Flower', makes a similar point.

93 Peter Anyang 'Nyong'o, 'Democratization Processes in Africa', *Review of African Political Economy*, no. 54, July 1992, p. 98.

94 Claude Ake, 'Rethinking African Democracy', *Journal of Democracy*, vol. 2, no. 1, Winter 1991, p. 32.

95 Henry S. Kariel (ed.), 'Introduction', *Frontiers of Democratic Theory* (New York, Random House, 1970), p. ix.

96 Eric A. Nordlinger, *Soldiers in Politics: Military Coups and Governments* (Englewood Cliffs, Prentice-Hall, 1977), pp. 204-205.

97 Josiah Ober, *Mass and Elite in Democratic Athens: Rhetoric, Ideology, and the Power of the People* (Princeton, Princeton University Press, 1989), p. 3. The democracy of the ancient Athenians has also been much criticized in contemporary times for its exclusion of women, foreigners, and slaves from political participation. While not attempting to defend this, it is worth noting that such exclusionary practices can be attributed, at least in part, to the almost complete absence of a concept of human or natural rights, as well as a very narrow conception of citizenship. Notions of rights (which apply now to a much wider citizenry), are an indispensable ingredient of modern democracy.

98 Iain Hampsher-Monk, 'The Historical Study of Democracy' in Graeme Duncan (ed.), *Democratic Theory and Practice* (Cambridge, Cambridge University Press, 1983), p. 30.

99 Giovanni Sartori, *The Theory of Democracy Revisited* (Chatham, NJ, Chatham House, 1987), p. 3.

100 Ibid., p. 27.

101 Russell L. Hanson, 'Democracy' in Ball, Farr, and Hanson (eds), *Political Innovation and Conceptual Change*, p. 76.

102 John Hoffman, 'Capitalist Democracies and Democratic States: Oxymorons or Coherent Concepts?', *Political Studies*, vol. XXXIX, no. 2, June 1991, p. 342.

103 Williams, *Keywords*, p. 83.

104 W. B. Gallie, 'Essentially Contested Concepts', *Proceedings of the Aristotelian Society*, vol. 56, 1956, p. 184.

105 George Orwell, 'Politics and the English language', *Inside the Whale and Other Essays* (London, Penguin, 1957), p. 149.

106 See A. Mason, 'On Explaining Political Disagreement: The Notion of an Essentially Contested Concept', *Inquiry*, vol. 33, 1990, p. 84. See also J. N. Gray, 'On the Contestability of Social and Political Concepts', *Political Theory*, vol. 5, no. 3, 1977, pp. 331-348.

107 Gallie, 'Essentially Contested Concepts', p. 193. The argument against Gallie's position is set out in more detail in Lawson, 'Conceptual Issues'.

108 See Ferenc Feher, 'Between Relativism and Fundamentalism' in Deutsch (ed.), *Culture and Modernity*, p. 181.

109 See N. J. Rengger, 'No Time Like the Present? Postmodernism and Political Theory', *Political Studies*, vol. XL, no. 3, September 1992, p. 563.

110 Sartori, *The Theory of Democracy Revisited*, p. 4.

111 Ernest Gellner, 'The Politics of Anthropology', *Government and Opposition*, vol. 23, no. 3, 1988, pp. 299–300, 303.
112 Roger Keesing, 'Class, Culture, Custom' (paper presented to workshop on the Global Anthropology of Oceania, University of Lund, Sweden, October 1991), pp. 20–21.
113 Ibid., p. 22.
114 Ibid., p. 24.
115 David Held, *Introduction to Critical Theory: Horkheimer to Habermas* (Berkeley, University of California Press, 1980), p. 15.
116 See Sartori, *The Theory of Democracy Revisited*, p. 4.
117 Andrew J. Nathan, 'The Place of Values in Cross-Cultural Studies: The Example of Democracy and China' in Paul A. Cohen and Merle Goldman (eds), *Ideas Across Cultures: Essays on Chinese Thought in Honor of Benjamin I. Schwartz* (Cambridge, Mass., Council on East Asian Studies and Harvard University Press, 1990), p. 301.
118 Sartori, *The Theory of Democracy Revisited*, p. 206.
119 See Hans Kellner, ' "To Make Truth Laugh": Eco's The Name of the Rose' in M. Thomas Inge (ed.), *Naming the Rose: Essays on Eco's The Name of the Rose* (Jackson, University of Mississippi Press, 1988), p. 4.
120 Quentin Skinner, 'Language and Political Change' in Ball, Farr and Hanson (eds), *Political Innovation and Conceptual Change*, p. 10.

2   Fiji

1 David Routledge, *Matanitu: The Struggle for Power in Early Fiji* (Suva, Institute of Pacific Studies, 1985), p. 27.
2 These include Lau, Cakaudrove, Bua and Macuata (which together form the powerful Tovata confederacy), as well as Tailevu, Lomaiviti and Kadavu (which form part of the Kubuna confederacy).
3 T.P. Bayliss-Smith, Richard Bedford, Harold Brookfield and Marc Latham, *Islands, Islanders and the World: The Colonial and Post-Colonial Experience of Eastern Fiji* (Cambridge, Cambridge University Press, 1988), p. 4.
4 For a detailed discussion of this specific point, see Stephanie Lawson, 'The Myth of Cultural Homogeneity and its Implications for Chiefly Power and Politics in Fiji', *Comparative Studies in Society and History*, vol. 32, no. 4, October 1990, pp. 795–821.
5 Although I do not subscribe to the view that democracy is relative (nor to the view that the 1970 constitution was democratic in an unqualified sense), there are nonetheless degrees of 'democratic' and 'non-democratic'. In other words, I argue that the 1970 constitution was *more* democratic than the 1990 constitution rather than fully democratic.
6 See especially Brij V. Lal, *Power and Prejudice: The Making of the Fiji Crisis* (Wellington, New Zealand Institute of International Affairs, 1988); R.T. Robertson and Akosita Tamanisau, *Fiji: Shattered Coups* (Leichhardt, Pluto Press, 1988); Stephanie Hagan, 'Race, Politics and the Coup in Fiji' and Anthony van Fossen, 'Two Military Coups in Fiji' both in *Bulletin of Concerned Asian Scholars*, vol. 19, no. 4, October–December 1987. An exception is Deryck Scarr, *Fiji: The Politics of Illusion: The Military Coups in Fiji* (Kensington, University of New South Wales Press, 1988).
7 *Constitution of the Sovereign Democratic Republic of Fiji*, s. 21 (1). This follows Chapter II – 'Protection of Fundamental Rights and Freedoms of the Individual' – which, among other things, purports to guarantee 'protection from discrimination on the grounds of race' s. 16 (1). Rotumans are the

184 NOTES (PAGES 41–47)

indigenous people of a small island some 300 miles to the north of Fiji which was annexed by the British in 1879 and subsequently administered as a dependency of the Crown Colony of Fiji. Rotuma remained part of Fiji at independence.

8 Reported in the *Australian*, 23 July 1990, p. 6.
9 R. R. Nayacakalou, *Leadership in Fiji* (Melbourne, Oxford University Press, 1975), p. 133.
10 M. G. Smith, *Culture, Race and Class in the Commonwealth Caribbean* (Mona, University of the West Indies, 1984), p. 29.
11 See Burton Benedict, 'Pluralism and Stratification', in L. Plotnicov and A. Tuden (eds), *Essays in Comparative Social Stratification* (Pittsburgh, University of Pittsburgh Press, 1970); Judith A. Nagata (ed.), *Pluralism in Malaysia; Myth and Reality* (Leiden, E.J. Brill, 1975); Chandra Jayawardena, 'Culture and Ethnicity in Guyana and Fiji', *Man*, vol. 15, 1980; and David Nicholls, *Three Varieties of Pluralism* (London, Macmillan, 1974).
12 Donald L. Horowitz, *Ethnic Groups in Conflict* (Berkeley, University of California Press, 1985), p. 139.
13 Nicholls, *Three Varieties of Pluralism*, p. 56.
14 See especially Stephanie Hagan, 'The Party System, the Labour Party and the Plural Society Syndrome in Fiji', *Journal of Commonwealth and Comparative Politics*, vol. 25, no. 2, July 1987.
15 The idea that political conflict between groups in plural societies can only be managed rather than resolved is implicit in the theory of consociational democracy, especially as formulated by Arend Lijphart in *The Politics of Accommodation* (Berkeley, University of California Press, 1968).
16 Quoted in the *Sydney Morning Herald*, 21 July 1990, p. 66.
17 Quoted in Eddie Dean and Stan Ritova, *Rabuka: No Other Way* (Moorebank, Doubleday, 1988), p. 17.
18 Quoted in the *Sydney Morning Herald*, 21 July 1990, p. 66.
19 Bayliss-Smith et al., *Islands, Islanders and the World*, p. 46.
20 See James Calvert, *Fiji and the Fijians* (vol. 2 of *Mission History*, ed. G. S. Rowe), (London, Alexander Heylin, 1858), p. 6.
21 John Garrett, *To Live Among the Stars: Christian Origins in Oceania* (Geneva and Suva, World Council of Churches and Institute of Pacific Studies, 1982), p. 80.
22 Bayliss-Smith et al., *Islands, Islanders and the World*, p. 48.
23 See Peter France, *The Charter of the Land* (Melbourne, Oxford University Press, 1969), pp. 73–74.
24 For a more detailed discussion see Stephanie Lawson, *The Failure of Democratic Politics in Fiji* (Oxford, Clarendon Press, 1991), esp. pp. 48–58.
25 Great Britain, *Parliamentary Debates* (House of Lords), 17 July 1874, col. 182.
26 A. Todd, *Parliamentary Government in the Colonies* (2nd edn, London, Longman, Green, 1894), p. 25.
27 See Great Britain, Colonial Office, *Correspondence Relating to the Native Population of Fiji* (1887), no. 11, pp. 33–34.
28 Also often referred to as the Great Council of Chiefs or *Bose Levu Vakaturaga*.
29 See Lawson, 'The Myth of Cultural Homogeneity', pp. 800–801.
30 Cf. Terence Ranger in Eric Hobsbawm and Terence Ranger (eds), *The Invention of Tradition* (Cambridge, Cambridge University Press, 1983), pp. 250–251.
31 In his capacity as Advisor on Native Affairs, Sukuna was a member of the Legislative Council.
32 Fiji, *Legislative Council Debates*, 24 February 1944, p. 35.

33 Fiji, *Legislative Council Debates,* 6 November 1935, p. 176.
34 O. H. K. Spate, *The Fijian People: Economic Problems and Prospects* (published as *CP* 13/1959, Legislative Council of Fiji), p. 32.
35 Sir Alan Burns, *Fiji: Population and Resources* (published as *CP* 1/1960, Legislative Council of Fiji), p. 29.
36 See Nayacakalou, *Leadership in Fiji* , p. 134.
37 Ibid., p. 133.
38 Asesela Ravuvu, *Vaka i Taukei: The Fijian Way of Life* (Suva, Institute of Pacific Studies, 1983), p. 70.
39 Christina Toren, 'Making the Present, Revealing the Past: The Mutability and Continuity of Tradition as Process', *Man,* vol. 23, 1988, p. 708.
40 R. Gerard Ward, 'Land, Law and Custom: Diverging Realities in Fiji' in R. Gerard Ward and Elizabeth Kingdon (eds), *Land, Custom and Practice in the South Pacific* (Cambridge, Cambridge University Press, 1995). The quotations are from the draft chapter, and I am grateful to the author for permission to cite this material.
41 Ibid., p. 5.
42 Ibid., p. 7.
43 Ibid., p. 8.
44 France, *The Charter of the Land.*
45 Ward, 'Land, Law and Custom', p. 11.
46 S. Williksen-Bakker, 'Vanua – A Symbol with Many Ramifications in Fijian Culture', *Ethnos,* vol. 55, nos. 3–4, 1990, p. 232.
47 Ward, 'Land, Law and Custom', p. 39.
48 Reported in the *Fiji Times,* 14 March 1987, p. 1.
49 See Lawson, *The Failure of Democratic Politics,* pp. 85–90.
50 Ibid., p. 77.
51 Joseph Carens, *Democracy and Respect for Difference: The Case of Fiji* (published as issues 3 and 4, *University of Michigan Journal of Law Reform,* vol. 25, Spring and Summer, 1992), p. 601.
52 See Lawson, *The Failure of Democratic Politics,* p. 75; and R. G. Ward, 'Native Fijian Villages: A Questionable Future?' in Michael Taylor (ed.), *Fiji: Future Imperfect* (North Sydney, Allen & Unwin, 1987), p. 39.
53 See Lawson, *The Failure of Democratic Politics,* p. 80.
54 Accurate figures are not available, but since the coup (and with a higher than usual rate of Fiji Indian emigration) Fijians and Fiji Indians both now represent about 45–46 per cent of the population.
55 Brij V. Lal, *Broken Waves: A History of the Fiji Islands in the Twentieth Century* (Honolulu, University of Hawaii Press, 1992), p. 75.
56 Carens makes the point that an appeal by indigenous Fijians to the Deed's supposed guarantee of paramountcy is not a plausible justification for the subordination of the Fiji Indian community because Britain had no moral right to make (or keep) a promise that entailed such subordination. Furthermore, it is doubtful whether Gordon and his successors actually intended that indigenous Fijians enjoy the kind of dominance now claimed by some of them. At a later point in the discussion, he canvasses the problem of the relevance of history in the moral analysis of the goal of cultural preservation, and notes that both Fijians and Fiji Indians can make plausible moral claims based on history. See Carens, *Democracy and Respect for Difference,* pp. 580, 585.
57 Great Britain, *Public (Emigration) Despatch to India,* no. 39 dated 24 March 1875, para. 17 (emphasis added).
58 Great Britain, Parliament, *Report of the the Committee on Emigration from India*

to the Crown Colonies and Protectorates, Cd. 5192, June 1910, para. 358. This document is commonly referred to as the Sanderson Report.

59 It should be noted that, since the coups, the Council has been restructured so as to exclude many of the capable, but non-chiefly Fijians who had been incorporated in earlier years, thereby strengthening the role of the traditional chiefly elite. See Nicholas Thomas, 'Regional Politics, Ethnicity, and Custom in Fiji', *The Contemporary Pacific*, vol. 2, no. 1, Spring 1990, p. 136.

60 Nayacakalou, *Leadership in Fiji*, pp. 33, 35.

61 Ibid., p. 81.

62 The sociopolitical typology based on the Polynesia/Melanesia division was first set out explicitly by Marshall Sahlins in 'Poor Man, Rich Man, Big Man, Chief: Political Types in Melanesia and Polynesia', *Comparative Studies in Society and History*, vol. 5, no. 3, 1963, pp. 285–303. It has since been criticized on a number of grounds. See, for example, Nicholas Thomas, 'The Force of Ethnology: Origins and Significance of the Melanesia/Polynesia Division', *Current Anthropology*, vol. 30, no. 1, 1989, pp. 27–34. George Marcus in 'Chieftainship' in A. Howard and R. Borofsky (eds), *Developments in Polynesian Ethnography* (Honolulu, University of Hawaii Press, 1989), sets up a 'kingly/populist continuum' for Polynesian chieftainship which, he says, 'effectively collapses the chief/bigman distinction used by Sahlins' (p. 180). Despite these criticisms, I have argued that the basic distinctions between political types remains useful for the analysis of politics in Fiji: See Lawson, 'The Myth of Cultural Homogeneity', esp. pp. 801–802.

63 Scarr, *Fiji: The Politics of Illusion: The Military Coups in Fiji*, p. 3.

64 See Robert Norton, *Race and Politics in Fiji* (2nd edn, St Lucia, University of Queensland Press, 1990), p. 61.

65 Toren, 'Making the Present', pp. 697–700.

66 Shelley Ann Sayes, 'Changing Paths of the Land: Early Political Hierarchies in Cakaudrove, Fiji', *Journal of Pacific History*, vol. 19, no. 1, 1984, p. 3.

67 For a detailed discussion on this issue see Lawson, 'The Myth of Cultural Homogeneity'. See also John Clammer, 'Colonialism and the Perception of Tradition in Fiji', in T. Asad (ed.), *Anthropology and the Colonial Encounter*, London, Ithaca, 1973, pp. 199–220.

68 See R. Handler and J. Linnekin quoted in Allan Hanson, 'The Making of the Maori: Culture Invention and Its Logic', *American Anthropologist*, vol. 91, 1989, p. 898.

69 Roger M. Keesing, 'Creating the Past: Custom and Identity in the Contemporary Pacific', *The Contemporary Pacific*, vol. 1, no. 1 and 2, Spring and Fall, 1989, p. 19.

70 Cf. Hanson, 'The Making of the Maori', p. 898.

71 Martha Kaplan, '*Luve Ni Wai* as the British Saw It: Constructions of Custom and Disorder in Colonial Fiji', *Ethnohistory*, vol. 36, no. 4, Fall, 1989, p. 358.

72 Fiji, *Report on the Census of the Population*, (*PP* 13/1976), Table 1.

73 It should be noted here that the 1970 constitution, through sections 45(1); 53(4); 67(2), (3), (4) and (5), and 68(1) together provided for the triple entrenchment of indigenous Fijian rights. It should also be pointed out, however, that at the time of the 1987 coup this constitution had never been translated into the Fijian language, and most Fijians were unaware of the extent to which their rights were protected.

74 See Lal, *Power and Prejudice*, p. 72.

75 See Hagan, 'Race, Politics and the Coup', pp. 12–13.

76 See S.A. de Smith, *The New Commonwealth and its Constitutions* (London, Stevens & Sons, 1964), p. 118.

77 Robert Norton, 'Ethnic Divisions and Elite Conciliation' in Brij Lal (ed.), *Politics in Fiji* (North Sydney, Allen & Unwin, 1986), p. 57.

78 *Fiji Times*, 29 November 1965, p. 3.

79 For further details on divisions and differences among Fiji Indians, see A. C. Mayer, *Peasants in the Pacific: A Study of Fiji Indian Rural Society* (London, Routledge and Kegan Paul, 1961); K. L. Gillion, *The Fiji Indians: Challenge to European Domination 1920–1946* (Melbourne, Oxford University Press, 1977); Lawson, *The Failure of Democratic Politics*, esp. pp. 144–148; and Lal, *Broken Waves*, esp. pp. 76–79.

80 See Hagan, 'Race, Politics and the Coup', p. 9.

81 The main point of the program was in fact to reveal some rather dubious practices allegedly pursued by the Alliance during the campaign.

82 Quoted from the full transcript of the 'Four Corners' program broadcast in Australia on ABC Television on 3 July 1982, reproduced in Fiji, Parliament, *Report of the Royal Commission into the 1982 Fiji General Election*, published as *PP* 74/1983, p. 145 (emphasis added).

83 *Fiji Times*, 17 July 1982, p. 7.

84 *Islands Business News*, 8 August 1982, p. 13.

85 See R. T. Robertson, 'The Formation of the Fiji Labour Party', *New Zealand Monthly Review*, October 1985, pp. 3–4.

86 *Fiji Sun*, 20 September 1986, p. 1.

87 Senator Inoke Tabua (a nominee of the Council of Chiefs), reported in *Fiji Sun*, 20 September 1986, p. 4.

88 *Fiji Times*, 31 March 1987, p. 12.

89 See Lawson, *The Failure of Democratic Politics*, pp. 245–246.

90 For a general discussion of this problem, see Ward, 'Land, Law and Custom'.

91 Robertson and Tamanisau, *Fiji: Shattered Coups*, pp. 122, 137.

92 A small percentage of Fiji Indians are Muslim, and an even smaller number are Christian.

93 Dean and Ritova, *Rabuka*, p. 126.

94 Ibid., p. 104.

95 *Canberra Times*, 26 July 1990, p. 7.

96 Sub-sections 156(b) and (c) define 'Rotumans' and 'Indians'. The same section also provides that where the identity of the father is unknown, 'the male progenitors of that person may instead be traced through that person's mother'.

97 Iva Tora, 'So, Who Really is a Fijian'?', *Islands Business Pacific*, February 1992, pp. 19–20, 23.

98 Thomas, 'Regional Politics', p. 137.

99 Republic of Fiji, *Report of the Fiji Constitution Inquiry and Advisory Committee*, August 1989, p. 15. The outcome is of some importance since the Great Council of Chiefs has a number of important new functions under the republican constitution. Apart from the power to nominate the majority of members in the new upper house, the Great Council of Chiefs is charged with appointing (and possibly removing) the president.

100 Thomas, 'Regional Politics', p. 137.

101 Tora is something of a political eclectic whose career has spanned any number of policy stances and political parties. His most recent political affiliation had been with the Alliance, but he had also been involved with the NFP in earlier years.

102 Twelve-Member Committee of the Western Confederacy, *Submission on the 1988 Draft Constitution*, 16 May 1988.

103 Twelve-Member Committee, pp. 5 *et seq.*

104 Radio New Zealand, Transcript of Interview with Major-General Rabuka, 21 May 1989.

105 The Fijian Nationalist Party was formed in the 1970s under the leadership of Sakeasi Butadroka, a former Alliance politician. Although this party has frequently called for the repatriation of Fiji Indians, much of its invective has been directed against the eastern chiefly establishment.

106 Soqosoqo ni Vakavulewa ni Taukei, *Constitution/Manifesto* (circa. 1990), p. 1.

107 *Pacific Islands Monthly*, vol. 60, no. 7, July 1990, p. 14.

108 See *Fiji Voice*, no. 22, July/August 1992, p. 2.

109 The statistics presented here have been calculated on the basis of detailed results published in the *Fiji Times*, 1 June 1992, and the discussion is based on my previously published paper, Lawson, *Ethnic Politics and the State in Fiji* (Working Paper No. 135, Canberra, Peace Research Centre, Australian National University, 1993).

110 Mosese Velia, 'SVT, Feds Taste Election Defeat', *Fiji Times*, 1 June 1992, p. 3.

111 'Fiji: Back to the Future ... Again', *Pacific Islands Monthly*, January 1994, p. 17.

112 Wainikiti Waqa, 'Chiefs Back Rabuka', *Pacific Islands Monthly*, January 1994, p. 21.

113 *Daily Post* (Fiji), 28 February 1994, pp. 1–5.

114 Ibid., p. 3.

115 Ibid., p. 4.

116 Only 8 of the 31 SVT parliamentarians are chiefs. Five of the twelve cabinet posts are held by chiefs, and one of these is an independent (Ratu Jo Nacola).

117 One General seat was won by an ANC member which was something of an upset considering that a General communal seat had never been lost by the General Electors' Association or its successor party.

118 See Robert Keith-Reid, 'Island Overture: Rabuka Offers an Olive Branch to Ethnic Indians', *Far Eastern Economic Review*, 17 March 1994, p. 22.

119 Yash Ghai, 'Themes for the Consultation', *Report of a Consultation on the National Agenda* (Suva and London, School of Social and Economic Development, University of the South Pacific, and International Alert, December 1993), p. 5.

3   Tonga

1 Emiliana Afeaki, 'Tonga: The Last Pacific Kingdom' in Ron Crocombe and Ahmed Ali (eds), *Politics in Polynesia* (Suva, Institute of Pacific Studies, University of the South Pacific, 1983), p. 57.

2 Malakai Koloamatangi, 'The Balance of Power within the Tongan Political Structure: Who Has What Power in Tongan Politics' (paper presented to the Pacific Islands Political Studies Association Conference, Monash University, December 1991), p. 12.

3 See Hans Kohn, *Nationalism: Its Meaning and History* (rev. edn, Malabar, Robert E. Krieger, 1982), p. 9.

4 Christine Ward Gailey, 'State Formation, Development, and Social Change in Tonga' in Albert B. Robillard (ed.), *Social Change in the Pacific Islands* (London, Kegan Paul International, 1992), p. 345.

5 I. C. Campbell, 'The Emergence of Parliamentary Politics in Tonga', *Pacific Studies*, vol. 15, no. 1, March 1992, p. 77.

6 Norman and Ngaire Douglas (eds), *Pacific Islands Yearbook* (North Ryde, NSW, Angus & Robertson, 1989), p. 552.

7 Jens Poulsen, 'Archaeology and Prehistory' in Noel Rutherford (ed.), *A History of Tonga* (Melbourne, Oxford University Press, 1977), pp. 7–8.

8 H. G. Cummins, 'Tongan Society at the Time of European Contact' in Rutherford (ed.), *History of Tonga*, p. 64.

9 Patricia Ledyard, *The Tongan Past* (Vava'u, Government Printing Office, 1982), p. 15. See Ian Campbell, *Island Kingdom: Tonga Ancient and Modern* (Christchurch, Canterbury University Press, 1992), esp. ch. 1 on the difficulties of reconstructing accurate lineages.

10 Cummins, 'Tongan Society', p. 63.

11 Niel Gunson, 'The Coming of Foreigners' in Rutherford (ed.), *History of Tonga*, pp. 91–92.

12 See Robert W. Williamson, *The Social and Political Systems of Central Polynesia* (Oosterhout, Anthropological Publications [1924] 1967), vol. 1, pp. 138–141.

13 See George E. Marcus, 'Chieftainship' in Alan Howard and Robert Borofsky (eds), *Developments in Polynesian Ethnology* (Honolulu, University of Hawaii Press, 1989), esp. pp. 189–90.

14 Marshall Sahlins, *Islands of History* (London, Tavistock, 1987), see especially ch. 3, 'The Stranger-King; or Dumézil among the Fijians'. The quotation is from p. 73.

15 Edwin N. Ferdon, *Early Tonga: As the Explorers Saw It 1616–1810* (Tucson, University of Arizona Press, 1987), p. 30.

16 Cummins, 'Tongan Society', p. 64.

17 George E. Marcus, *The Nobility and the Chiefly Tradition in the Modern Kingdom of Tonga* (Wellington, The Polynesian Society, 1980), p. 5.

18 Campbell, *Island Kingdom*, pp. 11–13.

19 Ibid., p. 13.

20 Guy Powles (personal correspondence) has pointed out to me that because the history of Tonga was entirely oral until Europeans arrived, accounts of Tongan society that were passed down from one generation to the next could easily be changed and distorted by the ruling branch or dynasty of a particular period. The hierarchy may therefore have been much less stable than surviving oral accounts suggest, and there is no reason to believe that the violent contests for supremacy that marked later periods (such as in the eighteenth century), were not also characteristic of some earlier times. This point has some relevance for the comparisons (and contrasts) that are often drawn between Tonga and Samoa in pre-contact times. These comparisons have been made in the context of post-contact observations, and are not necessarily accurate in depicting the two systems as showing wide divergence in terms of centralized versus decentralized polities.

21 Irving Goldman, *Ancient Polynesian Society* (Chicago, University of Chicago Press, 1970), p. 303.

22 Cummins, 'Tongan Society', pp. 64–67; Ledyard, *The Tongan Past*, p. 18; George E. Marcus, 'Contemporary Tonga: The Background of Social and Cultural Change' in Rutherford (ed.), *History of Tonga*, p. 212.

23 Cummins, 'Tongan Society', p. 77.

24 Sione Latukefu, *Church and State in Tonga* (Canberra, Australian National University Press, 1974), p. 1.

25 Ledyard, *The Tongan Past*, p. 70.

26 Edward Winslow Gifford, *Tongan Society* (Honolulu, *Bernice P. Bishop Museum Bulletin* 61, 1929), p. 127. Gifford may be mistaken in this account, however,

for it would be difficult for cooks to work effectively with one arm (and the purpose in doing this was to distinguish these cooks from others, rather than to punish them for some misdemeanour). Siosuia Lafitani has suggested to me that it was more likely that only one finger was cut off.

27 Goldman, *Ancient Polynesian Society*, p. 302.

28 Sione Latukefu, *The Tongan Constitution: A Brief History to Celebrate its Centenary* (Nuku'alofa, Tongan Traditions Committee, 1975), p. 9.

29 See Aletta Biersack, 'Blood and Garland: Duality in Tongan History' in Phyllis Herda, Jennifer Terrell and Niel Gunson (eds), *Tongan Culture and History* (Canberra, Department of Pacific and Southeast Asian History, Australian National University, 1990), p. 49.

30 Aletta Biersack, 'Under the *Toa* Tree: The Genealogy of the Tongan Chiefs' in Jukka Siikala (ed.), *Culture and History in the Pacific* (Helsinki, Transactions of the Finnish Anthropological Society, no. 27, 1990), p. 95.

31 Laki M. Niu, 'The Constitution and Traditional Political System in Tonga' in Yash Ghai (ed.), *Law, Politics and Government in the Pacific Island States* (Suva, Institute of Pacific Studies, University of the South Pacific, 1988), p. 308. The term does not necessarily imply enforced obedience since it also encapsulates a sense of obligation based on loyalty and devotion. I am grateful to Barbara McGrath for pointing this out.

32 I. F. Helu, 'The Rise of the Critical Spirit' (unpublished paper, Atenisi Institute, August 1993).

33 Remark made by Sione Latukefu during discussion at the Tongan History Association Conference, Nuku'alofa, 23–29 June 1993.

34 See Adrienne L. Kaeppler, 'Art, Aesthetics, and Social Structure' in Herda, Terrell and Gunson (eds), *Tongan Culture and History*, pp. 59–61.

35 I. F. Helu, 'Democracy Bug Bites Tonga' in Ron Crocombe, Uentaba Neemia, Asesela Ravuvu, and Werner Vom Busch (eds), *Culture and Democracy in the South Pacific* (Suva, Institute of Pacific Studies, University of the South Pacific, 1992), p. 140.

36 Cited in Pesi Fonua, 'Constitutional Convention: Debating the Future of the Tongan Monarchy', *Matangi Tonga*, vol. 7, no. 5, Sept.–Nov. 1992, p. 11. The interpretation of this concept, however, is ambiguous: *fa'iteliha* is often taken to be a negative quality in that a person who acts in an unrestrained or *fa'iteliha* manner is seen to be securing his/her own interests at the expense of others. For clarification of this point I am grateful to Siosuia Lafitani.

37 Epeli Hau'ofa, 'The Pangs of Transition: Kinship and Economy in Tonga, *Australian and New Zealand Journal of Sociology*, vol. 14, no. 2, June 1978, p. 164.

38 All such standard accounts, however, need to be treated with caution rather than accepted as fact. In discussions on this point, Siosuia Lafitani has suggested that the concept of *mana* was not necessarily well developed in the context of pre-Christian Tongan culture, and that its prominence in discussions of tradition now is largely due to the work of anthropologists and Christian missionaries.

39 Latukefu, *The Tongan Constitution*, p. 13.

40 Ledyard, *The Tongan Past*, p. 16.

41 S. L. Kavaliku, 'Ofa! The Treasure of Tonga', *Pacific Perspective*, vol. 6, no. 2, 1977, p. 48.

42 Max Weber, 'The Social Psychology of the World Religions' in H. H. Gerth and C. Wright Mills (eds), *From Max Weber: Essays in Sociology* (London, Routledge and Kegan Paul, 1948), p. 296.

43 Latukefu, *Church and State*, p. 4.
44 Gifford, *Tongan Society*, pp. 317–318.
45 Latukefu, *Church and State*, pp. 8–9.
46 Afeaki, 'Tonga', p. 57.
47 See Rodney C. Hills, *Tonga's Constitution and the Changing State* (Discussion Paper No. 4, Series on Regime Change and Regime Maintenance in Asia and the Pacific, Canberra, Department of Political and Social Change, Australian National University, 1991), p. 8.
48 Christine Ward Gailey, *Kinship to Kingship: Gender Hierarchy and State Formation in the Tongan Islands* (Austin, University of Texas Press, 1987), p. 146.
49 Ibid., p. 169.
50 Ibid., p. 179.
51 Sione Latukefu, 'The Wesleyan Mission' in Rutherford (ed.), *History of Tonga*, pp. 124–125.
52 Ibid., p. 129.
53 John Garrett, *To Live Among the Stars: Christian Origins in Oceania* (Geneva and Suva, World Council of Churches and Institute of Pacific Studies, University of the South Pacific, 1982), p. 80.
54 The missionary papers of Rev. Peter Turner indicate that he chose the name George at his baptism in 1831 'because he said he heard so many good things spoken about of the good King of England and he wished to imitate him'. See *Sources of Tongan History*, p. 61.
55 'The Code of Vava'u' reproduced in *Sources of Tongan History: A Collection of Documents, Extracts and Contemporary Opinions in Tongan Political History 1616–1900* compiled by H.G. Cummins (private publication, 1972), p. 105.
56 I. F. Helu, 'Cultural Survival' (Opening Address to the University of the South Pacific Cultural Program, 27 April 1991), p. 2.
57 Helu, 'The Rise of the Critical Spirit', p. 2.
58 Epeli Hau'ofa, 'Thy Kingdom Come: The Democratisation of Aristocratic Tonga', Plenary Address delivered to the Conference of the Association for Social Anthropology in Oceania, Kona, Hawaii, 24–28 March 1993.
59 Gailey, *Kinship to Kingship*, p. 171.
60 Hau'ofa, 'Thy Kingdom Come', p. 2.
61 See Aletta Biersack, 'Kava'onau and the Tongan Chiefs', *Journal of the Polynesian Society*, vol. 100, no. 3, 1991, p. 238.
62 Ferdon, *Early Tonga*, pp. 286–7.
63 Ledyard, *The Tongan Past*, p. 57.
64 'Tonga Circuit Report 1862' in *Sources of Tongan History*, p. 153.
65 Latukefu, *Church and State*, p. 206. Attention has also been given to this point by the Hon. Tutoatasi Fakafanua, Minister for Labour (Tonga), who remarked 'how rare for an individual to limit his own rights', and suggested that divine guidance must have been influential. Fakafanua went on to suggest that the justification for people being free comes from God, whereas the humanism implicit in such formulations as 'we the people' is an inferior rendering because it is not based on God's word. (From notes taken at Hon. Tutoatasi Fakafanua's address entitled 'Change: Constitutional and Economical' at the Tongan History Association Conference, Nuku'alofa, 23–29 June 1993.)
66 Marcus, 'Contemporary Tonga', p. 212.
67 Ibid., p. 215. There were originally 20 nobles appointed in 1875, and Tupou I added another 10 in 1880. Tupou II later introduced a further two noble

titles and Queen Salote one more, bringing the present number to 33. Not all titles, however, are necessarily active at any given time since male lines sometimes 'fail' and the title reverts to the monarch's control until a new noble is appointed. Occasionally, an individual can hold more than one title at a time. See Kerry James, 'Princes and Power: Rank, Title and Leadership in Contemporary Tonga' (paper presented at the Conference of the Association for Social Anthropology in Oceania, Kona, Hawaii 24–28 March 1993).

68 Latukefu, *Church and State,* pp. 3, 15.
69 James, 'Princes and Power', p. 3.
70 Guy Powles, 'The Common Law as a Source of Law in the South Pacific: Experiences in Western Polynesia', *University of Hawaii Law Review,* vol. 10, no. 105, 1988, p. 117.
71 Ibid., p. 118.
72 Guy Powles, 'The Early Accommodation of Traditional and English Law in Tonga' in Herda, Terrell and Gunson (eds), *Tongan Culture and History,* p. 145.
73 Powles, 'The Common Law as a Source of Law', p. 119.
74 See *The Constitution of Tonga* reproduced in C. Wylie (ed.), *The Law of Tonga* (rev. edn, vol. 1, Tonga, Government Printer, 1967). On the issue of land, James notes that the land tenure system enshrined in the original version of the constitution was meant to prevent abuse by nobles, but subsequent amendments have weakened its efficacy in this respect, creating increasing resentment among commoners, especially since access to land is becoming more difficult. See James, 'Princes and Power', p. 4.
75 See Hills, *Tonga's Constitution,* pp. 5–6.
76 Guy Powles, 'The Tongan Constitution: Some Realities' (paper prepared for the Convention on the Tongan Constitution and Democracy, Nuku'alofa, November 1992).
77 Hills, *Tonga's Constitution,* p. 8.
78 *The Constitution of Tonga,* Part 1:4.
79 Powles, 'The Early Accommodation of Traditional and English Law', p. 155.
80 Gailey, 'State Formation', p. 322.
81 Latukefu, *Church and State,* p. 209.
82 Quoted in W. P. Morrell, *Britain in the Pacific Islands* (Oxford, Clarendon Press, 1960), p. 312.
83 Niu, 'The Constitution and Traditional Political System', p. 306.
84 Garrett, *To Live Among the Stars,* p. 274.
85 'Eseta Fusitu'a and Noel Rutherford, 'George Tupou II and the British Protectorate' in Rutherford (ed.), *History of Tonga,* p. 187.
86 Powles, 'The Common Law as a Source of Law', p. 120.
87 C. Hartley Grattan, *The Southwest Pacific Since 1900* (Ann Arbor, University of Michigan Press, 1963), p. 391.
88 *Survey of British and Commonwealth Affairs,* vol. 4, no. 14, July 1970, p. 606.
89 Ferdon, *Early Tonga,* p. 287.
90 See Hills, *Tonga's Constitution,* p. 15.
91 Powles, 'The Tongan Constitution: Some Realities', p. 3.
92 Guy Powles, 'Tonga' in Michael A. Ntumy (ed.), *South Pacific Legal Systems* (Honolulu, University of Hawaii Press, 1993), p. 317.
93 Marcus, 'Contemporary Tonga', pp. 210–11.
94 Marcus, *The Nobility and the Chiefly Tradition,* p. 9.

95 Marcus, 'Chieftainship', p. 201.
96 Phyllis S. Herda, 'Genealogy in the Tongan Construction of the Past' in Herda, Terrell and Gunson (eds), *Tongan Culture and History*, p. 21.
97 Marcus, 'Chieftainship', p. 201.
98 A. H. Wood and Elizabeth Wood Ellem, 'Queen Salote Tupou III' in Rutherford (ed.), *History of Tonga*, p. 194.
99 Herda, 'Genealogy', p. 27.
100 Sione Latukefu, 'Tonga after Queen Salote', *Journal of Pacific History*, vol. 2, 1967, p. 159.
101 Marcus, 'Chieftainship', p. 201.
102 Hau'ofa, 'The Pangs of Transition', p. 160.
103 Small newspapers and magazines with limited circulation had existed before – and as far back as the late 1900s – but they were produced and controlled either by the churches or the government. See Helu, 'The Rise of the Critical Spirit', pp. 7–8.
104 Tavake Fusimalohi, 'Communication' (paper presented to the Tongan History Association Conference, Nuku'alofa, 23–29 June 1993), p. 1.
105 'Amanaki Taulahi, *His Majesty King Taufa'ahau Tupou IV of the Kingdom of Tonga: A Biography* (Suva, Institute of Pacific Studies, University of the South Pacific, 1979), p. 10.
106 Campbell, 'The Emergence of Parliamentary Politics', p. 79.
107 Marcus, *The Nobility and the Chiefly Tradition*, p. 51.
108 Powles, 'The Persistence of Chiefly Power and Its Implications for Law and Political Organization in Western Polynesia' (PhD thesis, Canberra, Australian National University, 1979), p. 365.
109 Hau'ofa, 'Thy Kingdom Come', p. 3.
110 Ibid., p. 3.
111 Ibid., p. 3.
112 See Marcus, 'Contemporary Tonga', p. 211.
113 Pesi Fonua, 'At Last a Woman', *Matangi Tonga*, vol. 8, no. 1, March–April 1993, p. 22.
114 For an account of development in Tonga since the ascension of Tupou IV, see Campbell, *Island Kingdom*, esp. ch. 14.
115 Ibid., p. 222.
116 Helu, 'The Rise of the Critical Spirit', p. 4. 'Atenisi' is the Tongan rendering of 'Athens' and this designation reflects the concern of Helu to promote 'the classical principles of criticism, dialogue and analysis' which characterized education in the ancient Athenian system.
117 Okusitino Mahina, 'The Tongan Traditional History Tala-E-Fonua: A Vernacular Ecology-Centred Historico-Cultural Concept' (PhD thesis, Canberra, Australian National University, 1992), p. 15. Emphasis in original.
118 Hau'ofa, 'Thy Kingdom Come', p. 9.
119 Helu, 'Democracy Bug Bites Tonga', p. 145.
120 Campbell, 'The Emergence of Parliamentary Politics', p. 81.
121 'The Quiet Crusader', *Pacific Islands Monthly*, May 1991, p. 14.
122 Quoted in Akilisi Pohiva, 'Monarchy Versus Democracy' (paper presented to a meeting of the Australian Institute of International Affairs, Canberra, 20 October 1993), pp. 2–3
123 Campbell, 'The Emergence of Parliamentary Politics', p. 86.
124 Campbell, *Island Kingdom*, p. 219.
125 Campbell, 'The Emergence of Parliamentary Politics', p. 88.

126 Campbell, *Island Kingdom*, p. 220.
127 Rodney C. Hills, 'The 1990 Elections in Tonga', *The Contemporary Pacific*, vol. 33, no. 2, Fall 1991, p. 359.
128 Campbell, 'The Emergence of Parliamentary Politics', pp. 89–90; Hills, 'The 1990 Elections in Tonga', p. 360.
129 See Danny Gittins, 'Tonga's Missing Millions', *Pacific Islands Monthly*, May 1991, pp. 10–14.
130 'The Quiet Crusader', *Pacific Islands Monthly*, May 1991, p. 14.
131 Gailey, 'Keeping Kinship Alive', *Cultural Survival Quarterly*, Winter 1992, p. 48.
132 Quoted ibid., p. 48.
133 Pohiva, 'Monarchy Versus Democracy', pp. 5–6.
134 Hills, 'The 1990 Elections in Tonga', p. 365.
135 Ibid., p. 366.
136 Campbell, 'The Emergence of Parliamentary Politics', p. 94.
137 Hills, 'The 1990 Elections in Tonga', p. 371.
138 Helu, 'Democracy Bug Bites Tonga', p. 147.
139 Reported in *Matangi Tonga*, vol. 7, no. 4, July–August 1992, p. 6.
140 Ulafala Aiavao, 'Tonga's Great Democracy Debate', *Islands Business Pacific*, December 1992, p. 31.
141 Reported in Lopeti Senituli, 'Tonga: The Pro-Democracy Convention and its Aftermath' in *Tok Blong SPPF*, no. 42, February 1993, p. 22.
142 See Garrett, *To Live Among the Stars*, p. 273.
143 Reported in Fonua, 'Constitutional Convention: Debating the Future of the Tongan Monarchy', p. 9.
144 Ulafala Aiavao, 'Tonga's Great Democracy Debate', p. 33.
145 An expression used by Malakai Koloamatangi in 'The Balance of Power', p. 11.
146 Aiavao, 'Tonga's Great Democracy Debate', p. 32.
147 Powles, 'The Tongan Constitution: Some Realities', p. 8.
148 Hau'ofa, 'Thy Kingdom Come', p. 1.
149 Senituli, 'Tonga: The Pro-Democracy Convention', p. 22.
150 Martin Tiffany, 'Tonga's Call for Democracy', *Pacific Islands Monthly*, January 1993, p. 17.
151 Ibid., p. 18.
152 Quoted in 'The Quiet Crusader', p. 14.
153 'Tongan Briefs', *Matangi Tonga*, vol. 7, no. 5, Sept.– Nov. 1992, p. 5.
154 'Election of Representatives', *Pacific Islands Monthly*, January 1993, p. 19.
155 Pesi Fonua, 'The Bishop of Tonga, Patelisio Finau', *Pacific Islands Monthly*, April 1991, p. 54.
156 Reported in Ulafala Aiavao, 'Tonga's Pro-Change Lobby Gains Support', But Change May Take Time', *Islands Business Pacific*, March 1993, p. 33.
157 Reported in Aiavao, 'Tonga's Pro-Change Lobby Gains Support', p. 54.
158 Bill Morton, 'A Question of Time', *Pacific Islands Monthly*, March 1993, p. 11.
159 See Pesi Fonua, 'A Bitter Contest for Minority Seats', *Matangi Tonga*, vol. 8, no. 1, March–April 1993, pp. 20–22.
160 Bill Morton, 'Spreading the Word', *Pacific Islands Monthly*, February 1993, p. 13.
161 Interview with Masao Pa'asi, PR for Vava'u, Neiafu, Vava'u, 25 June 1993.

162 Young woman, Neiafu, Vava'u, 24 June 1993.
163 Middle-aged professional man, Nuku'alofa, 21 June 1993.
164 Young male taxi-driver, Nuku'alofa, 27 June 1993.
165 Akilisi Pohiva, Interview, Nuku'alofa, 27 June 1993.
166 Quoted in Morton, 'A Question of Time', p. 11.
167 Reported in Aiavao, 'Tonga's Pro-Change Lobby Gains Support', p. 33.
168 Senituli, 'Tonga: The Pro-Democracy Convention', p. 24.
169 Quoted in James, 'Princes and Power', p. 1.
170 Futa Helu, 'Those Infernal Constitutions', *Pacific Islands Monthly*, February 1993, p. 43.
171 Morton, 'Spreading the Word', p. 13.
172 Morton, 'Behind the Elections', *Pacific Islands Monthly*, March 1993, p. 13.
173 Aiavao, 'Tonga's Pro-Change Lobby Gains Support', p. 33.
174 Morton, 'Behind the Elections', p. 13.
175 Futa Helu, 'The People Want Changes', *Pacific Islands Monthly*, March 1993, p. 23.
176 Morton, 'Behind the Elections', p. 13.
177 Morton, 'A Question of Time', p. 12.
178 'Kava Better than War, Warns Minister', *Matangi Tonga*, vol. 8, no. 1, March–April 1993, p. 23.
179 'Hereditary Titles Unfortunate', *Matangi Tonga*, vol. 7, no. 5, Sept.–Nov. 1992, p. 12.
180 See Giovanni Sartori, *The Theory of Democracy Revisited* (New Jersey, Chatham House, 1987), p. 42.
181 'Speaking up for the Royal Way of Rule', *Islands Business Pacific*, December 1992, pp. 33–34.
182 Richard J. Bernstein, *Beyond Objectivism and Relativism: Science, Hermeneutics, and Praxis* (Oxford, Basil Blackwell, 1983), pp. 143 and 167.
183 'Time to Watch the Manioke Grow', *Pacific Islands Monthly*, October 1991, p. 14.
184 Ibid., p. 15.
185 Akilisi Pohiva, Interview, Nuku'alofa, 27 June 1993.
186 James, 'Princes and Power', p. 1.
187 Hau'ofa, 'Thy Kingdom Come', p. 12.
188 See Epeli Hau'ofa, 'The New South Pacific Society: Integration and Independence' in Antony Hooper, Steve Britton, Ron Crocombe, Judith Huntsman, and Cluny Macpherson (eds), *Class and Culture in the South Pacific* (Auckland and Suva, Centre for Pacific Studies of the University of Auckland and Institute of Pacific Studies of the University of the South Pacific, 1987), p. 4. This point is supported as well by James, 'Princes and Power', p. 5.
189 F.O. Kolo, 'Historiography: The Myth of Indigenous Authenticity' in Herda, Terrell and Gunson (eds), *Tongan Culture and History*, p. 3.
190 Ibid., p. 3.
191 See Roger M. Keesing, 'Class, Culture, Custom' (paper presented to the workshop on the Global Anthropology of Oceania, University of Lund, Sweden, October 1991), p. 4.
192 Helu, 'Democracy Bug Bites Tonga', p. 142.
193 Hau'ofa, 'Thy Kingdom Come', p. 11.
194 Hills, *Tonga's Constitution*, p. 10.

4 Western Samoa

1 See Norman and Ngaire Douglas, *Pacific Islands Yearbook* (16th edn, North Ryde NSW, Angus and Robertson, 1989), pp. 16, 636.
2 See Patrick V. Kirch, 'A Brief History of Lapita Archaeology' in Patrick V. Kirch and Terry L. Hunt (eds), *Archaeology of the Lapita Cultural Complex: A Critical Review* (Seattle, Thomas Burke, Washington State Museum Research Report No. 5, 1988), pp. 4–5.
3 These limitations had applied to the 45 territorial constituencies in which those enrolled on the Matai Voters' Roll voted. Two other seats are set aside for people enrolled on the Individual Voters' Roll, who consist mainly of part-Europeans, Chinese and others.
4 The constitution itself did not actually entrench *matai*-only suffrage and eligibility for candidature. This was left to electoral regulations which could be changed by an Act of Parliament.
5 Quoted in J.W. Davidson, *Samoa Mo Samoa: The Emergence of the Independent State of Western Samoa* (Melbourne, Oxford University Press, 1967), p. 328.
6 Asofou So'o, *Universal Suffrage in Western Samoa: The 1991 General Elections* (Canberra, Department of Political and Social Change, Australian National University, Discussion Paper no. 10, Series on Regime Change and Regime Maintenance in Asia and the Pacific, 1993), p. 1.
7 Davidson, *Samoa Mo Samoa*, p. 30.
8 Independent MP, Le Tagaloa Pita quoted in Ulafala Aiavao, 'Chance for Democracy', *Pacific Islands Monthly,* July 1990, p. 17.
9 R.P. Gilson, *Samoa 1830 to 1900: The Politics of a Multi-cultural Community* (Melbourne, Oxford University Press, 1970), p. 9.
10 A point made explicitly by Guy Powles in 'Law and Authority in Pacific Island Decision Making', *Pacific Perspective,* vol. 9, no. 2, 1980, p. 49.
11 Guy Powles, personal communication, September 1993.
12 Malama Meleisea, *The Making of Modern Samoa: Traditional Authority and Colonial Administration in the Modern History of Western Samoa* (Suva, Institute of Pacific Studies, University of the South Pacific, 1987), p. 5.
13 Although in many respects it makes sense to speak of these structures in the present tense, since units like the *nu'u* still function in much the same way, the past tense is used to indicate that the discussion here is directed more to the historical than the contemporary context.
14 Malama Meleisea and Penelope Schoeffel, 'Western Samoa: "Like a Slippery Fish"', in Ron Crocombe and Ahmed Ali (eds), *Politics in Polynesia* (Suva, Institute of Pacific Studies, University of the South Pacific, 1983), p. 84.
15 Meleisea, *The Making of Modern Samoa*, p. 6.
16 Charles Guy Powles, 'The Persistence of Chiefly Power and Its Implications for Law and Political Organization in Western Polynesian' (PhD thesis, Canberra, Australian National University, 1979), p. 19. The non-localized nature of the '*aiga* meant that each family group could, and usually did, have branches in many *nu'u*. Clearly, this means that '*aiga* and *nu'u* are not coterminous.
17 Krämer quoted in Powles, 'The Persistence of Chiefly Power', p. 19.
18 Davidson, *Samoa Mo Samoa*, p. 17.
19 Meleisea and Schoeffel, 'Western Samoa', pp. 83–4.
20 Davidson, *Samoa Mo Samoa*, p. 19.
21 Meleisea, *The Making of Modern Samoa*, p. 9.
22 Davidson, *Samoa Mo Samoa*, p. 19. Asofou So'o (personal communication, January 1994) has also pointed out that *ali'i* and *tulafale* can both be heads

of *'aiga*. Also, the term *'aiga* is a broad one which can mean different things in different contexts, depending on whether one is referring to the nuclear family or the *'aiga potopoto* (extended family), or the *'aiga* as in a lineage group of common descent, or *'aiga* as the collective term for all the *ali'i* in a village council.

23 Malama Meleisea, *Change and Adaptations in Western Samoa* (Christchurch, Macmillan Brown Centre for Pacific Studies, 1988), p. 15.

24 Penelope Schoeffel, 'Rank, Gender and Politics in Ancient Samoa: The Genealogy of Salamasina O Le Tafa'ifa', *Journal of Pacific History*, vol. 22, no. 4, October 1987, p. 185.

25 Robert Norton, 'Titles, Wealth and Faction: Electoral Politics in a Samoan Village', *Oceania*, vol. 55, no. 1, September 1984, p. 103.

26 Meleisea, *The Making of Modern Samoa*, pp. 8–9.

27 F. J. West, *Political Advancement in the South Pacific: A Comparative Study of Colonial Practice in Fiji, Tahiti and American Samoa* (Melbourne, Oxford University Press, 1961), p. 128.

28 Sharon W. Tiffany, 'The Land and Titles Court and the Regulation of Customary Titles Successions and Removals in Western Samoa', *Journal of the Polynesian Society*, vol. 83, no. 1, March 1974, p. 36. But see Schoeffel, 'Rank, Gender and Politics', esp. p. 190 where she argues that gender was much more crucial than is often assumed, and that in the pre-Christian period, genealogical connection through maternal rank was often decisive for status attribution.

29 Margaret Mead, 'The Role of the Individual in Samoan Culture' in Alan Howard (ed.), *Polynesia: Readings on a Cultural Area* (Scranton, Chandler Publishing, 1971), p. 165. (Mead's paper was originally written in 1928.)

30 Aiono Fanaafi Le Tagaloa, 'The Samoan Culture and Government' in Ron Crocombe, Uentaba Neemia, Asesela Ravuvu, and Werner Vom Busch (eds), *Culture and Democracy in the South Pacific* (Suva, Institute of Pacific Studies, University of the South Pacific, 1992), p. 117.

31 Robert W. Franco, 'Schooling and Transformations in Samoan Social Status in Hawai'i' in Albert B. Robillard, *Social Change in the Pacific Islands* (London, Kegan Paul International, 1992), p. 305.

32 Mead, 'The Role of the Individual', pp. 167, 169.

33 Lowell D. Holmes, 'Factors Contributing to the Cultural Stability of Samoa', *Anthropological Quarterly*, vol. 53, no. 3, 1980, p. 195.

34 Meleisea, *Change and Adaptations*, p. 24

35 Meleisea, *The Making of Modern Samoa*, p. 6.

36 Meleisea, *Change and Adaptations*, p. 24

37 Robert Louis Stevenson, *A Footnote to History: Eight Years of Trouble in Samoa* (London, Cassell & Company, 1892), pp. 2–4.

38 Meleisea, *The Making of Modern Samoa*, pp. 1–2.

39 Ibid., p. 2.

40 Ibid., p. 11.

41 Morgan Tuimaleali'ifano, *Samoans in Fiji: Migration, Identity and Communication* (Suva, Institute of Pacific Studies, University of the South Pacific, 1990), p. 30. Tuimaleali'ifano's account indicates, however, that extensive kinship ties remained important and that intermarriage, especially between high-ranking Tongans and Samoans continued throughout the ensuing centuries. One Tu'i Tonga is said to have married Salamasina's mother.

42 Irving Goldman, *Ancient Polynesian Society* (Chicago, University of Chicago Press, 1970), p. 248.

13 Derek Freeman, 'Some Observations on Kinship and Political Authority in Samoa' in Howard (ed.), *Polynesia*, p. 95.

44 Schoeffel, 'Rank, Gender and Politics', p. 183.

45 Asofou So'o, 'Modern Political Parties and Leadership in Western Samoa' (paper presented at the IXth Pacific History Conference, Macmillan Brown Centre for Pacific Studies, University of Canterbury, Christchurch, New Zealand, 2–5 December 1992), p. 6. In relation to this point, it should be noted that other scholars refer to *tafaifa* as the name, not of a person, but of the four titles collectively. See Derek Freeman, *Margaret Mead and Samoa: The Making and Unmaking of an Anthropological Myth* (Canberra, Australian National University Press, 1983), p. 134. See also Meleisea, *The Making of Modern Samoa*, p. 11.

46 Gilson, *Samoa 1830 to 1900*, p. 61.

47 Freeman, *Margaret Mead and Samoa*, p. 134.

48 So'o (personal communication) says that *Tumua*, as understood by Samoans now, includes Leulumoega, Lufilufi, Tuisamau, and Aumatagi; the last two referring to Afega and Malie (both in the Tuamasaga District) respectively.

49 Davidson, *Samoa Mo Samoa*, p. 27.

50 Robert W. Williamson, *The Social and Political Systems of Central Polynesia*, (Oosterhout, Anthropological Publications, [1924], 1967), vol. II, p. 217.

51 Williamson, *The Social and Political Systems of Central Polynesia*, p. 219.

52 Gilson, *Samoa 1830 to 1900*, p. 40.

53 Meleisea, *Change and Adaptations*, p. 16.

54 Gilson, *Samoa 1830 to 1900*, p. 23.

55 Ibid., pp. 23–4.

56 Meleisea, *The Making of Modern Samoa*, p. 133.

57 F. J. H. Grattan, *An Introduction to Samoan Custom* (Papakura, NZ, R. McMillan, 1948), p. 127.

58 George Turner, *Samoa: A Hundred Years Ago and Long Before* (Suva, Institute of Pacific Studies, University of the South Pacific, [1884] 1984), p. 21.

59 West, *Political Advancement*, p. 131.

60 Gilson, *Samoa 1830 to 1900*, p. 23.

61 Ibid., p. 28.

62 Meleisea, *Change and Adaptations*, p. 22.

63 Ibid., p. 22

64 Ibid., p. 23.

65 Feleti E. Ngan-Woo, *FaaSamoa: The World of Samoans* (Wellington, Office of the Race Relations Conciliator, 1985), p. 35:

66 Gilson, *Samoa 1830–1900*, p. 68.

67 John Garrett, *To Live Among the Stars: Christian Origins in Oceania* (Geneva and Suva, World Council of Churches and Institute of Pacific Studies, University of the South Pacific, 1982), p. 121. The term *papalagi* translates literally as 'sky-burster' and refers to the manner in which European ships appeared to 'burst' through the horizon on the ocean.

68 W. P Morrell, *Britain in the Pacific Islands* (Oxford, Clarendon Press, 1960), p. 54.

69 West, *Political Advancement*, p. 129.

70 Peter Hempenstall and Noel Rutherford, *Protest and Dissent in the Colonial Pacific* (Suva, Institute of Pacific Studies, University of the South Pacific, 1984), pp. 20–21.

71 Davidson, *Samoa Mo Samoa*, p. 41.

72 Ibid., p. 42.

73 Ibid., pp. 44–5.
74 Meleisea, *The Making of Modern Samoa*, p. 36.
75 Ibid., pp. 38–42.
76 Ibid., p. 42. See also Cluny Macpherson, 'The Continuity of Chiefly Authority in Western Samoa: Some Thoughts on its Persistence' (paper presented to the Pacific Islands Political Studies Association, Rarotonga, Cook Islands, December 1993), p. 14, whose analysis also supports this point.
77 Peter J. Hempenstall, *Pacific Islanders Under German Rule: A Study in the Meaning of Colonial Rule* (Canberra, Australian National University Press, 1978), p. 32.
78 Michael J. Field, *Mau: Samoa's Struggle for Freedom* (Auckland, Polynesian Press, 1991), p. 26.
79 Quoted ibid., p. 26.
80 Hempenstall, *Pacific Islanders Under German Rule*, p. 33.
81 With respect to land, however, alienation was stopped, first by the Berlin Act of 1889 (with the agreement of the other major powers then still in Samoa). A 1900 Constitution Order also forbade alienation except under specific circumstances, a policy continued later by New Zealand. See R. R. Nayacakalou, 'Land Tenure and Social Organisation in Western Samoa', *Journal of the Polynesian Society*, vol. 69, no. 2, 1960, p. 104.
82 Davidson, *Samoa Mo Samoa*, p. 79.
83 It was later renamed the Native Land and Titles Court. In 1935 the 'Native' was replaced by 'Samoan'. From 1964, the Land and Titles Court and the Supreme Court together formed the Justice Department. In 1981, the Land and Titles Court was established as a separate department by the Land and Titles Act. See Western Samoa, Legislative Assembly, *Report of the Department of the Land and Titles Court for 1983 and 1984*, p. 1. For a brief account of the history of the court, see Aeau Semi Epati, 'Lawyers and Customary Land: The Western Samoa Land and Titles Court', *Pacific Perspective*, vol. 10, no. 1, 1981, pp. 65–71.
84 Davidson, *Samoa Mo Samoa*, p. 81.
85 See C. Guy Powles, 'Western Samoa' in Michael A. Ntumy (ed.), *South Pacific Legal Systems* (Honolulu, University of Hawaii Press, 1993), p. 397; J. Tim O'Meara, 'From Corporate to Individual Land Tenure in Western Samoa' in R. Gerard Ward and E. Kingdon (eds), *Land, Custom and Practice in the South Pacific*, (Cambridge, Cambridge University Press, in press) pp. 109–156.
86 The treatment of Chinese indentured labourers by both Germans and the New Zealand administration was just as appalling as that meted out to Indians in Fiji. For an account of the rampant racism of the New Zealand regime, especially in relation to the forced breaking-up of Samoan/Chinese marriages, see Field, *Mau*, pp. 30–33.
87 See Mary Boyd, 'The Record in Western Samoa to 1945' in Angus Ross (ed.), *New Zealand's Record in the Pacific Islands* (Auckland and London, Longman Paul and C. Hurst, 1969), pp. 115–120.
88 Field, *Mau*, p. 29.
89 For a detailed account of this event, and others concerning the Mau movement, see especially Field, *Mau*.
90 A. H. McDonald (ed.), *Trusteeship in the Pacific* (Sydney, Angus and Robertson, 1949), p. 53.
91 Boyd, 'The Record in Western Samoa Since 1945' in Ross (ed.), *New Zealand's Record*, p. 190.

92 Boyd, 'The Record in Western Samoa Since 1945', p. 204.
93 Talaolevavau in Western Samoa, Legislative Council, *Constitutional Convention 1954* (publ. 1955), *Papers and Proceedings*, vol. 2, p. 268. The reference to virginity brings to mind the famous Mead/Freeman debate which, although not a concern of the present discussion, is worth noting. See Margaret Mead, *Coming of Age in Western Samoa: A Psychological Study of Primitive Youth for Western Civilization* (New York, Mentor Books, [1928], 1949), and Derek Freeman, *Margaret Mead and Samoa: The Making and Unmaking of an Anthropological Myth* (Canberra, Australian National University Press, 1983).
94 S. Maulolo in *Constitutional Convention 1954*, vol. 2, p. 267.
95 Davidson, *Samoa Mo Samoa*, p. 316. Note that this resonates very clearly with conservative Fijian opinion on the prospects for the eventual introduction of a common roll.
96 Boyd, 'The Record in Western Samoa Since 1945', p. 208.
97 *Constitutional Convention 1954*, vol. 2, p. 264.
98 Western Samoa, *Statement to be Presented to the Trusteeship Council by the Samoan Members of the New Zealand Delegation*, July 1958, see pp. 3–5.
99 Davidson, *Samoa Mo Samoa*, p. 333.
100 New Zealand, Department of Island Territories, *Report by the New Zealand Government to the General Assembly of the United Nations on the Administration of Western Samoa for the Calendar Year 1960* (Wellington, 1961), ch. 5.
101 Davidson, *Samoa Mo Samoa*, pp. 389–390.
102 See R.A. Herr, 'A Minor Ornament: The Diplomatic Decisions of Western Samoa at Independence', *Australian Outlook*, vol. 29, no. 3, December 1975, p. 308.
103 Davidson, *Samoa Mo Samoa*, p. 404.
104 Alison Quentin-Baxter, 'The Independence of Western Samoa – Some Conceptual Issues', *Victoria University of Wellington Law Review*, vol. 17, no. 4, September 1987, p. 356.
105 Tasi Malifa, 'The Franchise in the Constitution of Western Samoa: Towards a Theory of the Constitution Incomplete' (LLM thesis, Harvard Law School, 1988), p. 2.
106 Preamble to *Constitution of the Independent State of Western Samoa*.
107 Powles, 'Western Samoa' in Michael A. Ntumy (ed.) *South Pacific Islands Legal Systems* (Honolulu, University of Hawaii Press, 1993), p. 399.
108 Ibid., p. 399.
109 Ibid., p. 399.
110 Epati, 'Lawyers and Customary Land: The Western Samoa Land and Titles Court', p. 66.
111 Western Samoa, Legislative Assembly, *Report of the Department of the Land and Titles Court for 1983 and 1984*, p. 4.
112 See Tiffany, 'The Land and Titles Court', p. 47. On the occasions when the Court rules in favour of splitting a title, however, it is usually only between two people, and on the condition that it reverts to a single holder on the death of one of the incumbents.
113 David Pitt, *Tradition and Economic Progress in Samoa: A Case Study of Traditional Social Institutions in Economic Development* (Oxford, Clarendon Press, 1970), p. 38.
114 Meleisea, *Change and Adaptations*, p. 59.
115 Powles, 'Law and Authority', p. 49.
116 Ibid., pp. 49–50.
117 G. Powles, 'Traditional Institutions in Pacific Constitutional Systems: Better

Late or Never?' in Peter Sack (ed.), *Pacific Constitutions* (Canberra, Australian National University, 1983), p. 355.

118 Western Samoa, Legislative Assembly, *Tupua Tamasese Report*, 1976, pp. 2–3.

119 Ibid., pp. 4–5.

120 Ibid., p. 5.

121 Ibid., p. 5.

122 Ibid., p. 5.

123 Ibid., p. 6.

124 Ibid., p. 6.

125 Tiffany, 'The Land and Titles Court', p. 42.

126 *Tupua Tamasese Report*, pp. 6–7.

127 Powles, 'The Persistence of Chiefly Power', p. 38.

128 Alessandro Duranti, *Launga and Talanoaga: Structure and Variation in the Language of a Samoan Speech Event* (Sociolinguistic Working Paper no. 72, Austin, Texas, Southwest Educational Development Laboratory, April 1980), p. 3. So'o (personal communication) adds that some *matai* don't understand the special language either.

129 *Tupua Tamasese Report*, pp. 7–8.

130 Ibid., p. 15.

131 Foreword to Western Samoa, Legislative Assembly, *Report of the Committee Appointed by Cabinet to Consider the Report of the 1975 Committee on Matai Titles, Customary Lands and the Samoan Land and Titles Court*, Parliamentary Paper no. 12, 1979.

132 Ibid., p. 3.

133 Ibid., p. 3.

134 Ibid., p. 3.

135 Ibid., p. 9. The major recommendations of the report in fact dealt with problems with the Land and Titles Court, including the capacity of its judges, understaffing, the increasing burden of demands on the Court, and the poor facilities with which the Court was required to carry out its functions. It further recommended that the Court operate as a completely independent institution.

136 *Constitution of the Independent State of Western Samoa*, Part II.

137 For a more detailed analysis see Peter J. Bayne, 'The Constitution and the Franchise in Western Samoa', *Qld. Institute of Technology Law Journal*, vol. 1, 1985, pp. 201–223.

138 Ibid., p. 221.

139 Quoted ibid., p. 221. It is worth noting here Meleisea's objection to the 'uncritically accepted assumption' put forward by scholars such as Gilson and Davidson, and accepted by St John, that 'traditional Samoan political systems did not envisage a national form of government'. Meleisea recounts the times during Samoan history when centralized authority did emerge (at least at a ceremonial level), and argues further that 'the notion that Samoan political institutions had always been the way … the Europeans first found and recorded them gives an absurdly unreal picture of a society which remained static over two thousand years'. See Meleisea, *The Making of Modern Samoa*, p. 225. Meleisea's argument is supported by Goldman, who says that the Samoan idea of a single founding lineage implies a sense of all-Samoan unity and that 'the sense of oneness under a god-descended founder is thoroughly traditional'. Further, this provides the basis for the conception of an 'all-Samoan Great Fono'. See Goldman, *Ancient Polynesian Society*, pp. 271–72.

140 Quoted in Bayne, 'Constitution and the Franchise', p. 221.
141 Quoted ibid., p. 221.
142 Quentin-Baxter, 'The Independence of Western Samoa', p. 358. In further explanation of this remark, Quentin-Baxter states in a later passage her view that: 'In relation to the right to vote, the Constitution could do no more than set standards at which to aim'.
143 Quoted ibid., p. 358.
144 Leulu F. Va'a, 'The Emergence and Significance of New Political Parties in Western Samoa' (unpublished paper, December 1989), p. 1.
145 Ibid., p. 7.
146 Ata Ma'ia'i, 'Western Samoa's General Election 1973', *Journal of Pacific History*, vol. 9, 1974, p. 147.
147 Tupua Tamasese Lealofi IV, *Western Samoa Faces the Modern World* (Wellington, New Zealand Institute of International Affairs, 1970), p. 3.
148 So'o, 'Modern Political Parties and Traditional Leadership', p. 20.
149 Ibid., pp. 20–21. By this time, Tupuola Efi had had the title Tupua Tamasese bestowed on him (having succeeded his cousin, and former political rival). To illustrate the complexity that can be created in the process of accumulating titles, it should be noted that this particular person was first known as Tufuga Efi, then Tupuola Efi, then Tupua Tamasese Efi, and now as Tuiatua Tupua Tamasese Efi. Moreover, references to him in various reports may use only some of these titles. For example, he is often now referred to simply as Tupua Tamasese, but this tends to cause confusion with previous holders of that title.
150 Tialetagi Poumau, 'Reclaiming our Cultural Memory' in David Robie (ed.), *Tu Galala: Social Change in the Pacific* (Wellington and Annandale, Bridget Williams Books and Pluto Press, 1992), p. 198.
151 David Robie, 'Eti Landslides Home', *Islands Business*, March 1985, p. 17.
152 'It's Democracy Samoan Style', *Islands Business*, September 1986, p. 56.
153 Ibid., p. 56.
154 Reported in 'Registrar of Land and Titles Court Reports on Problems in that Department', *Savali*, 31 July 1989, pp. 1–2.
155 On bribery and *fa'a Samoa* see Ma'ia'i, 'Western Samoa's General Election 1973', p. 151.
156 So'o, *Universal Suffrage in Western Samoa*, p. 4. At the same time, the government announced that it would include a further question in the plebiscite to determine public opinion on whether an upper house of parliament should be introduced.
157 Ibid., p. 5. The individual voters' roll, however, was not affected.
158 Martin Robinson, 'Women on the March', *Islands Business*, February 1991, p. 28.
159 Fata Sano Malifa, 'Why Tofilau Won, Tupua Lost', *Islands Business Pacific*, April 1991, p. 5.
160 Aiono Fana'afi Le Tagaloa, Interview, Apia, 16 June 1993.
161 Le Tagaloa Pita MP, Interview, Apia, 17 June 1993.
162 Ibid.
163 *Savali*, 15 April 1991, p. 6. It should be noted, however, that Tupua Tamasese Efi later returned to parliament after a complicated round of electoral protests and by-elections in the seat.
164 Tunumafono A. Aiavo, 'The House Without Tuiatua Tupua Tamasese Efi', *Savali*, 29 April 1991, p. 4.
165 Tunumafono Apelu Aiavo, 'Tuiatua Tupua Tamasese Efi – The Politician and the Paramount Chief', *Savali*, 25 November 1991, pp. 3–4.

166 Aiono Fana'afi Le Tagaloa, Interview, Apia, 16 June 1993.
167 Le Tagaloa Pita, MP, Interview, Apia, 17 June 1993.
168 Netina Galumalemana, Registrar of Land and Titles Court, Interview, Apia, 17 June 1993.
169 Leota Siaki (Matai Afioga, Solosolo village), former MP, served three years in colonial government and a further period from 1966–69. Later a member of HRPP.
170 Cluny Macpherson and La'avasa Macpherson, 'Towards an Explanation of Recent Trends in Suicide in Western Samoa', *Man*, vol. 22, no. 2, June 1987, p. 311.
171 Macpherson and Macpherson, pp. 311–312.
172 In the interests of brevity, no attempt is made here to set out the full case made by the authors in support of these hypotheses.
173 Poumau, 'Reclaiming our Cultural Memory', p. 200.
174 Robert Norton, 'Chiefs, Adolescent Suicide and the Transformation of Chiefly Authority in Western Samoa' (Correspondence), *Man*, vol. 23, 1988, pp. 759–760. Commenting generally on the issue of suicide, So'o (personal communication) says that the relatively high rate may have less to do with *fa'amatai* as such, and more to do with the social control exercised by parents in their homes (and not all parents are *matai*). On Norton's point about the uncertainty of status, So'o thinks, from his own experience, that if a chief is uncertain about it, then s/he has all the more reason *not* to assert it.
175 Meleisea, *The Making of Modern Samoa*, p. 208.
176 Katherine T. Nakata, 'The Costs of Fa'a Samoa Political Culture's Complementarity with the Modern World System' in *Evolving Political Cultures in the Pacific Islands* (Proceedings of the 1982 Politics Conference, Laie, Institute of Polynesian Studies, Brigham Young University – Hawaii Campus, 1982), p. 334.
177 Felise Va'a, 'Western Samoa: A New Zealand Experiment' in F. P. King (ed.), *Oceania and Beyond: Essays on the Pacific Since 1945* (Westport, Greenwood Press, 1976), p. 135.
178 *New Zealand Herald*, 30 September 1993, p. 1, and 1 October 1993, p. 20.
179 *Dominion*, 2 October 1993, p. 10.
180 *Dominion Sunday Times*, 17 October 1993, editorial, cited in Guy Powles, 'Unpredictable Dimensions of Change: Judges, Courts and Formal Law in Western Samoa and Tonga' (paper delivered to the Workshop on 'Traditional and Modern in Contemporary Pacific Island Politics', Australian National University, Canberra, 21–22 October 1993).
181 Powles, 'Unpredictable Dimensions of Change'. (NB: This paper was delivered verbally with reference to a written outline. The comments cited here are based largely on the verbal presentation.)
182 Guy Powles, 'Legal Systems and Political Cultures: Competition for Political Dominance in Western Samoa' in Peter Sack and Elizabeth Minchin (eds), *Legal Pluralism: Proceedings of the Canberra Law Workshop VII* (Law Department, Research School of Social Sciences, Australian National University, Canberra, 1986), p. 206; and Macpherson, 'The Continuity of Chiefly Authority', p. 41.
183 Macpherson, 'The Continuity of Chiefly Authority', p. 41. It should be noted, however, that a right of appeal against any punishment was provided for, but the court in this case was to be the Land and Titles Court and not a civil court. See Macpherson, p. 42. In any case, this was clearly of no help to Matautia.

184 *Dominion Sunday Times*, 3 October 1993, p. 3.

185 Tim O'Meara, '"Individualism" in a "Communal" Society: A Social Impact Analysis of Fa'amatai Authority in Samoa' (seminar presentation, Research School of Pacific Studies, Australian National University, October 1993).

186 Powles, 'Unpredictable Dimensions of Change' (verbal comments).

187 So'o, *Universal Suffrage in Western Samoa*, p. 11.

188 Meleisea, *Change and Adaptations*, p. 5.

5 Conclusion: Tradition Versus the West

1 Michael A. Ntumy, 'Introduction' in Michael A. Ntumy (ed.), *South Pacific Legal Systems* (Honolulu, University of Hawaii Press, 1993), p. xix.

2 For a brief commentary of mine on some of the implications of the Malaysian position, see Lawson, 'Malaysian-Australian Relations: Much Ado About Recalcitrance', *Pacific Research*, vol. 7, no. 1, February 1994, pp. 21–22.

3 Robert Keith-Reid, 'So Why Can't Pacific Islanders Face up to Criticism Too?' *Islands Business*, January 1991, p. 9.

4 Ibid., p. 9.

5 Ibid., p. 9.

6 Okusitino Mahina, 'The Tongan Traditional History Tala-E-Fonua: A Vernacular Ecology-Centred Historico-Cultural Concept' (PhD thesis, Australian National University, Canberra, 1992), p. 10. Mahina defines *tala-e-fonua* as, literally, the telling-of-the-land-[and-its]-people – a vernacular, ecology-centred concept of culture and history. See p. 1.

7 Aiono Fanaafi Le Tagaloa, 'The Samoan Culture and Government' in Ron Crocombe, Uentaba Neemia, Asesela Ravuvu, and Werner Vom Busch (eds), *Culture and Democracy in the South Pacific* (Suva, Institute of Pacific Studies, University of the South Pacific, 1992), p. 131.

8 J. H. Plumb, *The Death of the Past* (London, Macmillan, 1969), p. 45.

9 Peter Larmour, '"A Foreign Flower?" Democracy in the South Pacific', *Pacific Studies*, vol. 17, no. 1, March 1994, p. 45.

10 Robert T. Robertson with Akosita Tamanisau, 'Pacific Overview: Not So New World Order' in David Robie (ed.), *Tu Galala: Social Change in the Pacific* (Wellington and Annandale, Bridget Williams Books and Pluto Press, 1992), p. 27.

11 Edward W. Said, *Culture and Imperialism* (London, Vintage, 1994), p. xiii.

12 Asesela Ravuvu, *The Facade of Democracy: Fijian Struggles for Political Control 1830–1987* (Suva, Reader Publishing House, 1991), p. xi.

13 Ibid., pp. 58, 60.

14 Larmour, '"A Foreign Flower?"', p. 47.

15 These remarks were made by the Hon. Fusitu'a in response to a question by the author during a meeting with a delegation of Tongan parliamentarians, Australian National University, 17 December 1993.

16 Michael Goldsmith, 'The Great Pacific Democracy Debate' (paper presented to the conference of the Pacific Islands Political Studies Association, Rarotonga, Cook Islands, December 1993), p. 1.

17 Ibid., p. 1.

18 Goldsmith, 'The Great Pacific Democracy Debate', p. 2.

19 Asesela Ravuvu, introductory remarks to a session of the Colloquy on Democracy and Economic Development in the Asia-Pacific Region – The Role of Parliamentary Institutions, Strasbourg Conference on Parliamentary Democracy, Parliament House, Canberra, 22–23 October 1992, pub-

lished as *Colloquy Report* (Strasbourg, Secretariat, Council of Europe, 1992), p. 59.

20　See Donald Lawrence Brenneis and Fred R. Myers, 'Introduction' in Donald Lawrence Brenneis and Fred R. Myers (eds), *Dangerous Words: Language and Politics in the Pacific* (New York, New York University Press, 1984), p. 27.

21　Jaroslav Pelikan, *The Vindication of Tradition* (New Haven, Yale University Press, 1948), pp. 15–16.

22　A similar argument can be employed in the face of accusations about ethnocentricity on the part of those 'outsiders' who prescribe a return to the (relatively) more democratic institutions established under the 1970 constitution.

23　It is especially interesting to note that the Great Council of Chiefs is itself a colonial institution. It was originally set up to provide a forum for chiefs at a national level which in turn provided a convenient point of contact for the colonial administration. No such body had existed previously, of course, because there was really no sense in which Fiji was a 'nation' at the time of colonization. The report of the CIAC nonetheless refers to the Great Council of Chiefs in terms of its 'age-old authority and functions on traditional and customary matters' (p. 24).

24　J. J. Smolicz, 'Tradition, Core Values and Intercultural Development in Plural Societies', *Ethnic and Racial Studies,* vol. 11, no. 4, November 1988, p. 390.

25　Margaret Jolly, 'Custom and the Way of the Land: Past and Present in Vanuatu and Fiji', *Oceania,* vol. 62, no. 4, June 1992, p .2.

26　Allan Hanson, 'The Making of the Maori: Cultural Invention and its Logic', *American Anthropologist'*, vol. 91, 1989, p. 890.

27　Simione Durutalo, reported in Council of Europe Strasbourg Conference, *Colloquy Report* (1992) p. 69.

28　Reported in the *Sydney Morning Herald,* 25 June 1987, p.13.

29　In any case, 'democracy has only recently become a good thing' in the West – see Iain Hampsher-Monk, 'The Historical Study of Democracy', in Graeme Duncan (ed.), *Democratic Theory and Practice* (Cambridge, Cambridge University Press, 1983), p. 30.

30　Ian Hamnett, *Chieftainship and Legitimacy: An Anthropological Study of Executive Law in Lesotho* (London, Routledge and Kegan Paul, 1975), p. 15.

31　Richard J. Bernstein, 'Incommensurability and Otherness Revisited' in Eliot Deutsch (ed.) *Culture and Modernity: East–West Philosophic Perspectives* (Honolulu, University of Hawaii Press, 1991), p. 93.

32　Said, *Culture and Imperialism,* p. xiv.

33　This observation has been made in similar terms by Jocelyn Linnekin, 'On the Theory and Politics of Cultural Construction in the Pacific', *Oceania,* vol. 62, no. 4, June 1992, p. 6.

34　George Orwell, 'Notes on Nationalism' in *Decline of the English Murder and Other Essays* (Harmondsworth, Penguin, 1965), p. 167.

Bibliography

Acton, H. B., 'Tradition and Some Other Forms of Order', *Proceedings of the Aristotelian Society,* vol. LIII, 1952–53.

Afeaki, Emiliana, 'Tonga: The Last Pacific Kingdom' in Ron Crocombe and Ahmed Ali (eds), *Politics in Polynesia* (Suva, Institute of Pacific Studies, University of the South Pacific, 1983).

Aiavo, Tunumafono Apelu, 'The House Without Tuiatua Tupua Tamasese Efi', *Savali,* 29 April 1991.

Aiavo, Tunumafono Apelu, 'Tuiatua Tupua Tamasese Efi – The Politician and the Paramount Chief', *Savali,* 25 November 1991.

Aiavao, Ulafala, 'Tonga's Great Democracy Debate', *Islands Business Pacific,* December 1992.

Aiavao, Ulafala, 'Tonga's Pro-Change Lobby Gains Support, But Change May Take Time', *Islands Business Pacific,* March 1993.

Ake, Claude, 'Rethinking African Democracy', *Journal of Democracy,* vol. 2, no. 1, Winter 1991.

Al-Azmeh, Aziz, 'The Discourse of Cultural Authenticity: Islamist Revivalism and Enlightenment Universalism' in Eliot Deutsch (ed.), *Culture and Modernity: East–West Philosophic Perspectives* (Honolulu, University of Hawaii Press, 1991).

Aleck, Jonathan, 'Traditional Law and Legal Traditions in Papua New Guinea: A Reappraisal of the Relationship Between Law and Custom' (paper presented to the 49th Annual Conference of the Australasian Law Teachers' Association, Canberra, September 1990).

Babadzan, Alain, '*Kastom* and Nation Building in the Pacific' in Remo Guidieri, Francesco Pellizi, and Stanley J. Tambiah (eds), *Ethnicities and Nations: Processes of Interethnic Relations in Latin America, Southeast Asia, and the Pacific* (Austin, University of Texas Press, 1988).

Balandier, Georges, *Political Anthropology* (transl. A. M. Sheridan Smith, New York, Pantheon, 1970).

Ball, Terence, James Farr and Russell L. Hanson (eds), *Political Innovation and Conceptual Change* (Cambridge, Cambridge University Press, 1989).

Bayliss-Smith, T. P., Richard Bedford, Harold Brookfield and Marc Latham, *Islands, Islanders and the World: The Colonial and Post-Colonial Experience of Eastern Fiji* (Cambridge, Cambridge University Press, 1988).

Bayne, Peter J., 'The Constitution and the Franchise in Western Samoa', *Queensland Institute of Technology Law Journal*, vol. 1, 1985.

Benedict, Burton, 'Pluralism and Stratification', in L. Plotnicov and A. Tuden (eds), *Essays in Comparative Social Stratification* (Pittsburgh, University of Pittsburgh Press, 1970).

Bernstein, Richard J., *Beyond Objectivism and Relativism: Science, Hermeneutics, and Praxis* (Oxford, Basil Blackwell, 1983).

Bernstein, Richard J., 'Incommensurability and Otherness Revisited' in Eliot Deutsch (ed.), *Culture and Modernity: East-West Philosophic Perspectives* (Honolulu, University of Hawaii Press, 1991).

Biersack, Aletta, 'Under the *Toa* Tree: The Genealogy of the Tongan Chiefs' in Jukka Siikala (ed.), *Culture and History in the Pacific* (Helsinki, Transactions of the Finnish Anthropological Society, no. 27, 1990).

Biersack, Aletta, 'Blood and Garland: Duality in Tongan History' in Phyllis Herda, Jennifer Terrell and Neil Gunson (eds), *Tongan Culture and History* (Canberra, Department of Pacific and Southeast Asian History, Australian National University, 1990).

Biersack, Aletta, 'Kava'onau and the Tongan Chiefs', *Journal of the Polynesian Society*, vol. 100, no. 3, 1991.

Boyd, Mary, 'The Record in Western Samoa Since 1945' in Angus Ross (ed.), *New Zealand's Record in the Pacific Islands in the Twentieth Century* (Auckland and London, Longman Paul and C. Hurst, 1969).

Brenneis, Donald Lawrence, and Fred R. Myers (eds), *Dangerous Words: Language and Politics in the Pacific* (New York, New York University Press, 1984).

Burling, Robbins, *The Passage of Power: Studies in Political Succession* (New York, Academic Press, 1974).

Callick, Rowan, 'Forward to the Past?', *Australian Left Review*, no. 131, August 1991).

Calvert, James, *Fiji and the Fijians* (vol. 2 of *Mission History*, ed. G.S. Rowe, London, Alexander Heylin, 1858).

Campbell, I. C., 'The Emergence of Parliamentary Politics in Tonga', *Pacific Studies*, vol. 15, no. 1, March 1992.

Campbell, Ian, *Island Kingdom: Tonga Ancient and Modern* (Christchurch, Canterbury University Press, 1992).

Carens, Joseph, 'Democracy and Respect for Difference: The Case of Fiji', *University of Michigan Journal of Law Reform*, vol. 25, issues 3 and 4, Spring and Summer, 1992.

Carrier, James (ed.), *History and Tradition in Melanesian Anthropology* (Berkeley, University of California Press, 1992).

Carrier, James, 'Occidentalism: The World Turned Upside Down', *American Anthropologist*, vol. 19, no. 2, May 1992.

Clammer, John, 'Colonialism and the Perception of Tradition in Fiji', in T. Asad (ed.), *Anthropology and the Colonial Encounter* (London, Ithaca, 1973).

Clifford, James, *The Predicament of Culture: Twentieth-Century Ethnography, Literature, and Art* (Cambridge (Mass.), Harvard University Press, 1988).

Cohen, Paul A., and Merle Goldman (eds), *Ideas Across Cultures: Essays on Chinese Thought in Honor of Benjamin I. Schwartz* (Cambridge (Mass.), Council on East Asian Studies and Harvard University Press, 1990).

Colson, Elizabeth, *Tradition and Contract: The Problem of Order* (London, Heinemann, 1975).

Connolly, William, 'Appearance and Reality in Politics' in Michael T. Gibbons (ed.), *Interpreting Politics* (Oxford, Basil Blackwell, 1987).

Council of Europe, *Colloquy Report* (Strasbourg, Council of Europe Secretariat, 1992).

Cotton, James, 'The Limits to Liberalization in Industrializing Asia: Three Views of the State', *Pacific Affairs*, vol. 64, no. 3, Fall 1991.

Crocombe, Ron, *The Pacific Way: An Emerging Identity* (Suva, Lotu Pasifika, 1976).

Crocombe, Ron, and Ahmed Ali (eds), *Politics in Polynesia* (Suva, Institute of Pacific Studies, University of the South Pacific, 1983).

Crocombe, Ron, Uentaba Neemia, Asesela Ravuvu, and Werner Vom Busch (eds), *Culture and Democracy in the South Pacific* (Suva, Institute of Pacific Studies, University of the South Pacific, 1992).

Cummins, H. G., 'Tongan Society at the Time of European Contact' in Noel Rutherford (ed.), *A History of Tonga* (Melbourne, Oxford University Press, 1977).

Davidson, Alastair, 'European Democracy and the Pacific Way' (paper presented to the conference of the Pacific Islands Political Studies Association, Rarotonga, Cook Islands, December 1993).

Davidson, J. W., *Samoa Mo Samoa: The Emergence of the Independent State of Western Samoa* (Melbourne, Oxford University Press, 1967).

de Smith, S. A., *The New Commonwealth and its Constitutions* (London, Stevens & Sons, 1964).

Dean, Eddie and Stan Ritova, *Rabuka: No Other Way* (Moorebank, Doubleday, 1988).

Deutsch, Eliot (ed.), *Culture and Modernity: East–West Philosophic Perspectives* (Honolulu, University of Hawaii Press, 1991).

Douglas, Bronwen, 'Rank, Power, Authority: A Reassessment of Traditional Leadership in South Pacific Societies', *Journal of Pacific History*, vol. xiv, part I, 1979.

Douglas, Bronwen, 'Ritual and Politics in the Inaugural Meeting of High Chiefs from New Caledonia and the Loyalty Islands', *Social Analysis*, no. 18, December 1985.

Douglas, Norman, and Ngaire Douglas (eds), *Pacific Islands Yearbook* (North Ryde, Angus & Robertson, 1989).

Duncan, Graeme (ed.), *Democratic Theory and Practice* (Cambridge, Cambridge University Press, 1983).

Duranti, Alessandro, *Launga and Talanoaga: Structure and Variation in the Language of a Samoan Speech Event* (Sociolinguistic Working Paper no. 72, Austin (Texas), Southwest Educational Development Laboratory, April 1980).

Eccleshall, Robert, *Order and Reason in Politics: Theories of Absolute and Limited Monarchy in Early Modern England* (Oxford, Oxford University Press, 1978).

Eisenstadt, S. N., 'Post-Traditional Societies and the Continuity and Reconstruction of Tradition', *Daedalus*, vol. 102, no. 1, Winter 1973.

Epati, Aeau Semi, 'Lawyers and Customary Land: The Western Samoa Land and Titles Court', *Pacific Perspective*, vol. 10, no. 1, 1981.

Fakafanua, Tutoatasi, 'Change: Constitutional and Economical' (address to the Tongan History Association Conference, Nuku'alofa, 23–29 June 1993).

Feher, Ferenc, 'Between Relativism and Fundamentalism' in Eliot Deutsch (ed.), *Culture and Modernity: East–West Philosophic Perspectives* (Honolulu, University of Hawaii Press, 1991).

Ferdon, Edwin N., *Early Tonga: As the Explorers Saw It 1616–1810* (Tucson, University of Arizona Press, 1987).

Field, Michael J., *Mau: Samoa's Struggle for Freedom* (Auckland, Polynesian Press, 1991).

Fiji, *Constitution of Fiji*, 1970.

Fiji, *Legislative Council Debates*.

Fiji, Parliament, *Report of the Royal Commission into the 1982 Fiji General Election* (published as *PP* 74/1983).

Fiji Voice, no. 22, July/August 1992.

Fonua, Pesi, 'The Bishop of Tonga, Patelisio Finau', *Pacific Islands Monthly*, April 1991.

Fonua, Pesi, 'Constitutional Convention: Debating the Future of the Tongan Monarchy', *Matangi Tonga*, vol. 7, no. 5, Sept.–Nov. 1992.

Fonua, Pesi, 'A Bitter Contest for Minority Seats', *Matangi Tonga*, vol. 8, no. 1, March–April 1993.

Fonua, Pesi, 'At Last a Woman', *Matangi Tonga*, vol. 8, no. 1, March–April 1993.

France, Peter, *The Charter of the Land* (Melbourne, Oxford University Press, 1969).

Franco, Robert W., 'Schooling and Transformations in Samoan Social Status in Hawai'i' in Albert B. Robillard (ed.), *Social Change in the Pacific Islands* (London, Kegan Paul International, 1992).

Freeman, Derek, 'Some Observations on Kinship and Political Authority in Samoa' in Alan Howard (ed.), *Polynesia: Readings on a Cultural Area* (Scranton, Chandler Publishing, 1971).

Freeman, Derek, *Margaret Mead and Samoa: The Making and Unmaking of an Anthropological Myth* (Canberra, Australian National University Press, 1983).

Freeman, Michael, *Edmund Burke and the Critique of Political Radicalism* (Oxford, Basil Blackwell, 1980).

Friedman, Jonathan, 'Beyond Otherness or: The Spectacularization of Anthropology', *Telos*, No. 71, Spring 1987.

Friedrich, Carl J., *Tradition and Authority* (New York, Praeger, 1972).

Fusimalohi, Tavake, 'Communication' (paper presented to the Tongan History Association Conference, Nuku'alofa, 23–29 June 1993).

Fusitu'a, Eseta and Noel Rutherford, 'George Tupou II and the British Protectorate' in Noel Rutherford (ed.), *A History of Tonga* (Melbourne, Oxford University Press, 1977).

Gailey, Christine Ward, *Kinship to Kingship: Gender Hierarchy and State Formation in the Tongan Islands* (Austin, University of Texas Press, 1987).

Gailey, Christine Ward, 'Keeping Kinship Alive', *Cultural Survival Quarterly*, Winter 1992.

Gailey, Christine Ward, 'State Formation, Development, and Social Change in Tonga' in Albert B. Robillard (ed.), *Social Change in the Pacific Islands* (London, Kegan Paul International, 1992).

Gallie, W. B., 'Essentially Contested Concepts', *Proceedings of the Aristotelian Society*, vol. 56, 1956.

Garrett, John, *To Live Among the Stars: Christian Origins in Oceania* (Geneva and Suva, World Council of Churches and Institute of Pacific Studies, 1982).

Gellner, Ernest, 'Concepts and Society' in Bryan R. Wilson (ed.), *Rationality* (Oxford, Basil Blackwell, 1970).

Gellner, Ernest, 'The Politics of Anthropology', *Government and Opposition*, vol. 23, no. 3, 1988.

Gerth, H. H. and C. Wright Mills (eds), *From Max Weber: Essays in Sociology* (London, Routledge & Kegan Paul, 1948).

Gewertz, Deborah and Frederick Errington, 'We Think Therefore They Are? On Occidentalizing the World', *Anthropological Quarterly*, vol. 64, no. 2, April 1991.

Ghai, Yash (ed.), *Law, Politics and Government in the Pacific Island States* (Suva, Institute of Pacific Studies, University of the South Pacific, 1988).

Chai, Yash, 'Themes for the Consultation', *Report of a Consultation on the National Agenda* (Suva and London, School of Social and Economic Development, University of the South Pacific, and International Alert, December 1993).

Gibbons, Michael T., *Interpreting Politics* (Oxford, Basil Blackwell, 1987).

Gifford, Edward Winslow, *Tongan Society* (Honolulu, Bernice P. Bishop Museum Bulletin 61, 1929).

Gillion, K. L., *The Fiji Indians: Challenge to European Domination 1920–1946* (Melbourne, Oxford University Press, 1977).

Gilson, R. P., *Samoa 1830 to 1900: The Politics of a Multi-cultural Community* (Melbourne, Oxford University Press, 1970).

Gittins, Danny, 'Tonga's Missing Millions', *Pacific Islands Monthly*, May 1991.

Goldman, Irving, *Ancient Polynesian Society* (Chicago, University of Chicago Press, 1970).

Goldsmith, Michael, 'The Tradition of Invention' in Michael Goldsmith and Keith Barber (eds), *Sites: Social Anthropology and the Politics of Interpretation* (Palmerston North, Department of Social Anthropology, Massey University, 1992).

Goldsmith, Michael, 'The Great Pacific Democracy Debate' (paper presented to the conference of the Pacific Islands Political Studies Association, Rarotonga, Cook Islands, December 1993).

Goldsmith, Michael and Keith Barber (eds), *Sites: Social Anthropology and the Politics of Interpretation* (Palmerston North, Department of Social Anthropology, Massey University, 1992).

Gould, Stephen Jay, *Time's Arrow, Time's Cycle: Myth and Metaphor in the Discovery of Geological Time* (London, Penguin, 1987).

Gould, Stephen Jay, *Wonderful Life: The Burgess Shale and the Nature of History* (London, Penguin, 1989).

Grattan, F. J. H., *An Introduction to Samoan Custom* (Papakura (NZ), R. McMillan, 1948).

Grattan, C. Hartley, *The Southwest Pacific Since 1900* (Ann Arbor, University of Michigan Press, 1963).

Gray, J. N., 'On the Contestability of Social and Political Concepts', *Political Theory*, vol. 5, no. 3, 1977.

Great Britain, Colonial Office, *Correspondence Relating to the Native Population of Fiji* (no. 11, 1887).

Great Britain, *Parliamentary Debates* (House of Lords), 17 July 1874.

Great Britain, Parliament (Sanderson report) *Report of the the Committee on Emigration from India to the Crown Colonies and Protectorates* (Cd. 5192, June 1910).

Great Britian, *Public (Emigration) Despatch to India* (no. 39, 24 March 1875).

Guidieri, Remo, Francesco Pellizi, and Stanley J. Tambiah (eds), *Ethnicities and Nations: Processes of Interethnic Relations in Latin America, Southeast Asia, and the Pacific* (Austin, University of Texas Press, 1988).

Gunson, Neil, 'The Coming of Foreigners' in Noel Rutherford (ed.), *A History of Tonga* (Melbourne, Oxford University Press, 1977).

Hagan, Stephanie, 'The Party System, the Labour Party and the Plural Society Syndrome in Fiji', *Journal of Commonwealth and Comparative Politics*, vol. 25, no. 2, July 1987.

Hagan, Stephanie, 'Race, Politics and the Coup in Fiji', *Bulletin of Concerned Asian Scholars*, vol. 19, no. 4, October–December 1987.

Hamnett, Ian, *Chieftainship and Legitimacy: An Anthropological Study of Executive Law in Lesotho* (London, Routledge & Kegan Paul, 1975).

Hampsher-Monk, Iain, 'The Historical Study of Democracy' in Graeme Duncan (ed.), *Democratic Theory and Practice* (Cambridge, Cambridge University Press, 1983).

Hanson, Allan, 'The Making of the Maori: Culture Invention and Its Logic', *American Anthropologist*, vol. 91, 1989.

Hanson, Russell L., 'Democracy' in Terence Ball, James Farr, and Russell L. Hanson (eds), *Political Innovation and Conceptual Change* (Cambridge, Cambridge University Press, 1989).

Hau'ofa, Epeli, 'The Pangs of Transition: Kinship and Economy in Tonga', *Australian and New Zealand Journal of Sociology*, vol. 14, no. 2, June 1978.

Hau'ofa, Epeli, 'The New South Pacific Society: Integration and Independence' in Antony Hooper, Steve Britton, Ron Crocombe, Judith Huntsman and Cluny Macpherson (eds), *Class and Culture in the South Pacific* (Auckland and Suva, Centre for Pacific Studies, University of Auckland and Institute of Pacific Studies, University of the South Pacific, 1987).

Hau'ofa, Epeli, 'Thy Kingdom Come: The Democratisation of Aristocratic Tonga' (plenary address delivered to the Conference of the Association for Social Anthropology in Oceania, Kona, Hawaii, 24–28 March 1993).

Hayek, Friedrich A., *Law, Legislation and Liberty: A New Statement of the Liberal Principles of Justice and Political Economy* (vol. 1: *Rules and Order*, Chicago, University of Chicago Press, 1973).

Held, David, *Introduction to Critical Theory: Horkheimer to Habermas* (Berkeley, University of California Press, 1980).

Helu, Futa, 'Those Infernal Constitutions', *Pacific Islands Monthly*, February 1993.

Helu, Futa, 'The People Want Changes', *Pacific Islands Monthly*, March 1993.

Helu, I. F., 'Cultural Survival' (opening address at the University of the South Pacific Cultural Program Week, Suva, 27 April 1991).

Helu, I. F., 'Democracy Bug Bites Tonga' in Ron Crocombe, Uentaba Neemia, Asesela Ravuvu, and Werner Vom Busch (eds), *Culture and Democracy in the South Pacific* (Suva, Institute of Pacific Studies, University of the South Pacific, 1992).

Helu, I. F., 'The Rise of the Critical Spirit' (unpublished paper, Atenisi Institute, Tonga August 1993).

Hempenstall, Peter J., *Pacific Islanders Under German Rule: A Study in the Meaning of Colonial Rule* (Canberra, Australian National University Press, 1978).

Hempenstall, Peter, and Noel Rutherford, *Protest and Dissent in the Colonial Pacific* (Suva, Institute of Pacific Studies, University of the South Pacific, 1984).

Herda, Phyllis S., 'Genealogy in the Tongan Construction of the Past' in Phyllis Herda, Jennifer Terrell and Neil Gunson (eds), *Tongan Culture and History* (Canberra, Department of Pacific and Southeast Asian History, Australian National University, 1990).

Herda, Phyllis, Jennifer Terrell and Neil Gunson (eds), *Tongan Culture and History* (Canberra, Department of Pacific and Southeast Asian History, Australian National University, 1990).

Herr, R. A., 'A Minor Ornament: The Diplomatic Decisions of Western Samoa at Independence', *Australian Outlook*, vol. 29, no. 3, December 1975.

Hills, Rodney C., 'The 1990 Elections in Tonga', *The Contemporary Pacific*, vol. 33, no. 2, Fall 1991.

Hills, Rodney C., *Tonga's Constitution and the Changing State* (Discussion Paper No. 4, Series on Regime Change and Regime Maintenance in Asia and the Pacific, Canberra, Department of Political and Social Change, Australian National University, 1991).

Hobsbawm, Eric, 'Introduction. Inventing Tradition', in Eric Hobsbawm and Terence Ranger (eds), *The Invention of Tradition* (Cambridge, Cambridge University Press, 1983).

Hobsbawm, Eric and Terence Ranger (eds), *The Invention of Tradition* (Cambridge, Cambridge University Press, 1983).

Hoffman, John, 'Capitalist Democracies and Democratic States: Oxymorons or Coherent Concepts?', *Political Studies*, vol. XXXIX, no. 2, June 1991.

Holmes, Lowell D., 'Factors Contributing to the Cultural Stability of Samoa', *Anthropological Quarterly*, vol. 53, no. 3, 1980.

Hooper, Antony, Steve Britton, Ron Crocombe, Judith Huntsman, and Cluny Macpherson (eds), *Class and Culture in the South Pacific* (Auckland and Suva, Centre for Pacific Studies, University of Auckland and Institute of Pacific Studies, University of the South Pacific, 1987).

Hooper, Antony and Judith Huntsman (eds), *Transformations of Polynesian Culture* (Auckland, The Polynesian Society, 1985).

Horigan, Stephen, *Nature and Culture in Western Discourses* (London, Routledge, 1988).

Horowitz, Donald L., *Ethnic Groups in Conflict* (Berkeley, University of California Press, 1985).

Horton, Robin, 'African Traditional Thought and Western Science', *Africa*, vol. 37, no. 1, January 1967.

Howard, Michael C., *Fiji: Race and Politics in an Island State* (Vancouver, University of British Columbia Press, 1991).

Howard, Alan (ed.), *Polynesia: Readings on a Cultural Area* (Scranton, Chandler Publishing, 1971).

Inge, Thomas (ed.), *Naming the Rose: Essays on Eco's The Name of the Rose* (Jackson, University of Mississippi Press, 1988).

Islands Business Pacific, 'It's Democracy Samoan Style', September 1986.

Islands Business Pacific, 'Speaking up for the Royal Way of Rule', December 1992.

James, Kerry, 'Princes and Power: Rank, Title and Leadership in Contemporary Tonga' (paper presented at the Conference of the Association for Social Anthropology in Oceania, Kona, Hawaii, 24–28 March 1993).

Jarvie, I. C., 'Explaining Cargo Cults' in Bryan R. Wilson (ed.), *Rationality* (Oxford, Basil Blackwell, 1970).

Jayawardena, Chandra, 'Culture and Ethnicity in Guyana and Fiji', *Man*, vol. 15, 1980.

Jolly, Margaret, 'Custom and the Way of the Land: Past and Present in Vanuatu and Fiji', *Oceania*, vol. 62, no. 4, June 1992.

Jolly, Margaret, 'Introduction' in Elizabeth Tonkin, Maryon McDonald and Malcolm Chapman (eds), *History and Ethnicity* (London, Routledge, 1989).

Jolly, Margaret, 'Specters of Inauthenticity', *The Contemporary Pacific*, vol. 1, nos 1–2.

Kaeppler, Adrienne L., 'Art, Aesthetics, and Social Structure' in Phyllis Herda, Jennifer Terrell and Neil Gunson (eds), *Tongan Culture and History* (Canberra, Department of Pacific and Southeast Asian History, Australian National University, 1990).

Kapferer, Bruce, 'Nationalist Ideology and a Comparative Anthropology', *Ethnos*, vol. 54, nos, III–IV, 1989.

Kaplan, Martha, '*Luve Ni Wai* as the British Saw It: Constructions of Custom and Disorder in Colonial Fiji', *Ethnohistory*, vol. 36, no. 4, Fall, 1989.

Kariel, Henry S. (ed.), *Frontiers of Democratic Theory* (New York, Random House, 1970).

Kavaliku, S.L., 'Ofa! The Treasure of Tonga', *Pacific Perspective*, vol. 6, no. 2, 1977.

Keesing, Roger M., 'Creating the Past: Custom and Identity in the Contemporary Pacific', *The Contemporary Pacific*, vol. 1, nos. 1 and 2, Spring and Fall, 1989.

Keesing, Roger M., 'Theories of Culture Revisited', *Canberra Anthropology*, vol. 13, no. 2, 1990.

Keesing, Roger M., 'Class, Culture, Custom' (paper presented to workshop on the Global Anthropology of Oceania, University of Lund, Sweden, October 1991)

Keesing, Roger M., and Robert Tonkinson (eds), *Reinventing Traditional Culture: The Politics of Kastom in Island Melanesia, Mankind*, vol. 13, no. 4, August 1982.

Keith-Reid, Robert, 'So Why Can't Pacific Islanders Face up to Criticism Too?', *Islands Business*, January 1991.

Keith-Reid, Robert, 'Island Overture: Rabuka Offers an Olive Branch to Ethnic Indians', *Far Eastern Economic Review*, 17 March 1994.

Kellner, Hans, '"To Make Truth Laugh": Eco's The Name of the Rose' in Thomas Inge (ed.), *Naming the Rose: Essays on Eco's The Name of the Rose* (Jackson, University of Mississippi Press, 1988).

King, F. P. (ed.), *Oceania and Beyond: Essays on the Pacific Since 1945* (Westport, Greenwood Press, 1976).

Kirch, Patrick V., 'A Brief History of Lapita Archaeology' in Patrick V. Kirch and Terry L. Hunt (eds), *Archaeology of the Lapita Cultural Complex: A Critical Review* (Washington State Museum Research Report No. 5, Seattle, Thomas Burke, 1988).

Kohn, Hans, *Nationalism: Its Meaning and History* (rev. edn, Malabar, Robert E. Krieger, 1982).

Kolo, F. O., 'Historiography: The Myth of Indigenous Authenticity' in Phyllis Herda, Jennifer Terrell and Neil Gunson (eds), *Tongan Culture and History* (Canberra, Department of Pacific and Southeast Asian History, Australian National University, 1990).

Koloamatangi, Malakai, 'The Balance of Power within the Tongan Political Structure: Who Has What Power in Tongan Politics' (paper presented to the Pacific Islands Political Studies Association Conference, Monash University, Melbourne, December 1991).

Krygier, Martin, 'Law as Tradition', *Law and Philosophy*, vol. 5, 1986.

Lal, Brij V., *Power and Prejudice: The Making of the Fiji Crisis* (Wellington, New Zealand Institute of International Affairs, 1988).

Lal, Brij V., *Broken Waves: A History of the Fiji Islands in the Twentieth Century* (Honolulu, University of Hawaii Press, 1992).

Lal, Brij V. (ed.), *Politics in Fiji* (North Sydney, Allen & Unwin, 1986).

Larmour, Peter, '"A Foreign Flower?" Democracy in the South Pacific', *Pacific Studies*, vol. 17, no. 1, March 1994.

Latukefu, Sione, 'Tonga after Queen Salote', *Journal of Pacific History*, vol. 2, 1967.

Latukefu, Sione, *Church and State in Tonga* (Canberra, Australian National University Press, 1974).

Latukefu, Sione, *The Tongan Constitution: A Brief History to Celebrate its Centenary* (Nuku'alofa, Tongan Traditions Committee, 1975).

Latukefu, Sione, 'The Wesleyan Mission' in Noel Rutherford (ed.), *A History of Tonga* (Melbourne, Oxford University Press, 1977).

Lawson, Stephanie, 'The Myth of Cultural Homogeneity and its Implications for Chiefly Power and Politics in Fiji', *Comparative Studies in Society and History*, vol. 32, no. 4, October 1990.

Lawson, Stephanie, 'The Authentic State: History and Tradition in the Ideology of Ethnonationalism' (paper presented at the conference on 'The State in Transition', La Trobe University, Melbourne, 6–8 August 1993).

Lawson, Stephanie, 'Conceptual Issues in the Comparative Study of Regime Change and Democratization', *Comparative Politics*, vol. 25, no. 2, January 1993.

Lawson, Stephanie, *Ethnic Politics and the State in Fiji* (Working Paper No. 135, Canberra, Peace Research Centre, Australian National University, 1993).

Lawson, Stephanie, *The Failure of Democratic Politics in Fiji* (Oxford, Clarendon Press, 1991).

Lawson, Stephanie, 'Institutionalizing Peaceful Conflict: Political Opposition and the Challenge of Democratisation in Asia', *Australian Journal of International Affairs*, vol. 47, no. 1, May 1993.

Lawson, Stephanie, 'The Tyranny of Tradition: Chiefs and Politics in Contemporary Fiji' (paper presented at a symposium on 'Chiefs Today', Association for Social Anthropology in Oceania, Kona, Hawaii, 24–28 March 1993).

Lawson, Stephanie, 'Malaysian-Australian Relations: Much Ado About Recalcitrance', *Pacific Research*, vol. 7, no. 1, February 1994.

Leach, Edmund, 'Concluding Remarks' in Antony Hooper and Judith Huntsman (eds), *Transformations of Polynesian Culture* (Auckland, The Polynesian Society, 1985).

Lealofi, Tupua Tamasese IV, *Western Samoa Faces the Modern World* (Wellington, New Zealand Institute of International Affairs, 1970).

Ledyard, Patricia, *The Tongan Past* (Vava'u, Government Printing Office, 1982).

Lijphart, Arend, *The Politics of Accommodation* (Berkeley, University of California Press, 1968).

Linnekin, Jocelyn, 'On the Theory and Politics of Cultural Construction in the Pacific', *Oceania*, vol. 62, no. 4, June 1992.

Macpherson, Cluny, 'The Continuity of Chiefly Authority in Western Samoa: Some Thoughts on its Persistence' (paper presented to the Pacific Islands Political Studies Association, Rarotonga, Cook Islands, December 1993).

Macpherson, Cluny and La'avasa Macpherson, 'Towards an Explanation of Recent Trends in Suicide in Western Samoa', *Man*, vol. 22, no. 2, June 1987.

Maddox, Graham, 'Constitution' in Terence Ball, James Farr and Russell L. Hanson (eds), *Political Innovation and Conceptual Change* (Cambridge, Cambridge University Press, 1989).

Mahina, Okusitino, 'The Tongan Traditional History Tala-E-Fonua: A Vernacular Ecology-Centred Historico-Cultural Concept' (PhD thesis, Canberra, Australian National University, 1992).

Ma'ia'i, Ata, 'Western Samoa's General Election 1973', *Journal of Pacific History*, vol. 9, 1974.

Malifa, Tasi, 'The Franchise in the Constitution of Western Samoa: Towards a Theory of the Constitution Incomplete' (LL.M. Thesis, Harvard Law School, 1988).

Malifa, Fata Sano, 'Why Tofilau Won, Tupua Lost', *Islands Business Pacific*, April 1991.

Marable, Manning, *African and Caribbean Politics: From Kwame Nkrumah to the Grenada Revolution* (London, Verso, 1987).

Marcus, George E., 'Contemporary Tonga: The Background of Social and Cultural Change' in Noel Rutherford (ed.), *A History of Tonga* (Melbourne, Oxford University Press, 1977).

Marcus, George E., *The Nobility and the Chiefly Tradition in the Modern Kingdom of Tonga* (Wellington, The Polynesian Society, 1980).

Marcus, George, 'Chieftainship' in A. Howard and R. Borofsky (eds), *Developments in Polynesian Ethnography* (Honolulu, University of Hawaii Press, 1989).

Mason, A., 'On Explaining Political Disagreement: The Notion of an Essentially Contested Concept', *Inquiry*, vol. 33, 1990.

Mataitoga, Isikeli, 'Westminster Style Democracy and Cultural Diversity: A Critique of the Fijian Experience' in Ron Crocombe, Uentaba Neemia, Asesela Ravuvu, and Werner Vom Busch (eds), *Culture and Democracy in the South Pacific* (Suva, Institute of Pacific Studies, University of the South Pacific, 1992).

Matangi Tonga, 'Hereditary Titles Unfortunate', vol. 7, no. 5, Sept.–Nov. 1992.

Matangi Tonga, 'Kava Better than War, Warns Minister', vol. 8, no. 1, March–April 1993.

Matangi Tonga, 'Tongan Briefs', vol. 7, no. 5, Sept.- Nov. 1992.

Mayer, A. C., *Peasants in the Pacific: A Study of Fiji Indian Rural Society* (London, Routledge & Kegan Paul, 1961).

McDonald, A. H. (ed.), *Trusteeship in the Pacific* (Sydney, Angus & Robertson, 1949).

McDonald, Graham, and Philip Pettit, *Semantics and Social Science* (London, Routledge & Kegan Paul, 1981).

Mead, Margaret, *Coming of Age in Western Samoa: A Psychological Study of Primitive Youth for Western Civilization* (New York, Mentor Books, [1928] 1949).

Mead, Margaret, 'The Role of the Individual in Samoan Culture' in Alan Howard (ed.), *Polynesia: Readings on a Cultural Area* (Scranton, Chandler Publishing, 1971).

Meleisea, Malama, *The Making of Modern Samoa: Traditional Authority and Colonial Administration in the Modern History of Western Samoa* (Suva, Institute of Pacific Studies, University of the South Pacific, 1987).

Meleisea, Malama, *Change and Adaptations in Western Samoa* (Christchurch, Macmillan Brown Centre for Pacific Studies, 1988).

Meleisea, Malama and Penelope Schoeffel, 'Western Samoa: "Like a Slippery Fish"', in Ron Crocombe and Ahmed Ali (eds), *Politics in Polynesia* (Suva, Institute of Pacific Studies, University of the South Pacific, 1983).

Melman, Billie, 'Claiming the Nation's Past: The Invention of an Anglo-Saxon Tradition', *Journal of Contemporary History*, vol. 26, nos 3 and 4, September 1991.

Montagu, Ashley, *Man's Most Dangerous Myth: The Fallacy of Race* (4th edn, Cleveland, World Publishing Company, 1964).

Moorehead, Alan, *The Fatal Impact: The Invasion of the Pacific 1767–1840* (rev. edn, Sydney, Mead and Beckett, 1987).

Morrell, W. P., *Britain in the Pacific Islands* (Oxford, Clarendon Press, 1960).

Morton, Bill, 'Spreading the Word', *Pacific Islands Monthly*, February 1993.

Morton, Bill, 'A Question of Time', *Pacific Islands Monthly*, March 1993.

Morton, Bill, 'Behind the Elections', *Pacific Islands Monthly*, March 1993.

Mulgan, Richard, 'Peoples of the South Pacific and Their Rights' in Ramesh Thakur (ed.), *The South Pacific: Problems, Issues and Prospects* (Houndmills, Macmillan, 1991).

Nagata Judith A. (ed.), *Pluralism in Malaysia; Myth and Reality* (Leiden, E.J. Brill, 1975).

Nakata, Katherine T., 'The Costs of Fa'a Samoa Political Culture's Complementarity with the Modern World System' in *Evolving Political Cultures in the Pacific Islands* (Proceedings of the 1982 Politics Conference, Laie, Institute of Polynesian Studies, Brigham Young University – Hawaii Campus, 1982).

Narokobi, Bernard, *The Melanesian Way* (rev. edn, Boroko and Suva, Institute of Papua New Guinea Studies and Institute of Pacific Studies, 1983).

Nathan, Andrew J., 'The Place of Values in Cross-Cultural Studies. The Example of Democracy and China' in Paul A. Cohen and Merle Goldman (eds), *Ideas Across Cultures: Essays on Chinese Thought in Honor of Benjamin I. Schwartz* (Cambridge (Mass.), Council on East Asian Studies and Harvard University Press, 1990).

Nayacakalou, R. R., 'Land Tenure and Social Organisation in Western Samoa', *Journal of the Polynesian Society*, vol. 69, no. 2, 1960.

Nayacakalou, R. R., *Leadership in Fiji* (Melbourne, Oxford University Press, 1975).

Neemia, Uentabo, 'Decolonization and Democracy in the South Pacific' in Ron Crocombe, Uentaba Neemia, Asesela Ravuvu, and Werner Vom Busch (eds), *Culture and Democracy in the South Pacific* (Suva, Institute of Pacific Studies, University of the South Pacific, 1992).

New Zealand, Department of Island Territories, *Report by the New Zealand Government to the General Assembly of the United Nations on the Administration of Western Samoa for the Calendar Year 1960* (Wellington, 1961).

Ngan-Woo, Feleti E., *Fa'a Samoa: The World of the Samoans* (Wellington, Office of the Race Relations Conciliator, 1985).

Nicholls, David, *Three Varieties of Pluralism* (London, Macmillan, 1974).

Nisbet, Robert, *Conservatism* (Milton Keynes, Open University Press, 1986).

Niu, Laki M., 'The Constitution and Traditional Political System in Tonga' in Yash Ghai (ed.), *Law, Politics and Government in the Pacific Island States* (Suva, Institute of Pacific Studies, University of the South Pacific, 1988).

Nordlinger, Eric A., *Soldiers in Politics: Military Coups and Governments* (Englewood Cliffs, Prentice-Hall, 1977).

Norton, Robert, 'Titles, Wealth and Faction: Electoral Politics in a Samoan Village', *Oceania*, vol. 55, no. 1, September 1984.

Norton, Robert, 'Ethnic Divisions and Elite Conciliation' in Brij Lal (ed.), *Politics in Fiji* (North Sydney, Allen & Unwin, 1986).

Norton, Robert, 'Chiefs, Adolescent Suicide and the Transformation of Chiefly Authority in Western Samoa', *Man*, vol. 23, 1988.

Norton, Robert, *Race and Politics in Fiji* (2nd edn, St Lucia, University of Queensland Press, 1990).

Ntumy, Michael A., 'Introduction' in Michael A. Ntumy (ed.), *South Pacific Islands Legal Systems* (Honolulu, University of Hawaii Press, 1993).

Ntumy, Michael A. (ed.), *South Pacific Islands Legal Systems* (Honolulu, University of Hawaii Press, 1993).

Nursey-Bray, Paul, 'Consensus and Community: African One-Party Democracy' in Graeme Duncan (ed.), *Democratic Theory and Practice* (Cambridge, Cambridge University Press, 1983).

'Nyong'o, Peter Anyang, 'Democratization Processes in Africa', *Review of African Political Economy*, no. 54, July 1992.

O'Meara, J. Tim, '"Individualism" in a "Communal" Society: A Social Impact Analysis of Fa'amatai Authority in Samoa' (seminar presentation, Research School of Pacific Studies, Australian National University, Canberra, October 1993).

O'Meara, J. Tim, 'From Corporate to Individual Land Tenure' in R. G. Ward and E. Kingdon (eds), *Land, Custom and Practice in the South Pacific* (Cambridge, Cambridge University Press, 1995) pp. 109–156.

Oakeshott, Michael, *Rationalism in Politics* (London, Methuen, 1962).

Ober, Josiah, *Mass and Elite in Democratic Athens: Rhetoric, Ideology, and the Power of the People* (Princeton, Princeton University Press, 1989).

Orwell, George, 'Politics and the English language', in *Inside the Whale and Other Essays* (London, Penguin, 1957).

Orwell, George, 'Notes on Nationalism' in *Decline of the English Murder and Other Essays* (Harmondsworth, Penguin, 1965).

Pacific Islands Monthly, 'The Quiet Crusader', May 1991.

Pacific Islands Monthly, 'Time to Watch the Manioke Grow', October 1991.

Pacific Islands Monthly, 'Election of Representatives', January 1993.

Pelikan, Jaroslav, *The Vindication of Tradition* (New Haven, Yale University Press, 1948).

Pitt, David, *Tradition and Economic Progress in Samoa: A Case Study of Traditional Social Institutions in Economic Development* (Oxford, Clarendon Press, 1970).

Plotnicov L. and A. Tuden (eds), *Essays in Comparative Social Stratification* (Pittsburgh, University of Pittsburgh Press, 1970).

Plumb, J. H., *The Death of the Past* (London, Macmillan, 1969).

Pocock, J. G. A., *The Machiavellian Moment: Florentine Political Thought and the Atlantic Republican Tradition* (Princeton, Princeton University Press, 1975).

Pohiva, Akilisi, 'Monarchy Versus Democracy' (paper read to a meeting of the Australian Institute of International Affairs, Canberra, 20 October 1993).

Popper, Karl R., *Conjectures and Refutations; The Growth of Scientific Knowledge* (4th edn, London, Routledge & Kegan Paul, 1972).

Poulsen, Jens, 'Archaeology and Prehistory' in Noel Rutherford (ed.), *A History of Tonga* (Melbourne, Oxford University Press, 1977).

Poumau, Tialetagi, 'Reclaiming our Cultural Memory' in David Robie (ed.), *Tu Galala: Social Change in the Pacific* (Wellington and Annandale, Bridget Williams Books and Pluto Press, 1992).

Powles, [Charles] Guy, 'The Persistence of Chiefly Power and Its Implications for Law and Political Organization in Western Polynesia' (PhD thesis, Australian National University, Canberra, 1979).

Powles, G., 'Law and Authority: Pacific Island Decision Making', *Pacific Perspective*, vol. 9, no. 2, 1980.

Powles, G., 'Traditional Institutions in Pacific Constitutional Systems: Better Late or Never?' in Peter Sack (ed.), *Pacific Constitutions* (Canberra, Research School of Social Sciences, Australian National University, 1983).

Powles, Guy, 'Legal Systems and Political Cultures: Competition for Political Dominance in Western Samoa' in Peter Sack and Elizabeth Minchin (eds), *Legal Pluralism: Proceedings of the Canberra Law Workshop VII*, (Law Department, Research School of Social Sciences, Australian National University, Canberra, 1986).

Powles, Guy, 'The Common Law as a Source of Law in the South Pacific: Experiences in Western Polynesia', *University of Hawaii Law Review*, vol. 10, no. 105, 1988.

Powles, Guy, 'The Early Accommodation of Traditional and English Law in Tonga' in Phyllis Herda, Jennifer Terrell and Neil Gunson (eds), *Tongan Culture and History* (Canberra, Department of Pacific and Southeast Asian History, Australian National University, 1990).

Powles, Guy, 'The Tongan Constitution: Some Realities' (paper prepared for the Convention on the Tongan Constitution and Democracy, Nuku'alofa, November 1992).

Powles, [C.] Guy, 'Tonga' in Michael A. Ntumy (ed.), *South Pacific Islands Legal Systems* (Honolulu, University of Hawaii Press, 1993).

Powles, [C.] Guy, 'Western Samoa' in Michael A. Ntumy (ed.), *South Pacific Islands Legal Systems* (Honolulu, University of Hawaii Press, 1993).

Quentin-Baxter, Alison, 'The Independence of Western Samoa – Some Conceptual Issues', *Victoria University of Wellington Law Review*, vol. 17, no. 4, September 1987.

Radio New Zealand, Transcript of Interview with Major-General Rabuka, 21 May 1989.

Ravuvu, Asesela, *Vaka i Taukei: The Fijian Way of Life* (Suva, Institute of Pacific Studies, University of the South Pacific, 1983).

Ravuvu, Asesela D., *The Fijian Ethos* (Suva, Institute of Pacific Studies, University of the South Pacific, 1987).

Ravuvu, Asesela, *The Facade of Democracy: Fijian Struggles for Political Control 1830–1987* (Suva, Reader Publishing House, 1991).

Ravuvu, Asesela, 'Culture and Traditions: Implications for Modern Nation Building' in Ron Crocombe, Uentaba Neemia, Asesela Ravuvu, and Werner Vom Busch (eds), *Culture and Democracy in the South Pacific* (Suva, Institute of Pacific Studies, University of the South Pacific, 1992).

Rengger, N. J., 'No Time Like the Present? Postmodernism and Political Theory', *Political Studies,* vol. XL, no. 3, September 1992.

Republic of Fiji, *Report of the Fiji Constitution Inquiry and Advisory Committee* (August 1989).

Republic of Fiji, *Constitution of the Sovereign Democratic Republic of Fiji* (1990).

Robertson, R. T., 'The Formation of the Fiji Labour Party', *New Zealand Monthly Review,* October 1985.

Robertson, R. T. and Akosita Tamanisau, *Fiji: Shattered Coups* (Leichhardt, Pluto Press, 1988).

Robertson, Robert T. with Akosita Tamanisau, 'Pacific Overview: Not So New World Order' in David Robie (ed.), *Tu Galala: Social Change in the Pacific* (Wellington and Annandale, Bridget Williams Books and Pluto Press, 1992).

Robie, David (ed.), *Tu Galala: Social Change in the Pacific* (Wellington and Annandale, Bridget Williams Books and Pluto Press, 1992).

Robie, David, 'Eti Landslides Home', *Islands Business,* March 1985.

Robillard, Albert B. (ed.), *Social Change in the Pacific Islands* (London, Kegan Paul International, 1992).

Robinson, Martin, 'Women on the March', *Islands Business,* February 1991.

Ross, Angus (ed.), *New Zealand's Record in the Pacific Islands* (Auckland and London, Longman Paul and C. Hurst, 1969).

Routledge, David, *Matanitu: The Struggle for Power in Early Fiji* (Suva, Institute of Pacific Studies, University of the South Pacific, 1985).

Rutherford, Noel (ed.), *A History of Tonga* (Melbourne, Oxford University Press, 1977).

Sabine, George H., *A History of Political Thought* (London, George G. Harrap & Co., 1948).

Sahlins, Marshall, 'Poor Man, Rich Man, Big Man, Chief: Political Types in Melanesia and Polynesia', *Comparative Studies in Society and History,* vol. 5, no. 3, 1963.

Said, Edward, *Orientalism* (New York, Vintage 1978).

Said, Edward, *Culture and Imperialism* (London, Vintage, 1993).

Sanderson Report, *see* Great Britain, Parliament.

Sartori, Giovanni, *The Theory of Democracy Revisited* (Chatham (NJ), Chatham House, 1987).

Savali, 'Registrar of Land and Titles Court Reports on Problems in that Department', 31 July 1989.

Sayes, Shelley Ann, 'Changing Paths of the Land: Early Political Hierarchies in Cakaudrove, Fiji', *Journal of Pacific History,* vol. 19, no. 1, 1984.

Scarr, Deryck, *Fiji: The Politics of Illusion: The Military Coups in Fiji* (Kensington, University of New South Wales Press, 1988).

Schoeffel, Penelope, 'Rank, Gender and Politics in Ancient Samoa: The

Genealogy of Salamasina O Le Tafa'ifa', *Journal of Pacific History*, vol. 22, no. 4, October 1987.

Senituli, Lopeti, 'Tonga: The Pro-Democracy Convention and its Aftermath', *Tok Blong SPPF*, no. 42, February 1993.

Shils, Edward, *Tradition* (London, Faber & Faber, 1981).

Siikala, Jukka (ed.), *Culture and History in the Pacific* (Helsinki, Transactions of the Finnish Anthropological Society, no. 27, 1990).

Sinclair, T. A., *A History of Greek Political Thought* (London, Routledge & Kegan Paul, 1951).

Skinner, Quentin, 'Language and Political Change' in Terence Ball, James Farr and Russell L. Hanson (eds), *Political Innovation and Conceptual Change* (Cambridge, Cambridge University Press, 1989).

Smith, M. G., *Culture, Race and Class in the Commonwealth Caribbean* (Mona, University of the West Indies, 1984).

Smolicz, J. J., 'Tradition, Core Values and Intercultural Development in Plural Societies', *Ethnic and Racial Studies*, vol. 11, no. 4, November 1988.

Sokomanu, Ati George, 'Government in Vanuatu: The Place of Culture and Tradition' in Ron Crocombe, Uentaba Neemia, Asesela Ravuvu, and Werner Vom Busch (eds), *Culture and Democracy in the South Pacific* (Suva, Institute of Pacific Studies, University of the South Pacific, 1992).

So'o, Asofou, 'Modern Political Parties and Leadership in Western Samoa' (paper presented to the IXth Pacific History Conference, Macmillan Brown Centre for Pacific Studies, University of Canterbury, Christchurch, New Zealand, 2–5 December 1992).

So'o, Asofou, *Universal Suffrage in Western Samoa: The 1991 General Elections* (Canberra, Department of Political and Social Change, Australian National University, Discussion Paper no. 10, Series on Regime Change and Regime Maintenance in Asia and the Pacific, 1993).

Sources of Tongan History: A Collection of Documents, Extracts and Contemporary Opinions in Tongan Political History 1616–1900 compiled by H. G. Cummins (private publication, 1972).

Soqosoqo ni Vakavulewa ni Taukei, *Constitution/Manifesto* (circa. 1990).

Spate, O. H. K., (The Spate Report) *The Fijian People: Economic Problems and Prospects* (published as *CP* 13/1959, Legislative Council of Fiji).

Spence, Donald P., 'Saying Goodbye to Historical Truth', *Philosophy of the Social Sciences*, vol. 21, no. 2, June 1992.

Stevenson, Robert Louis, *A Footnote to History: Eight Years of Trouble in Samoa* (London, Cassell & Company, 1892).

Survey of British and Commonwealth Affairs, vol. 4. no. 14, July 1970.

Tagaloa, Aiono Fanaafi Le, 'The Samoan Culture and Government' in Ron Crocombe, Uentaba Neemia, Asesela Ravuvu, and Werner Vom Busch (eds), *Culture and Democracy in the South Pacific* (Suva, Institute of Pacific Studies, University of the South Pacific, 1992).

Taulahi, Amanaki, *His Majesty King Taufa'ahau Tupou IV of the Kingdom of Tonga: A Biography* (Suva, Institute of Pacific Studies, University of the South Pacific, 1979).

Thakur, Ramesh (ed.), *The South Pacific: Problems, Issues and Prospects* (Houndmills, Macmillan, 1991).

Thomas, Nicholas, 'The Force of Ethnology: Origins and Significance of the Melanesia/Polynesia Division', *Current Anthropology*, vol. 30, no. 1, 1989.

Thomas, Nicholas, 'Regional Politics, Ethnicity, and Custom in Fiji', *The Contemporary Pacific*, vol. 2, no.1, Spring 1990.

Thomas, Nicholas, *Entangled Objects. Exchange, Material Culture, and Colonialism in the Pacific* (Cambridge (Mass.), Harvard University Press, 1991).

Tiffany, Martin, 'Tonga's Call for Democracy', *Pacific Islands Monthly*, January 1993.

Tiffany, Sharon W., 'The Land and Titles Court and the Regulation of Customary Titles Successions and Removals in Western Samoa', *Journal of the Polynesian Society*, vol. 83, no. 1, March 1974.

Todd, A., *Parliamentary Government in the Colonies* (2nd edn, London, Longman, Green & Co., 1894).

Tonkin, Elizabeth, Maryon McDonald and Malcolm Chapman (eds), *History and Ethnicity* (London, Routledge, 1989).

Tora, Iva, 'So, Who Really is a Fijian?', *Islands Business Pacific*, February 1992.

Toren, Christina, 'Making the Present, Revealing the Past: The Mutability and Continuity of Tradition as Process', *Man*, vol. 23, 1988.

Tuimaleali'ifano, Morgan, *Samoans in Fiji: Migration, Identity and Communication* (Suva, Institute of Pacific Studies, University of the South Pacific, 1990).

Turner, George, *Samoa: A Hundred Years Ago and Long Before* (Suva, Institute of Pacific Studies, University of the South Pacific, [1884] 1984).

Twelve Member Committee of the Western Confederacy (Fiji), *Submission on the 1988 Draft Constitution* (16 May 1988).

Ullmann, Walter, *Medieval Political Thought* (Harmondsworth, Peregrine, 1975).

Va'a, Felise, 'Western Samoa: A New Zealand Experiment' in F.P. King (ed.), *Oceania and Beyond: Essays on the Pacific Since 1945* (Westport, Greenwood Press, 1976).

Va'a, Leulu F., 'The Emergence and Significance of New Political Parties in Western Samoa' (unpublished paper, December 1989).

van Fossen, Anthony, 'Two Military Coups in Fiji', *Bulletin of Concerned Asian Scholars*, vol. 19, no. 4, October-December 1987.

Velia, Mosese, 'SVT, Feds Taste Election Defeat', *Fiji Times*, 1 June 1992.

Walzer, Michael, *The Revolution of the Saints: A Study in the Origins of Radical Politics* (New York, Atheneum, 1974).

Ward, Alan, 'The Crisis of our Times: Ethnic Resurgence and the Liberal Ideal', *Journal of Pacific History*, vol. 27, no. 1, June 1992.

Ward, R. Gerard, 'Native Fijian Villages: A Questionable Future?' in Michael Taylor (ed.), *Fiji: Future Imperfect* (North Sydney, Allen & Unwin, 1987).

Ward, R. Gerard, 'Land, Law and Custom: Diverging Realities in Fiji' in R. Gerard Ward and Elizabeth Kingdon (eds), *Land, Custom and Practice in the South Pacific* (Cambridge, Cambridge University Press, 1995).

Ward, R. Gerard and Elizabeth Kingdon (eds), *Land, Custom and Practice in the South Pacific* (Cambridge, Cambridge University Press, 1995).

Weber, Max, 'The Social Psychology of the World Religions' in H.H. Gerth and C. Wright Mills (eds), *From Max Weber: Essays in Sociology* (London, Routledge & Kegan Paul, 1948).

Weisbrot, David, 'Custom, Pluralism, and Realism in Vanuatu: Legal Development and the Role of Customary Law', *Pacific Studies*, vol. 13, no. 1, November 1989.

West, F. J., *Political Advancement in the South Pacific: A Comparative Study of Colonial Practice in Fiji, Tahiti and American Samoa* (Melbourne, Oxford University Press, 1961).

Western Samoa Legislative Council, *Constitutional Convention 1954* (*Papers and Proceedings*, vol. 2, 1955).

Western Samoa, Legislative Assembly, *Report of the Committee Appointed by Cabinet to Consider the Report of the 1975 Committee on Matai Titles, Customary Lands and the Samoan Land and Titles Court* (Parliamentary Paper no. 12, 1979).

Western Samoa, *Constitution of the Independent State of Western Samoa.*

Western Samoa, Legislative Assembly, *Report of the Department of the Land and Titles Court for 1983 and 1984.*

Western Samoa, Legislative Assembly, *Tupua Tamasese Report* (1976).

Western Samoa, *Statement to be Presented to the Trusteeship Council by the Samoan Members of the New Zealand Delegation* (July 1958).

Williksen-Bakker, S., 'Vanua–A Symbol with Many Ramifications in Fijian Culture', *Ethnos*, vol. 55, nos 3–4, 1990.

Williams, Raymond, *Keywords: A Vocabulary of Culture and Society* (London, Fontana, 1976).

Williamson, Robert W., *The Social and Political Systems of Central Polynesia* (Oosterhout, Anthropological Publications [1924] 1967), vol. 1.

Wilson, H.T., *Tradition and Innovation: The Idea of Civilization as Culture and its Significance* (London, Routledge & Kegan Paul, 1984).

Wood, A. H. and Elizabeth Wood Ellem, 'Queen Salote Tupou III' in Noel Rutherford (ed.), *A History of Tonga* (Melbourne, Oxford University Press, 1977).

Wylie, C. (ed.), *The Law of Tonga* (rev. edn, vol. I, Tonga, Government Printer, 1967).

Index

Afeaki, Viliami 107
Africa 2, 4, 15, 28
  tradition 1, 12, 21, 46
Akau'ola, Father Selwyn 104
All Nationals Congress (ANC) (Fiji) 68
Alliance Party (Fiji) 43, 48, 50, 56, 60, 62, 72
  1987 elections 59–60, 63, 66, 67
  1992 elections 71
  chiefs 59, 60, 61, 63
  indigenous Fijians 57
  land and 58
anthropology, ethnography 2, 14, 16, 23, 25
Apolima 117, 127
aristocracy 5, 31 *see also* chiefs; elites; *matai*; nobility
Asia Pacific Economic Cooperation (APEC) 163
Asia 12, 15
Atenisi Institute 100, 101
Australia 42, 44, 51 163
authenticity *see* tradition
authoritarianism 7, 44
authority
  government 18
  tradition 13, 15, 17, 20

Babadzan, Alain 15
Baker, Reverend Shirley 95
Bau 45, 46
Bavadra government 40, 56
Bavadra, Dr Timoci and Adi Kuini 39, 62
Bayne, Peter J. 145–146
Biersack, Aletta 85
Bose Levu Vakaturaga (BLV) 67, 69 *see also* Great Council of Chiefs
Boyd, Mary 136
Bua 68, 71
Burke, Edmund 16, 19, 20, 26

Burling, Robbins 23
Butadroka, Sakeasi 73

Cakaudrove 45, 55, 71, 73
Cakobau, Ratu Seru 45
Cakobau, Ratu Sir George 38
Campbell, Ian 83, 100
capitalism 29
Carens, Joseph 50, 51
Caribbean 2
Carrier, James 3, 14, 25
Césaire, Aimé 2
chauvinism *see* ethnocentrism
chiefs 4, 5, 19, 161, 170, 172, 173
  Fijian 5, 8, 44, 46, 50, 61, 62, 67, 68–69 74, 161
    elections, 63, 72, 73
    Fijian Nationalist Party and, 69
    function/nature of 47, 48, 53-57
    land 48, 49, 51
    see also Great Council of Chiefs
  Tongan 84, 90, 97, 103, 113, 114, 170
    Christianity, 88, 90
    control 83, 85
    customs 82
    divine right of 86–87, 89, 105
    power 80, 85, 91–94, 97, 161
    see also nobility
  Western Samoan *see matai*
Chinese indentured labourers 134
Christian Democratic Party (CDP) (Western Samoa) 148
Christianity
  Fiji 44, 46, 54, 55, 64, 130
  South Pacific 44, 160, 170, 171
  Tonga 44, 82, 84, 87, 88–90, 91, 95, 104–105, 106–107, 109
  Western Samoa 120, 128–129, 130, 131, 132–133, 140

Clausewitz, Karl von 111
colonialism 1, 4, 21, 168
  Fiji 44-48, 168
  Tonga 8
  see also democracy
Colson, Elizabeth 21
communalism 76
conservatism 7, 17, 21, 136, 166
Constitution Inquiry and Advisory
    Committee (CIAC) (Fiji) 64, 67, 69
Constitutional Review Committee (CRC)
    (Fiji) 64
constitutionalism 27, 167
Cook, Captain James 88
Cook Islands 131
criticism, role of 6–7, 34, 100, 163
Crocombe, Ron 2
culture see identity; relativism; tradition
Cummins, H. G. 84
custom
  Fijian 41, 45, 52, 62, 66
  Tongan 82, 96, 97, 103, 110
  Western Samoan 124, 134, 136, 144, 151,
      153, 156
    matai system 138–145
    suffrage 137, 138, 141, 143, 145, 149
  see also kastom; tradition
customary law see law, customary

Davidson, J. W. 111, 119, 131, 136, 137, 145
democracy 8, 11, 13, 20, 24, 26, 27, 29,
    108
  colonialism 28, 167
  concepts of 26–33, 167–172
  elites 4–5, 167, 169, 171, 172
  Fiji 6, 44, 66, 67, 69, 75, 163, 169, 171
  South Pacific 4, 29, 162, 166, 171
  as indigenous 27, 165, 168–169
  Tonga 81, 90, 104–6, 108, 112, 113, 168,
      169, 170
    Christianity and 90
  Western Samoa 119, 138, 141, 148, 150,
      164, 168
democratization 6, 7, 9, 11, 29, 167
  Tonga 6, 101, 108, 113
  Western Samoa 6, 9, 118, 148, 149, 152,
      157, 158
development 2, 5, 24
  Fiji 37, 47, 51
  Tonga 90, 98, 100, 108
divine right, authority see chiefs; monarchy
Durutalo, Simione 171

education 12, 108, 165
  Eisenstadt S.N., 21
  in South Pacific 7, 12, 75, 100, 153

elections
  Fijian 67, 69
    1982 61
    1987 50, 57, 62–64, 67
    1992 70-72
    1994 73-74
  Tongan 80, 100, 101, 102, 103–104 107,
      108, 109–112
  Western Samoan 142, 143, 147–148,
      149–150, 157
    matai-only suffrage 135–137, 139, 141,
      142, 149, 153, 155, 165
elites 4–5, 7, 12, 161, 163–166
  Fijian 41, 43, 53, 56, 169
  Tongan 80, 92, 102, 110, 114, 171
  Westernization 108, 113
  see also democracy; tradition
Emancipation Edict of 1862 (Tonga) 91,
    99
Enlightenment 16, 20
essentialism 2, 172
ethnicity 40, 50, 57
ethnocentrism, eurocentrism, 23, 32, 33,
    35, 162
Europe 17, 18, 19, 27, 28
  expectations/perceptions 124, 125,
      126
  Fiji 44, 45, 51, 57–58, 59
  South Pacific 160
  Tonga 88–90, 94, 120
  Western Samoa 120, 122, 127, 130–138,
      146, 158
Evans, Gareth 164
explorers 82, 120

fa'amatai 119, 122–124, 131, 138, 150, 165
  sociopolitical value system, 151–155,
      157–158
fa'aSamoa 20, 117, 119, 122, 124, 129, 138,
    144
  sociopolitical value system 118, 138, 147,
      149, 151–155, 157–158
Faumuina 135
Ferdon, Edwin N. 90
feudalism 124
Fiji
  colonial rule 28, 38, 44–48, 161
  constitutions
    1970 40, 41, 53, 57–60, 75
    1990 20, 39, 40, 41, 43, 53, 55, 64–70,
        75, 163, 168
  coups 39, 40, 41, 43, 44, 53, 56, 63, 72,
      75, 164, 167, 168
  description 37–42, 51
  eastern provinces 46, 48, 54, 56, 59
    chiefs 38, 45, 66, 67, 171
    elections 71, 73

Fiji, cont.
  'Fijianness' 50, 66
  land and indigenous paramountcy
    48–53
  paramountcy doctrine of 52, 53, 57, 75
  party politics 59–64, 70–74
  plural society 8, 42–44, 56
  religion 64, 105, 128
  sociopolitical structures 53–57
  Tonga and 44, 66, 83
  see also chiefs: Fijian; Christianity;
    custom; democracy; elite; land; plural
    society; self-determination; tradition
Fiji Indians 11, 50, 52–53, 56, 63, 75, 163
  1987 coup 64
  1990 constitution 41, 65–67, 69
  elections 71, 74
  identity 50
  indigenous Fijian rights 39
  land 51
  Legislative Council 57, 58–59
  see also plural society; self-determination
Fiji Labour Party 59–60, 62, 64, 68, 69
  1990 constitution 41
  Alliance Party corruption 63
  communal interests 58
  elections 50, 70, 71, 72, 74
  formation of 61
Fiji National Congress 60
Fijian Administration 46–48
Fijian Association 60
Fijian Association Party (FAP) 73, 74
Fijian Nationalist Party 69, 73
Finau, Bishop Patelisio 107
France, Peter 49
Franco, Robert W. 123
Freeman, Derek 127
Friedrich, Carl J. 15, 20, 21
Fuko, Teisino 102
Fusimalohi, Tavake 98
Fusitu'a, Eseta 106, 109, 110, 111, 168,
  169
Fusitu'a, Mrs 'Ofa ki 'Okalani 100

Gailey, Christine Ward 88, 94, 103
Gallie, W. B. 31, 32
Ganilau, Ratu Sir Penaia 38, 64, 71, 171
Gellner, Ernest 23, 33
genealogical records 13, 53, 82, 97, 122, 126
General Electors' Association (Fiji) 60, 71
General Voters' Party (GVP) (Fiji) 71, 74
Germany 28, 132, 133–134
Gilson, R. P. 120, 128–129
Goldman, Irving 84, 85
Goldsmith, Michael 168–169
Gordon, Sir Arthur 45-46, 48, 51, 52, 133

Great Council of Chiefs 37, 30, 17, 53, 57,
  72, 74, 75
  1990 constitution, 64, 65, 67, 69, 70
  see also Bose Levu Vakaturaga (BLV);
    tradition

Ha'apai 79, 88, 93, 101, 102, 104, 107
Hanson, Allan 171
Hau'ofa, Epeli 4–5, 86, 90, 99, 100, 105,
  111, 113, 114
Helu, I. 86, 100, 110, 114
Henry, Geoffrey 163
Herda, Phyllis S. 97
Hills, Rodney C. 102
history, oral see oral tradition
Hobsbawm, Eric 21
Holmes, Lowell D. 124
Horowitz, Donald L. 43
Human Rights Protection Party (HRPP)
  (Western Samoa) 147, 148, 149–150,
  152, 157, 158, 164
human rights 27, 104, 112, 167

identity
  cultural 3, 20, 33, 113, 173
  Fiji 38, 50, 66
  Tonga, 20
  see also tradition
imperialism 3, 29, 34, 35, 160, 161
  anthropology and 14
  cultural 34
  South Pacific 8, 170
India 51, 57
insider/outsider dichotomy 5, 22, 33,
  163–166

James, Kerry 113
Jarvie, I. C. 15
Jolly, Margaret 22, 23, 25, 171

Kamikamica, Josevata 72, 73, 74
Kaplan, Martha 56
kastom 3 see also custom; tradition
Kata, Siaki 108
Katoa, 'Atunaisa 104
Kau'ulufonua 83, 84
Keesing, Roger M. 3, 21, 22, 23, 33
Keith-Reid, Robert 164
Kele'a 101, 104
Kolo, F. O. 114
Koloamatangi, Malakai 80
Krämer, Augustus F. 121

Lal, Brij V. 52
land
  control of, rights 22, 161

Fiji 39, 41, 48–53, 58–59, 63
  Tonga 80, 85, 91, 93, 95, 99, 101, 110
  Western Samoa 132, 134, 138, 139, 143,
    145, 153
Land Claims Commission (Fiji) 49
language 2
  in Tonga 86–87, 108
  in Western Samoa 120, 144
Lapita pottery 37, 82, 117
Larmour, Peter 167, 168
Latukefu, Sione 85, 89, 94, 97
Lau 45, 71, 74
Lauaki Namaluaulu Mamoe 134
law, customary 3, 22, 86, 145
Le Tagaloa, Aiono Fana'afi 150, 152
Le Tagaloa Pita 150, 152
Ledyard, Patricia 91
legitimacy see authority; chiefs; tradition
Leota Siaki 152, 153
Lini, Walter 24
Logan, General Robert 134
London Missionary Society 88, 128, 130,
  132

Ma'afu Tuku'i'aulahi 110
Ma'afu, 44, 45
Macpherson, Cluny 153, 154
Macpherson, La'avasa 153, 154
Mahathir, Dr Mohamed 163
Malietoa Tanumafili II 146
Malietoa Vainuupo 127, 130, 133
Manono 117, 127
Mao Tse-Tung 110
Mara, Ratu Finau 72, 73
Mara, Ratu Sir Kamisese 38, 43, 44, 60, 61
  1987 coup 64
  1994 elections 73
  corruption charges against 63
  'Pacific Way' 2, 4
  retirement of 70
  threats to land 62
Marcus, George E. 83, 91, 96-97, 98
Martin, Mr Justice 101
Mata'afa Faumuina Fiame Mulinu'u II
  146–147
Mata'afa, 134
matai
  democratic reform and 164
  divine authority 19, 121, 127, 129
  power of 138, 144, 155, 156–157, 161
  suffrage 111, 117, 118
  women 123
  see also matai system
matai system 5, 119, 136, 150, 153, 158
  democracy 146, 153
  pressures on 139, 140, 149
  sociopolitical organization 119

suffrage 118, 141–142
titles 126–127, 129, 138, 139, 144, 149
tradition 5, 138, 145, 152
women 150
see also matai
Matautia, Nu'utai Mafulu 155
Mau a Pule 134–135, 146, 168
Mea'ole, Tupua Tamasese 146
Mead, Margaret 123
Melanesia, 'Melanesian Way', the 2, 20,
  120
Meleisea, Malama 121, 122, 124, 125, 129,
  132–133, 140, 154
Micronesia 120
missionaries see Christianity
modernity 5
  Tonga, 96, 98, 100
  see also tradition
modernization 2, 13
monarchy 18, 30, 96, 98, 99, 113
  Tongan 5, 79, 80, 84, 88, 91, 98, 99, 161
    1993 elections 109, 110
    Christianity 89
    language 108
    power, 80, 91, 92, 93–4, 101, 105, 108,
      114

Nakata, Katherine T. 155
Nathan, Andrew J. 34
National Federation Party (NFP) (Fiji) 41,
  59, 60–62, 64, 69
    1987 elections 50
    1992 elections 70, 71
    1994 elections 74
nationalism 29, 33, 158
  Fijian 11, 38, 44, 56, 70, 75
  Tongan 81
  Western Samoan 20
Native Administration (Fiji) 39, 46
Native Lands Commission (Fiji) 49
Native Lands Trust Board (Fiji) 63
Nayacakalou, R. R. 47, 53
négritude movement 2, 3, 6
New Zealand 44, 51, 163
  Western Samoa and 28, 117, 134–135,
    136, 140, 155
Niu, Laki M. 95
nobility, Tongan 79, 88, 90, 91–92, 161
    1993 elections 109
    Christianity 89
    language 87
    power of 80, 99, 101
    Pro-Democracy Movement 80
    Tupou IV 98-99
    Westernization of 113
    see also monarchy
nomos 11, 12, 32

Oakeshott, Michael 16
oral tradition 7, 8, 83, 125, 126
Orientalism 14, 34, 172
Orwell, George 31, 174

Pacific Islanders 4, 24–26, 27, 33, 50, 160,
    163, 170
    see also tradition
Pacific region see South Pacific region
'Pacific Way', the 2, 3–4, 11, 163, 165–166
Paitomaleifi 137
plural society 47, 51
    Fiji 40, 42–44, 54, 56, 58, 59, 64, 69, 75
Pocock, J. G. A. 13, 14
Pohiva, 'Akilisi, 101–103, 104, 105, 106,
    108, 109, 110, 113
Polynesia 5, 18, 82, 83, 97, 120, 126, 127,
    154
Popper, Karl R. 15, 16
postmodernism 32
Powles, G. R. 135
Powles, Guy
    Tonga 92, 93–94, 96, 99, 105
    Western Samoa 120, 138–139, 139, 140,
        143
Pro-Democracy Movement (PDM)
    (Tonga) 101–108, 109, 112, 113, 163
progressivism 15

Rabuka, Sitiveni 38, 39, 70, 71, 72, 73,
    169
    1987 coup 64
    1990 constitution 58, 69
    endorsement by Council of Chiefs 53
    government 44, 58, 72
    race relations 43, 74
racism 2, 162
radicalism 16
Ranger, Terence 21
rationalism 16
Ravuvu, Asesela D. 19, 169, 170
Reddy, Jai Ram 74
relativism 29, 32, 33, 34, 111
    cultural 6, 23, 34
    democracy and 8, 169
    tradition and 23, 29, 162
Robertson, Robert T. 5, 167
Roggeveen, Jacob 130
Rotuma 65, 83
Routledge, David 37

Sabine, George H. 19
Sahlins, Marshall 82
Said, Edward W. 3, 14, 34, 167, 173
Salamasina 123, 126
Samoa Amendment Act 1947 135
Samoa, American 117, 123, 136, 140

Samoa see Western Samoa
Samoan Democratic Party 136
Samoan National Development Party
    (SNDP) 148, 157
Sartori, Giovanni 32
Savai'i 117, 120, 127, 130, 134
Scarr, Deryck 54
Schoeffel, Penelope 126
self-determination 167–168
    see also sovereignty
Skinner, Quentin 35
slavery 93
Smith, M. G. 42
So'o, Asofou 125, 147, 157
sociology 2
Solf, Dr William 133–134
Soqosoqo ni Vakavulewa ni Taukei (SVT)
    (Fiji) 69, 70–72, 73, 74
South Pacific region 160, 170
    Christianity 170, 171
    colonialism, imperialism 4, 8, 168, 170
    education 7,12, 75, 100, 153
    West and 3, 160, 162, 170, 171
    see also democracy; tradition;
        traditionalism
sovereignty 18, 34, 94, 168, 171
Spate Report 47
Stevenson, Robert Louis 124–125
suicide 153–154
Sukuna, Ratu Sir Lala 46, 47

Tagaloa 126, 127–128
Tahiti 128
Takalaua 83, 84
Talakuli, Adi Samanunu Cakobau 73
Taliai, Reverend Siupeli 104–105
tama-a-aiga 125, 146, 147, 151
Taufa'ahau 44, 86, 88, 89, 90, 111
Taufa'ahau Tupou IV 98
Taukei movement 58, 63
Thomas, Nicholas 23
Tofilau Eti Alesana 147, 148, 149, 150
Tonga
    constitution 81, 84, 88, 90–96, 99, 103,
        108, 111, 112
        1875 79–80, 84, 91, 93, 94–95, 104–106
    democratic reform 163
    description 79, 81
    Europe and 88–90, 98, 133
    Fiji and 44, 66, 83
    monarchy 94, 95, 96–101
    myths of 82–83, 114
    passports scandal 102–103
    Pro-Democracy Movement 8, 12, 80, 94,
        101–108
        1993 elections 109
        November 1992 conference 110

religion in 86, 87–88, 95, 105
  see also Christianity
sociopolitical system 79, 80, 81–88, 90,
  96, 100, 103, 107–108, 111
West and 11, 28, 170
Western Samoa and 120, 126
  see also colonialism; culture; custom;
    democracy; elites; identity; land;
    missionaries; modernity; monarchy;
    nobility; tradition; Tupou IV
Tonga Chronicle 98, 109
Tongatapu 79, 82, 88, 89, 102, 104, 107
Tonkinson, Robert 21
Tora, Apisai 68
traders 44, 46, 120
tradition 5, 8, 11, 172–173
  as ideology 17-20
  authenticity and 20–26, 56, 81, 125, 162,
    171, 174
  concept of 1, 3, 5, 7, 8, 10–13
  elites 4, 10, 12, 15, 22, 24, 171, 173
  Fiji 12, 38, 42, 45, 69, 75
    constitution 40
    Great Council of Chiefs 46
    land tenure in Fiji 48
    missionaries 55
    rights 41
    see also authenticity; chiefs: Fijian
  identity 11, 13, 173
  introduced concepts 170
  modernity 13-17, 162
  politics of 7, 20, 25, 33
  South Pacific region 1, 12, 22, 26, 34,
    160, 162
  Tonga 12, 81, 97, 98–99, 103, 109, 112,
    113, 171, 172
    criticism 96, 100
    see also authenticity; culture
  universal suffrage and 9
  Western Samoa 12, 151, 157, 172
    electoral system 118, 119, 141–144,
      149
    fa'amatai 152–153
    fa'aSamoa 119
    matai 138, 140
    politics 135, 136, 138, 147
    suffrage 136–137, 156, 158–159
    village *fono* 139
    see also authenticity; authority;
      education; modernity; relativism;
      traditionalism
traditionalism 2, 7, 17, 21, 24, 32, 173–174
  democracy, 20
  Fiji 76, 167
  nationalism and 158
  South Pacific 2, 17, 166
  Western Samoa 119

Tu'i Ha'atakalaua 83, 84, 90, 97
Tu'i Kanokupolu 84, 97, 111
Tu'i Tonga 7, 82–85, 86, 90, 97
Tu'ipeiehake, Prince Fatafehi III
Tufuga Efi 151
Tuimaleali'ifano 135
Tupou I, King George 88, 90, 91, 94, 95,
  97, 106
Tupou II 95, 96
Tupou III, Queen Salote 96–98
Tupou IV 98–101
Tupouto'a, Crown Prince 106, 107
Tupua Tamasese Leolofi III 135
Tupua Tamasese Leolofi IV 141, 146, 147
Tupua Tamasese Leolofiaana IV 151
Tupuola Efi 147, 148, 150, 151
tyranny 12, 31

Ulualofiaga Talamaiveo Niko 157
United Kingdom 42, 172
  Fiji and 38, 45, 161, 168
  Tonga and 94–95, 132, 161
  Western Samoa and 130, 131, 132, 135
United Nations 117, 135, 136, 137
UNESCO 29
UN, Trusteeship Council and
  Decolonization Committee of 96
United States of America 21, 31, 42, 131,
  132, 152
universalism 6, 34
University of the South Pacific 101, 111
Upolu 117, 127, 130

Va'ai Kolone 147, 148
Vaea, Baron 106, 110
Vanua Levu 37, 44, 45, 68
Vanuatu 20, 24, 83
Vava'u 79, 93, 104, 107
Vava'u Codes 91
Vesikula, Ratu Timoci 73–4
Viti Levu 37, 45, 54, 62, 68, 72

Walzer, Michael 13, 14
war
  Tonga 88, 89, 90, 110, 111
  Western Samoa 127, 130, 131, 132, 133,
    134
Ward, R. Gerard 49, 50
Weber, Max 13, 14, 87
West, F. J. 128, 129
West, the
  democracy 8, 12, 17, 27, 112, 119, 142,
    166
  Fiji and 40, 55, 75
  South Pacific and 3, 160, 162, 170, 171
  Tonga and 28, 109, 112

West, the, *cont.*
  tradition, authenticity 1, 11, 13, 14, 17,
    19, 22, 25, 26, 172
  values of 3, 20, 161, 170
  Western Samoa and 28, 132, 119, 142,
    148, 158
Western Samoa
  colonial rule 28
  constitution 111, 135, 137, 138, 150
  cultural heritage 20, 118, 119, 123, 136,
    140, 151, 157
  description 117, 120
  electoral system 117, 118, 119, 136,
    141–146, 152, 153
  Germany and 28, 132, 133–134
  Land and Titles Court, Act 1981, 118,
    134, 138, 139, 143, 145, 149, 152

oral tradition 7
religion 121, 127–129, 130
sociopolitical system 120–126, 126–129,
  135, 146
Tonga and 83, 120, 126
universal suffrage 9, 117–119, 135–138,
  139, 145, 148, 151, 152–153, 156, 157,
  158–159, 164
Village Fono Act 1990 139, 155-157
West and 11, 161, 170
see also divine right, authority; custom;
  democracy; democratization;
  fa'amatai; *fa'aSamoa*; land; *matai*; *matai*
  system; missionaries; self-
  determination; tradition
Williams, John 130
women 149–150, 164